GAIA COOPER
with Veronica Clark

MODERN
Slave

HARPER
element

This book is a work of non-fiction based on the author's experiences.
In order to protect privacy, names, identifying characteristics,
dialogue and details have been changed or reconstructed.

HarperElement
An imprint of HarperCollins*Publishers*
1 London Bridge Street
London SE1 9GF

www.harpercollins.co.uk

HarperCollins*Publishers*
Macken House, 39/40 Mayor Street Upper
Dublin 1, D01 C9W8, Ireland

First published by HarperElement 2024

1 3 5 7 9 10 8 6 4 2

© Gaia Cooper and Veronica Clark 2024

Gaia Cooper and Veronica Clark assert the moral right
to be identified as the authors of this work

A catalogue record of this book is
available from the British Library

ISBN 978-0-00-865043-8

Printed and bound in the UK using 100%
renewable electricity at CPI Group (UK) Ltd

This book contains FSC™ certified paper and other controlled
sources to ensure responsible forest management.

For more information visit: www.harpercollins.co.uk/green

CONTENTS

PROLOGUE

September 2015, 9.30 a.m.

The knock at the door had been unexpected.

I'd just finished hoovering the bedrooms and was about to tackle the downstairs rooms when I heard it. It was so loud that it made me stop dead in my tracks. Unplugging the hoover, I retracted the cord so I didn't trip over it and headed towards the top of the stairs.

It was still early morning; the kids had just left for school and the house was empty. I didn't realise it then, but each step I took would be a step closer to the moment my life would change forever. As I neared the bottom step I spotted the outlines of two people on the doorstep through the frosted-glass door pane. Expecting them to be Jehovah's Witnesses, I tried to think of an excuse to move them on. I fixed a polite smile on my face and opened the door, the lame excuse still dancing on the tip of my tongue. As I did, I came face to face with two women – a glamorous blonde and an older, stern-faced brunette, neither of whom I'd ever seen before. Both were dressed in smart, sombre work clothes and they were each holding a briefcase.

'Gaia Cooper?' the dark-haired woman asked.

I tried to second-guess who she was and what she wanted. The woman had a solemn face and an equally serious manner about her. I guessed she must have been in her mid-forties. She wore her hair in a severe mahogany-brown bob, which aged her prematurely. Clutching a red lanyard draped around her neck, she held it up towards me. It had an equally dowdy photograph of her, and underneath was her job title: *Police officer, National Crime Agency.*

'Can we come in?'

My mind scrambled as I tried to process what was written on her lanyard.

Why are two officers from the National Crime Agency knocking at my door early on a Monday morning?

Thoughts of my two young sons flashed through my mind as my stomach curdled with fear. I began to tremble. Her colleague noticed and tried to reassure me.

'Don't worry, Gaia, everything's okay. No one's been hurt,' she insisted, as she reached out towards me with a hand that didn't quite touch.

I sighed with relief, but my heart continued to clatter inside my chest.

What do they want?

Remembering my manners, I shifted over and invited them inside. Both officers found their way quickly to my front room, so quickly that, for a split second, I wondered if they'd been here before. Of course they hadn't. I wasn't like that anymore. I was a changed person and I'd left all that in the past.

They took a seat on the sofa and rested their briefcases on the ground by their feet. A tense silence followed, before it was broken by the younger, fair-haired officer.

'We knew your children would be at school, Gaia. That's why we've come so early. We didn't want you to get upset in front of them.'

Upset? Why the hell would I be upset, and why are two police officers sitting in my front room?

'We wanted you to have the rest of the day to try and process what we've come to ask you about.'

My mind raced, full of uncertainty.

'Why?' I said, interrupting her. 'What have you come to ask me?'

The officer seemed a little unsure of herself and turned to her older colleague for back-up. It became apparent the dark-haired woman was her boss, as she now stepped in and took charge.

'Gaia, could you please sit down for a moment?'

She gestured with a nod of her head to a chair directly behind me and, that's when I realised – I was still standing. I perched myself on the edge of the chair as I waited for them to say whatever it was they'd come to say.

'Could one of you just please tell me what this is about?'

The senior officer cleared her throat and began to explain.

'As officers with the National Crime Agency we have been investigating historical offences following the recent failings in both Rotherham and Rochdale. Our work is part of a special taskforce, and we've been looking into the historical sexual exploitation of girls.'

The breakfast I'd enjoyed only an hour earlier threatened to claw its way back up my throat. I listened in horror and tried hard not to vomit as a series of intrusive thoughts flashed across my mind.

Men ... lying on top of me. Hot breath clawing against the skin of my neck as I try to pull myself free. Black eyes, smashed glass on the floor ... a broom handle.

I gulped down a rising panic, and shook my head to try and rid it of the barbaric memories.

A wardrobe door ... a horrible crunching noise as it slams against my face – skin, tissue and bone disintegrating ... splintering.

I shuddered and tried to compose myself. A slick of sweat coated both hands and my skin grew clammy, as though a fever had just taken hold. I wrung both hands together anxiously as my face flushed and burned with ... what? Shame ... anger? I couldn't be sure, as the urge to vomit intensified.

These women – these strangers – were inside my home, discussing a past I'd spent years trying to erase. A past I'd buried deep within me. In the space of a few moments, that same past had risen to the surface, and was now living and breathing inside my front room. It had arrived unexpectedly with the knock at the door, and come kicking and screaming back into my life – the one I'd spent years painstakingly carving out for me and my boys. My hands trembled, and soon the rest of my body joined in.

I glanced up to find both officers staring straight at me. The dark-haired one had opened her mouth, as though she was about to say more. Instinctively, I closed my eyes and swallowed hard to try and prepare myself. There was worse to come.

'Gaia, we have been trawling through the records of hundreds of girls who had been reported missing in the late 1990s and early 2000s, and you have been identified to us as one of those girls.'

Subconsciously, I rubbed my fingers against my wrist as more memories rose to the surface.

Tight parcel tape, holding me down ... sprained wrists ...

'Gaia?'

It was the senior officer, but I couldn't answer her. My heart beat so fast that I was finding it difficult to breathe. The fussy wallpaper in my front room began to swirl, the walls bending and narrowing as though they were closing in on me. I panted, sweating with fear, and stumbling to my feet, I staggered over to the window.

Hot ... the room is too hot ... I can't breathe.

'Gaia, are you ...?' a voice started to say.

The intense heat faded as I rested my forehead against the cold, damp glass.

Breathe ... don't forget to breathe.

Outside it was a cold, fresh autumnal day, and right now I needed air. Turning the chrome latch, I pushed the window open. I wasn't sure what I needed to do first – breathe or throw up. A gust of air brushed against my face, calming me. I gulped it down greedily. Cold air flooded into the radiator-hot room, leaving a distinct chill, but I didn't care. I couldn't think straight because I was terrified of what they might say next. After a few moments, my heart had stopped galloping. I wandered back over to my seat and tried to pull myself together.

'Sorry ...' I mumbled.

The senior officer held up her hand as if to say no apology was needed.

I urged her to continue, even though I found it painful and shameful. But I *needed* to know. Staring hard at a pattern in the nap of the grey carpet, I tried my best to concentrate and avoid eye contact. I needed to focus and prepare myself for the next body blow.

'Are you okay, Gaia? Do you need a moment – or a glass of water?'

I shook my head, because I wanted it to be over and done with. I needed her to rip the plaster clean from the wound in one swift movement.

She clasped both hands together, leaned forward in her seat and began to speak.

'Okay, as I was saying, you were one of those girls who was repeatedly reported missing, from what we can see on the missing persons database. Gaia, the men you associated with at that time … well, the thing is, we believe you were a victim of both grooming and sexual exploitation.'

She paused as she said the word 'exploitation', and it hung in the air between us.

'Gaia, the men exploited you and, as a result, you got into a lot of trouble when you were still a child. But none of it – any of it – was your fault. You were groomed and exploited in the most horrible way.'

I gasped. Angry tears flooded my eyes, blurring my vision. My chest tightened like a snare drum as my heart hammered against it. Lifting the sleeve of my sweatshirt, I wiped both eyes defiantly and managed to choke back an unexpected wave of emotion. But I was fooling no one, least of all myself. The floodgates had burst open, and a lifetime of pent-up hurt and frustration came spilling out.

Years of being called a thief, a crook and a bad girl.

I sobbed as I remembered all the names, the sly remarks and the untrusting, sideways glances.

Look at her, the black sheep of the family. The fraudster, the slag ...

Each one punctured me like a shard of glass.

The room fell silent, apart from intermittent sobs as they wracked through my body. The officers looked on as I tried, but failed, to catch my breath. I combed my trembling fingers through my long, strawberry blonde hair. Twisting and knotting each strand, I pulled them taut around my fingers. I wanted, no, I *needed* to feel something – anything. Pain was good because pain reminded me of what I'd been through.

My home – my sanctuary – had instantly changed. Everything had changed, and I would never forget these two strangers with their briefcases and lanyards, or this moment. They had transported me right back there – a terrified fourteen-year-old child, the girl no one wanted to know, the girl no one trusted.

'Gaia, are you okay?'

The young officer stretched out a manicured hand towards me and I let her.

'Look,' her boss said, breaking the silence, 'we understand that this has come as a complete shock to you, but we really need your help.'

I wiped away the last angry tears in one sweep.

'I'm okay. It's just that ...'

'What? What is it, Gaia?'

I opened my mouth and took a deep breath of courage.

'It's just that nobody – not one person – has ever said that to me before – that none of this was my fault. But now you're here ...'

I glanced up at them both. '... and you're asking for my help?' I said, my voice incredulous.

The younger officer shifted uncomfortably in her seat and averted her eyes to the floor.

But I hadn't finished. I hadn't even started. They needed to know ... everyone needed to know. I pictured myself – a fourteen-year-old schoolgirl, travelling in a car with much older men. The police had pulled us over, but I'd been so drunk that I'd vomited all over the officer's shoes.

She can see I'm out of it and alone with those men, yet she laughs and sends me on my way.

The thought of it now made me boil with anger.

'Where were you?' I hissed, my eyes flashing with fury. 'Where were you back then when I was a fourteen-year-old child, begging for help? Where were you when I needed you?'

The senior officer glanced up. Our eyes locked as she looked me straight in the eye for the very first time.

'Gaia, we're here now.'

CHAPTER ONE

SHOES

Standing in the long grass at the side of the school field, I shielded a hand against my eyes to try and block out the brightness of the blistering morning sun. I glanced down at my feet. The glitter glistened between gaps in the wilted yellow blades of grass. Shuffling my feet, I pushed them deeper into the thick, messy undergrowth. I was still busy, looking down at them, when a voice snapped me back into the moment.

'Gaia Cooper, come over here right now.'

I raised my head and stared into the eyes of my teacher. She lifted a hand and beckoned me over towards her and the rest of the class, but I didn't want to move – not an inch – because if I did then everyone would see.

'Gaia, aren't you listening? Come over here right now,' the teacher said tersely.

My classmates looked over in bewilderment as they waited for me to do as I was told. But I couldn't step out of the long grass because if I did, they would all laugh at me.

Miss Brown's knee-length skirt rustled and her blouse twisted at the waistband as she marched over towards me. Her dark eyebrows knitted together in annoyance.

'Whatever's got into you this morning, Gaia?'

She cupped a hand around my shoulder and I felt a gentle push as she tried, but failed, to nudge me from the spot. Both feet remained firmly planted against the ground. I hoped it'd open up and swallow me whole.

'Please don't make me move,' I whispered.

My teacher sighed. Bending her long legs at the knees, she crouched down until she was eye-level with me.

'Why, Gaia? What is it?'

But I didn't know what to say or even where to begin so I shrugged.

'Look, whatever it is, you're just being silly. Now, be a good girl, go over there and join the rest of the class.'

Just then, I heard the voice of one of my classmates standing behind her.

'Miss, what's wrong with Gaia?'

The teacher twisted awkwardly as she crouched down. Wobbling slightly, she turned to my annoying classmate.

'Ellie, what have I told you? Now go back and join the rest of the class.'

Ellie shot me a hateful look and returned to the others as the rest of the class gawped impatiently. They were waiting to start the day's outdoor PE lesson. Some children love attention, but I wasn't one of them. In fact, I hated it.

'Come on,' Miss Brown said, standing up. 'I don't have time for this.'

Do it. Do it now! My heart fluttered like a wild bird inside my chest as my crippling embarrassment engulfed me. With my eyes scrunched tightly shut behind jam-jar spectacles, I stepped away from the long grass and back into the world.

The first snigger came quickly, followed by a crescendo of giggles. Soon, the whole class was laughing at me. Small fingers began to point down at my feet and Miss Brown's eyes followed. My once-perfect black plimsolls had been customised with lime-green elastic U-shapes (instead of the usual black), and the edge trim had been dipped in glue and glitter. The silver glitter glistened in the sunlight as though the glue underneath was still wet.

'Miss, why are Gaia's shoes all funny?'

It was Ellie again. She was a confident, pushy and popular girl – everything I was not. Ellie had everything her heart desired – she only had to say the word. She didn't know what it felt like to be me – none of them did, not even the poor ones. I remained standing there – my shoes aglow in the bright sunlight – as everyone sniggered and pointed.

For once, Miss Brown was lost for words.

'I, er, come on, Gaia,' she mumbled.

But I knew; I could tell by the way she'd wrapped a protective arm around my shoulders. I could hear it in her voice. Everyone who knew Mum, knew what she was like. She was different – quirky – and, by default, that made me the same. Miss Brown knew that anything she did say would make matters ten times worse. Turning to the rest of the class, she clapped her hands together to try and bring order.

'Okay, enough. Let's get the lesson started!'

Slowly, the children separated into different groups as I went over to find mine. I knew what they were thinking; it was obvious in the way they were all glancing at one another.

What has Gaia's mum made her wear now?

When Mum had first bought my plimsolls a few weeks earlier, I'd been ecstatic I finally had something 'normal' to wear. Smiling, I held them up against the light. I was dying to wear them because I wanted to belong.

'Put them back in the bag,' Mum nagged.

'But …'

'Do as I say.'

After I did, the pumps went missing. I searched everywhere, but I couldn't find them. When I finally asked her if she'd seen them, Mum's face had lit up with excitement.

'Well, it was supposed to be a surprise, but you might as well have them now.'

With that, she disappeared while I stood there waiting. I heard noises as she rummaged through a kitchen cupboard, so I wandered through to join her. She turned and triumphantly held the carrier bag up, then pulled out my newly decorated pair of plimsolls.

'Here you go!'

My mouth fell open with shock because she'd changed the elastic and coated the edges of the pumps with a crust of glitter.

I wanted to die.

'Lovely, aren't they?' Mum chirped. 'Took me ages.'

'I, er, I … I …'

For once, I was completely speechless.

'No need to thank me. No one else will have a pair like that, you know.'

Clearly delighted, she scrunched the carrier bag in her hands and popped it back inside a drawer.

She was right – no other child would want to wear something quite as awful.

As she plonked herself down onto a kitchen chair, I realised that she was waiting for me to thank her. But I was still dumbstruck.

They'll crucify me.

And they did, only not straight away. Over the next few weeks I kept the awful pumps strictly under wraps. Mum insisted I took them to school. I did, but I pushed them to the bottom of my PE bag and kept them hidden there. With no pumps, I'd run around the school hall and field barefoot. I didn't care how freezing and painful the cold floor and ground felt underfoot, that didn't matter because I knew it was better than the plimsolls.

Miss Brown quizzed me, asking where my plimsolls were. Each time I'd swear I'd forgotten them. It annoyed her – that, and all the verrucas I seemed to catch. The verrucas soon became a real problem. Mum seemed baffled how I'd managed to pick up so many in such a short space of time. She'd complain bitterly and soak my feet in a strange, orange-coloured chemical solution that smelled disgusting. It was so strong that it stained my skin bright orange. I wasn't sure which was worse, bright turmeric-coloured feet or the awful plimsolls. Eventually, Miss Brown became so fed up seeing my beacon feet that she threatened to contact Mum. That's when I knew the game was up. I'd have to wear them – and now I had.

'Miss, why does Gaia have funny stuff on her pumps?' Ellie asked again.

She was like a dog with a bone; she wouldn't give up. But the teacher didn't answer her.

She knew Mum was a hippy – all the teachers did – because I couldn't exactly hide it. Or her. Mum would come and pick me up from school in her battered yellow van. It would splutter and backfire loudly as it pulled up outside the school gates, drawing a crowd of its own. My mum wasn't anything like the other school mums. For starters, she had dreadlocked hair and wore charity-shop clothes. She'd dress me the same. My clothes had not only seen better days, they were decades out of fashion. Everything about her was different and, in turn, that made me different. But my humiliation didn't end after the PE lesson – I had to wear the stupid plimsolls for the rest of the school year. Every time I took them out of my bag the other kids would nudge and whisper. I was desperate to fit in, but the odds were stacked against me right away.

My inner-city London school was multicultural, but even against a backdrop of children of all ethnicities and social classes, I always stood out. It wasn't just my stupid, hippyish name that set me apart – everything about me was different, including the jam jar glasses I had to wear. I'd never been one of the pretty girls; I didn't even have a favourite doll.

Mum always said I was so hyperactive and naughty that she didn't know what to do with me. She coped by doing exactly what she wanted to do, namely dragging me along to Glastonbury or gigs by the band Pentangle. It was usually just the two of us, so I could never escape. My real dad had disappeared. She said he'd upped and left as soon as she'd told him she was pregnant with me. I'd always doubted her version of events but as there was no one else to ask, I had to accept it. However, something didn't quite fit.

My mother had a full-time job in a health food shop so she'd drop me at the childminder's house, which was just across the road. The childminder was strict, and one of my earliest memories was wetting myself after I'd been told not to move from my chair. I'd always been the sort of kid who didn't like to get into trouble. Although it had just been us, Mum didn't stay single for long. When I was six years old, she met my stepdad, Richard. I immediately warmed to Richard because he was everything Mum wasn't. For starters, he looked normal, like a dad should. Most of all, he seemed to take a genuine interest in what I had to say. Although he was divorced, he had two children of his own – a boy called Josh and a girl called Ruby. Having Josh and Ruby was like having two ready-made playmates. I'd sit by the front window, eagerly awaiting their arrival on the weekends that Richard had them. Like most brothers, Josh could be annoying. He was only four months older than me, but he'd decided he should be in charge. He'd terrorise me and Ruby, spitting chewed-up paper in our faces. Being a bit of a tomboy, I'd retaliate. Eventually, the three of us would end up collapsed on the floor in an exhausted heap, giggling. Until they arrived, I didn't realise quite how much I missed having siblings, even if they were only step ones. At least I wasn't alone now.

Unlike me, Ruby was close to both her mum and her dad. The girls at my school were the same. Although I was young, I would feel a weird pang of jealousy whenever the other girls bragged how they'd been shopping with their mums. My life wasn't like that because all my clothes came from jumble sales or charity shops. Apart from the customised plimsolls, I rarely received anything new. Other girls also seemed to have a closeness to their mums that I never had. It made me feel sad and lonely.

By the time I turned eight years old, I realised that Mum was at the root of all my problems – from all the strange clothes she made me wear to my odd home life. Unlike the other kids who ate burgers and chips, Mum would feed me healthy food all the time. I guess it went with the territory, but I must have been the only child who thought green beans were chips, or 'green chips' as Mum called them. I couldn't understand why all my friends raved about chips, until one day I tried the real thing at school.

'Are these like the green ones?' I asked the dinner lady.

She looked a little bemused, as though she didn't have a clue what I was talking about.

Unlike the rest of my classmates, I'd never eaten fast food. Sweet treats were almost non-existent in our house unless Ruby and Josh came to stay. At one point my craving for sweet things became so bad that I took to stealing. One afternoon, I'd been invited over to a friend's house for tea. After dinner, her mother brought out some Jammie Dodgers biscuits and placed them on the table. My eyes were on stalks as I watched my friend tuck in and eat as many as she wanted. An hour or so later we decided to go to the local park to play. I was carrying my school bag – a small drawstring bag – which I'd strapped to my back. However, as I scaled the climbing frame, the bag slipped off my shoulder, spilling the contents to the ground. The jammy biscuit centres glinted in the afternoon sun as a handful tumbled to the ground and rolled off in different directions. My friend stopped, looked down and pointed at them accusingly.

'Why have you taken all the biscuits?'

My face burned as my eyes shifted between her and them. I didn't know what to say because I couldn't tell her the real reason – that we never had nice things back home.

The following day during lunchtime, my friend watched me as she slowly ate one of the biscuits.

'You like these, Gaia, don't you?' she said pointedly.

Of course, it wasn't long before the rest of the class found out. Suddenly, the invites back home to different houses for tea dried up. It must have been obvious to everyone who cared to notice that I didn't have what the other children had. I couldn't understand why I was so different or why Mum would want me to be.

I didn't realise it then, but the graffitied plimsolls were just the start.

* * *

'Sing us a song, Gaia,' my classmate Abbie insisted.

Abbie and I sat next to each other on the same table at school. The other children glanced up from what they were doing. We were supposed to be copying out sentences into our jotters, but I'd been far too busy daydreaming, staring out of the classroom window.

'Hmm … what?' I mumbled.

The end of my chewed pencil had disintegrated into small wooden splinters inside my mouth. As I tried to wipe them away, I realised that everyone was staring, including Abbie.

'Me?'

Abbie rolled her eyes in annoyance.

'Yes, Gaia. I said, "Sing us a song."'

My stomach tightened with nerves as I tried to think of a song – any song – I knew. Of course, I knew all the

Pentangle and Jethro Tull songs off by heart because those were Mum's favourites, but a proper song?

Suddenly, something popped into my head. I grinned because I knew it off by heart – it was one of my stepdad's favourites. I closed my eyes and began to sing:

'A drop of Nelson's blood wouldn't do us any harm …'

The sea shanty began to stream from my mouth. It was a song about Lord Horatio Nelson, rum and the Battle of Trafalgar. To me, it was just a song and one I knew well. I wasn't a natural extrovert, which was why I'd shut my eyes; however, by the time I'd opened them I realised everyone was staring at me open-mouthed. That's when I knew – I'd done something weird again.

Abbie's face changed to one of utter confusion. In fact, everyone stayed silent. It was obvious that no one knew what to say or make of me and my strange little song.

'What was that?' someone called out.

'It's a sea shanty, it's about …'

Before I could answer, Abbie butted in.

'No, I mean, what was that?'

She looked across the table as everyone began to side-eye each other. Then they laughed. Embarrassment whooshed up from the soles of my feet right to my face as it began to redden.

'Okay, you sing a song,' I huffed, as I pointed at Abbie.

She smirked and cleared her throat. That's when I realised she already had something prepared. Abbie had a good singing voice, and she knew it. She pulled a serious face as she began to sing the opening lines of 'Chains' by Tina Arena. As soon as she reached the chorus, the others joined in. Everyone knew the words – everyone apart from me. Although the song was catchy, I'd never heard it before in my life.

'Well, I think it's a silly song,' I added.

Abbie stopped, looked at me and narrowed her eyes.

'Well, at least it's in the charts, unlike yours …'

That's when I realised it wasn't just my jumble-sale clothes or customised plimsolls that set me apart. Everything about me was wrong.

That afternoon, Mum waved as she climbed down from her van and parked outside the school gates. Although I couldn't hear what they were saying, I spotted the other mums standing in small groups, staring. Mum was wearing a long, flowery dress, a moth-eaten, knitted waistcoat and some old boots that she'd customised. Even though she was my mum and I loved her, I cringed because I was beginning to view her through other people's eyes.

'Good day at school?' she asked.

Her banana-coloured van was ancient and the wheel arches covered in large patches of orange rust. Metal groaned and creaked beneath us as we both climbed in. I could almost picture the rust flaking to the floor, leaving a trail of ginger dust as we drove off.

'Gaia, I asked you a question. I said, did you have a good day at school?'

'Hmmm …' I mumbled.

What could I say?

I stood out because I was weird Gaia Cooper – the girl with the strange name and strange clothes.

To try and fit in, I decided to stick to the other weird kids. Although she knew all the songs in the charts, Abbie's family seemed even stranger than mine because they were Jehovah's Witnesses. There seemed to be loads of things that she wasn't allowed, including immunisations at school.

'The stuff they put in the injections is made from dead babies,' Abbie said, her eyes wide with horror.

'What!'

Afterwards, I ran home to tell my parents.

'Don't be silly, Gaia, she's winding you up!' my stepdad chortled.

I was a gullible little girl, and everyone knew.

Despite this, I'd just begun to build up a small friendship group when, one day, completely out of the blue, Mum announced that we were moving. She'd just given birth to my half-sister Laura and had decided to finally marry my stepdad.

'I just don't think London is a safe place to bring kids up, especially not two little girls,' she insisted.

Although I'd had a difficult time, in many ways I loved my school and my friends because they were all different. My class was a melting pot of different cultures and it had taught me to accept everyone, no matter who they were or where they came from.

But, with Mum's mind firmly made up, a 'For Sale' sign was hammered into the ground outside in the garden and a few months later our house was sold.

To mark my departure, I asked Mum if I could make my teacher a leaving present. Mum opened up her craft boxes and, not long after, a beautiful necklace dangled from my fingers.

'She's going to love it,' my mother agreed.

I smiled. For once I'd done something good and that made me feel happy inside. Although the necklace was colourful, I felt it needed something else. I rummaged in the craft box until I spotted some star sequins. Grabbing the glue pot, I began to stick them to the beads as Mum nodded with approval.

The following morning, I couldn't wait to give Miss Brown her special homemade present. As soon as I did, her face lit up.

'Thank you, Gaia. I shall treasure it. I'll wear it every day.'

She pointed to the little stars.

'I especially love these.'

I left school that day feeling wonderful.

'Did she like it?' Mum asked, as she met me at the school gate.

'She loved it!'

During my final week, Miss Brown wore my home-made necklace, only I noticed that the sequin stars were missing.

'What happened?' I asked.

The teacher clasped a self-conscious hand against her neck.

'Oh, I loved them; I really did, Gaia,'

Red bloomed across her cheeks the more she tried to explain.

'It's just that the stars were a little scratchy against my neck, so I peeled them off.'

My face crumpled.

'But you said you loved them.'

'I did, it's just that …'

It was too late. Miss Brown had changed my necklace, just as Mum changed everything. I realised then that adults didn't always mean what they said. They could lie too.

CHAPTER TWO

SMALL TOWN

Everything about my new home was different, from the neat little garden at the front to the identikit houses lined up in ordered little red-bricked rows. There were no high-rise tower blocks like those that once dominated the skyline near my old home; the dust, noise and constant bustle of central London had disappeared, and along with them the excitement. Instead, I'd been transported to another world – a new town with fields, fresh air and a small, generic high street but very little else. Rather than being surrounded by diversity, the town was largely populated by a sea of white faces. It was a small town stuffed full of small-minded people. The school Mum had chosen for me wasn't much better. As soon as I walked into the classroom on my first day, I knew that no matter how hard I tried, I'd never fit in.

'Those are funny glasses. Why do you wear them?' a girl asked as I took a seat at a new table.

'Look at her funny dress,' her friend remarked.

She nudged her as the two girls covered their mouths and began to giggle.

I glanced down at my awful, old-fashioned dress; it was even older than I was. It was made from a horrible, bobbled, checked cloth. It had a huge patch pocket on the front with a worn-out transfer picture of a kitten stuck to it. Bizarrely, even though she'd bought it from a jumble sale, somehow Mum had managed to find two of the same dress in different sizes – one for me and one for my step-sister. Ruby hated hers on sight because we both realised how ridiculous we looked. I was older, so being dressed the same as my younger step-sister left me feeling foolish. Ruby was luckier than I was; she had her own mother, who immediately threw the awful dress in the bin. Sadly, I wasn't as fortunate and, with Mum breathing down my neck, I was forced to wear it, come rain or shine.

Not only did I not look like my classmates, the curriculum we'd followed in my previous school in London had also been entirely different. I was just nine years old but, when it came to reciting our times table, I didn't have a clue because we'd never memorised them.

One day, just after lunch I was sitting in class when the teacher decided to single me out.

'Gaia, please stand and say your nine times table.'

My mouth grew dry with anxiety.

'Er, erm …'

In a blind panic, I tried to stall for time. I stood there, umming and erring as the whole class waited.

'Gaia, you do know your times tables, don't you?' the teacher asked gently.

She arched an eyebrow hopefully. An excruciating silence followed as everyone waited for me to answer.

'I, erm, I …'

But I didn't, and the fact I didn't answer confirmed it.

'Okay,' she said, mercifully. 'You can sit back down.'

Tears pricked at the backs of my eyes as I willed them not to fall, but they did. Everyone in class turned to stare at the strange new girl, wearing the jam jar glasses, sobbing in her chair.

'Okay, class, everyone face the front.'

Although I was grateful, the teacher and I both knew I was way behind. My classmates were streets ahead of me, not only in the fashion stakes, but in every sense. When I later told Mum what had happened, she went out and bought a cassette tape for me so I could try and catch up.

Not long afterwards, I was playing with my baby sister in the kitchen when I heard the front door slam. Mum wandered through to join us. She was holding a bulging plastic carrier bag. I shuddered. It meant only one thing – she'd been to the car boot.

'I've got some right bargains,' she said excitedly.

She proceeded to pull out a series of awful, creased and unfashionable clothes. My eyes scoured the pile, looking for something half-decent.

'Oh, I nearly forgot,' she added, as her hand rustled in the bottom of the carrier bag.

'You said you wanted some Reebok trainers so, I got you these.'

In her hand were a pair of old Reeboks. They weren't perfect – the 'white' leather had yellowed – but at least they said Reebok, the trainers everyone wore at school. My heart galloped with excitement.

'Well, go on then. Don't just stand there, try them on.'

I couldn't stop smiling as I sat down on the kitchen chair and pulled them on. But my smile soon slipped.

'Lovely,' Mum remarked.

Then she spotted my face. I pulled off one of the trainers and loosened the laces a little to peer at the label
inside.

'They're a size five!'

I pointed to the label as my mother picked up her
glasses and came over to inspect it herself. She straightened up and thought for a moment.

'Don't worry, you'll soon grow into them.'

'But I'm only a three!'

She'd already stopped listening. She lifted a hand and
scratched her head with her stubby, bitten-back finger-
nails.

'Listen, you're almost a size five and, well, if they're
too big now then it won't be much longer before you
grow into them. Besides, I can't afford to spend money on
trainers that you won't wear. They're not that much
bigger; just wear thick socks with them.'

Even though they were two sizes too big and a funny
colour, at least I owned a pair of prized Reeboks – something the other kids had. But if I thought the trainers
would help me fit in, then I was wrong.

'Nice trainers, Gaia,' a boy smirked as I hobbled into
the classroom the next morning.

'Thanks,' I replied, beaming with joy.

The trainers were so big that they kept slipping off the
backs of my heels and they made me trip up over my own
feet. At first, I didn't understand why he was laughing.
Although the trainers had the right name written on
the side, they were worn out and stank of someone else's
foot odour.

'And you've got ginger hair …' the boy quipped.

'It's strawberry blonde.'

'And a funny name,' his mate chipped in.

Within the hour, my happiness had evaporated. The kids at my new school began to mock me and my clothes. It soon became a sport – a kind of *'What will Gaia wear next?'* joke.

Just like Reeboks, Kickers boots were all the rage at the time and all the popular girls wore them. I drove Mum crazy, begging her to buy me some, but they cost a small fortune. Mum begrudged spending money on new things when she could find perfectly good second-hand clothes and shoes at jumble sales. Shortly afterwards, she emerged triumphant from a local scout hall holding a pair of salmon pink, suede Kickers boots. They were so worn and dirty that they looked grey. While everyone else bombed around the playground in their brightly coloured trendy boots, I had to make do with a pair the colour of a well-used rag. She finally relented and gave me some money to buy another second-hand pair, only this time from a girl at school, called Annie. They'd also seen better days, but what made matters worse was the fact everyone knew they'd once belonged to her.

Occasionally there would be a bit of respite. It came in the form of my aunt and uncle, who lived in Newcastle. I loved it up there. Not only was it a big, friendly city with lots of stuff happening, but my aunt and I would catch a bus to the Metro Centre in nearby Gateshead, where she'd take me clothes shopping. Back home, I'd only ever get something new if it was my birthday. Even then, Mum would insist on taking me to somewhere like TK Maxx, where everything had been heavily discounted.

But Aunt Linda was different. As soon as I walked in through the door of her Newcastle home, she'd give me a cursory glance.

'Hang on, I'll just grab my coat,' she said one day, just after Mum had dropped me off.

'But I've only just got here,' I said, throwing my old school bag on the floor.

My aunt nodded, checked her watch and made her way over towards the door.

'Come on, if we're quick we'll be able to make the next bus.'

I stared at her blankly.

'Why?'

'Because I'm taking you shopping. This,' she said, tugging at my threadbare sleeve, 'has seen better days. And those,' she said, pointing down at Annie's old Kickers boots, 'deserve to live in the bin.'

My face broke into a smile. That day we caught the bus and trawled the shops, where she bought me a new coat and shoes.

'But what do I tell Mum?' I asked.

I was worried how I'd be able to explain it all away to my frugal mother. Aunt Linda was a kind but formidable woman. She also knew exactly what her sister was like.

'Tell her it's my treat – for your birthday.'

It was my turn to be confused.

'But that was months ago, and you sent me some money, remember?'

She rested a hand against her mouth.

'Did I? Ah well, it's the rest of your birthday present then.'

I grinned, delighted that I'd be able to keep all my lovely new things. True to her word, my stinky Reeboks and knackered Kickers boots went straight in the bin.

On my next visit, Aunt Linda bought me lots of lovely underwear from Marks & Spencer, some stationery, a pencil case, Parker ink pens and a trendy Kangol shoulder bag to carry all my school books in.

'We don't want everyone thinking you're poor now, do we?'

I loved my aunt and the novelty of having new things to wear. Not only that, everything fitted properly too and I'd been able to choose it. I was used to clothes being too big, too short, unfashionable or too garish. My aunt had offered a kind of normality I'd not known before, and I loved her for it.

My stepdad was kind, like my aunt, but he was too busy at work all day to notice my mother's growing indifference towards me. It reached a point where she even started to keep 'extra' food from me. If I took something from the fridge, Mum would go mad, scream and call me a thief. I couldn't win. Soon, I'd become so skinny that the school nurse flagged it up with the family GP. The doctor called me in for a check-up, along with Mum. He carried out a routine examination of my lungs, eyes and heart, then he recorded my height and asked me to stand on a set of weighing scales. He frowned as he slid the weight along a chest-height long metal pole. Then he logged all the information into a computer as Mum sat opposite him, watching like a hawk. The doctor nodded towards an empty chair and asked me to take a seat.

'It's like this, Mrs Cooper. Gaia is extremely underweight. I can see no obvious problems other than the fact she's far too thin for her age and height. She's eleven years old and, to be honest, she should weigh much more than she does.'

My mother stared at him in shock.

I have no food and it's all your fault, I thought bitterly.

Feeling annoyed, I bounced the heels of my shoes off the chair legs.

However, the doctor hadn't finished.

'I don't wish to worry you, but I suspect Gaia might have an eating disorder.'

Mum drew a sharp intake of breath. I watched as she held it inside her lungs before breathing out slowly.

'An eating disorder?'

The doctor nodded, and glanced from her to me and back again.

'Yes, I'm afraid so. It's unusual for girls of Gaia's age, as it often presents itself during the pubescent years, however it can and does happen. But don't worry. As long as we've identified it, then we can do something about it, can't we, Gaia? We can stop all this silly nonsense.'

The GP stared at me before turning his attention back to Mum, who twisted in her seat to look at me.

'I've tried everything, Doctor, but she's such a fussy eater.'

Liar . . ., I screamed silently inside my head.

My nails dug hard into the side of the plastic chair. I wanted to jump up onto it and shout as loud as my lungs would allow, *I'm skinny because she hardly gives me any food. When I try to take something from the fridge, she says I'm stealing*.

But I couldn't say it. I couldn't say anything because she was sitting right next to me. Besides, I knew she'd deny it and blame me.

Mum's answer to curing my 'eating disorder' was to place a Mars bar in my lunchbox the following morning for school. As soon as I spotted it, I gasped.

Maybe this is it? Maybe from now on things will be different.

I dared to hope. But my happiness was short-lived because she only did it once and never repeated it, although every now and again she'd throw in a few extra-cheap supermarket value snacks to keep me from becoming too emaciated.

My humiliation didn't end there. A short while later, I started my period. I was so shocked and underprepared that I ran straight home after school and picked up the phone to call Mum at work.

'It's Gaia. Can I speak to Mum, erm, Tracey Cooper, please?' I garbled down the phone to her male work colleague.

Moments later, I heard muffled voices and the rustling of paper as he passed her the receiver.

'Hello?'

'Mum, it's me, Gaia. I think I've started my period today. I was at school and …'

But she'd gone. I stood there and listened as she pulled the receiver away from her mouth to tell the rest of the shop the news.

'It's Gaia, she's just become a woman! Started her period today!'

I imagined the gasps, but all I could do was cringe on the other end of the line. I wanted to die.

Please don't.

Only it was too late.

'Yeah, she's eleven … today, apparently. Yeah … great, isn't it?'

I stared at the phone and slammed the receiver down in shock. Unsure what else to do, I went upstairs to Mum's bedroom. I knew she kept some sanitary pads in a bedside drawer, so I took a couple. Later that evening, when she returned home, I could barely look at her.

'Here, I bought you something,' she said.

With that, she tossed a packet of sanitary towels over to me.

'You know how to use them, right?'

I nodded as I flushed with embarrassment.

Only her temporary act of kindness had been too good to be true because once the packet ran out, she only bought a few more packs for me. Even then, they were a supermarket value brand that didn't stick and would fall out of my knickers. Soon, even these got used up and she stopped buying me anything. With nothing to protect my clothes, I did the only thing I could – I went back into her bedroom to take some of hers. When she later discovered what I'd done, she went crackers.

'Richard, she's been in our bedroom again. She's stolen from me, haven't you?'

Mum narrowed her eyes in annoyance.

I shook my head defiantly, because I didn't consider 'borrowing' a few sanitary towels the same as stealing.

'I only borrowed them,' I said, as I turned to look back at the TV.

I didn't want to say 'sanitary towel' because my stepfather was sitting just a few feet away.

'Things? *Things?* You've taken sanitary pads out of my bedside cabinet again, you little thief.'

My face burned as my stepdad looked away and pretended he hadn't heard. At that moment I hated her more than anything. I wanted to shout out that I wouldn't have to go into her bedroom if she'd just bought them, like other mums. But Mum hadn't finished.

'I always know when she's on her period, because all the toilet paper in this house goes.'

Tears pricked at the backs of my eyes and I ran shame-faced from the front room.

A few days later she fitted a lock on her bedroom door to try and keep me out. I passed her at the top of the stairs on my way to the loo. She'd just packed away the last of her tools and, as she straightened up, she dusted both hands against her long hippy skirt. Then she looked at me for a moment.

'You little thief! You won't be getting in my room any longer now, will you?'

I couldn't understand why she was being so mean to me. I also knew that if I was going to survive my periods then I'd have to come up with a plan. I didn't get any pocket money and now, with her bedroom out of bounds, I had no way of getting sanitary products.

Instead, whenever I knew my period was due, I'd try and bag an invite back to a friend's house for tea. Once inside, I'd ask to use the toilet and search through the bathroom cupboards for something – anything – I could use. I'd take my school bag up there with me and 'borrow' three or four pads – however many I thought I could get away with. Technically, I knew it was stealing, but I was desperate.

To try and boost my free supply of sanitary pads, I started to cut out coupons from inside women's maga-zines. I'd fill them in and send them off for free samples. Thankfully, they'd always be delivered in a small, discreet white box. I don't know how Mum thought I was coping or managing each month because she never asked. Besides, I didn't want to tell her where I was getting all the pads from. I realised it would be far too risky to throw the used ones into the bin in case she spotted them. Instead, I'd roll them up in a piece of tissue paper and hide them at the bottom of a cupboard in my bedroom. I loved my bedroom and, unlike other children my age, would keep it immaculate. I'd always been an unusually clean child. I often wonder if it's because it was the only thing I had any control over in my life. My bedroom was always spic and span, so I have no idea what made my mother search it one day but she was waiting for me when I came in from school.

'You dirty little cow!' she screamed.

I was still only halfway in through the door when she started on me.

'How could you be so disgusting? What the hell are these doing inside your cupboard?'

She held up a mound of creased tissues in her hand.

'I ... I ...'

My voice quivered and I began to stammer because I didn't have an answer. Instead, I stood there silently as I burned with shame.

'There's something wrong with you. You're not normal. Normal girls don't keep used sanitary towels in their bedroom cupboard. I'm seriously worried about you.'

She seemed manic, tapping a finger against the side of her head as though I'd lost the plot. But she knew why I'd done it. Almost overnight I'd become a frightened, anxious and secretive child. It was the only way I knew how to survive.

To try and blend in at school, I decided to knock around with the clever kids. I knew, without a doubt, that the popular ones would never accept me. However, if I hoped that some of their cleverness might rub off on me then I was wrong. Sitting with the swots didn't stop me from failing my 11-plus exam, much to my mother's disapproval. After the summer holidays, I was sent to a comprehensive instead of the more prestigious grammar school. However, instead of enrolling at the one right on our doorstep, Mum decided to send me to another school that was a thirty-minute walk and a bus ride away. Once again, I decided to knock around with the brainy kids, choosing the sort of friends a parent would choose for their own child.

I became particularly friendly with a girl called Savannah in the year above me. Savannah was clever and well liked, so I unexpectedly found myself in the popular set by default. I thought I'd made it, until one day she had a massive falling-out with a girl called Denise from a neighbouring school. A fight had been arranged between both girls but, for whatever reason, nothing happened. I was a natural peacemaker and I tried my best to smooth things over, but then I found myself drawn into their argument.

Savannah had accused me of taking Denise's side and soon I became persona non grata. Savannah was popular, so the other girls also turned against me. Things became so difficult that I began to knock around with the boys. I'd always been a natural tomboy anyway, and I realised they'd be a much safer option. Soon, the school broke up for half-term holidays. I was twelve years old, when one of my friends – a boy called Thomas – came to the house to look for me. Thomas was with his friends Neil and Luke when he knocked on my front door to ask if I wanted to go and hang out together.

Unfortunately, Mum reached the front door before me.

Thomas was a nice, clever boy and he came from a good family. He had impeccable manners, so nothing could have prepared him for what was about to follow. I'd been upstairs, listening to music in my bedroom, when I heard the knock on the door. I ran over to the window and spotted the three boys below. Mum answered the door and I realised I had to get down there fast.

'Yes,' I heard her say, as I charged down the stairs.

I could just imagine her eyes narrowing with suspicion as she took in my three friends on the doorstop.

I heard Thomas's voice as it floated through the open door.

'We just wondered if Gaia was in and if she wanted to come out for a while.'

I'd just reached the bottom step when Mum's reply stopped me dead in my tracks.

'Listen, I'm not having you lot knock round here, sniffing after her cunt …'

I froze. The bottom step faced the door, and I could see Thomas – the outline of his small frame and the tell-tale colour of his football shirt – distorted through the thick glass. I was just grateful he couldn't see my horrified face, or me his.

Oh my God!

I couldn't believe Mum would even think something like that, never mind say it. I felt sick with embarrassment, sick at the thought of ever having to face Thomas or the others again. He was a good boy from a nice family; I was certain he'd never heard language like that before.

Still, Mum slammed the door straight in his face as my stepfather came marching through into the hallway. It was obvious he'd also overheard.

'Tracey! What the hell?'

Richard's eyes flitted between me and her, as though searching for an answer. But I couldn't look at him – I couldn't look at anyone. Mum either didn't care or couldn't see what she'd done wrong. She simply shrugged her shoulders, pushed past us both and made her way through to the kitchen as though nothing weird had just happened.

Afterwards, Thomas and his friends stopped hanging around with me. In fact, no one did. Sadly, I still had to catch the bus to and from school, which meant a good thirty-minute walk into town. Other girls – friends of Savannah – would walk behind, taunting me.

'Look at the state of that,' one hissed.

My breath snagged inside my chest as my steps began to quicken.

'Yeah, she thinks she's so special but look at the state of her. I heard her mum's a weirdo too.'

The situation with Thomas had been bad enough, but things had grown even more toxic between Savannah and me. They became so bad that her older sister, who had already left school, got involved. She'd started to ring me at home just to threaten me down the phone.

'Wait till I get you on your own, you little bitch. Just wait till I catch you, you little slag. You dropped my sister for that cow Denise.'

The situation became so bad that I tried to do anything to get out of class, even explaining things to Mum – but she was less than sympathetic.

'You just can't keep running away from problems, Gaia. You have to face them head on.'

It was fine for her to say that, but she'd caused most of my problems. She wasn't the one who had to go to school either.

'Please don't send me back there, I'm frightened,' I begged.

However, she refused to listen or even offer support.

'Well, you wouldn't have to go there if you'd tried harder in your exams.'

Despite everything – and to her credit – she must have finally taken my fears onboard. Not long afterwards, Mum announced I'd be enrolling at the school around the corner. It wasn't a very academic school, and its students achieved much lower grades, but at least I knew I wouldn't have to spend the rest of the school year looking over my shoulder.

I'd just turned thirteen and this would be my fresh start.

CHAPTER THREE

FOOD AND TADPOLES

I found my teenage years particularly challenging. I also realised they were a time when a girl really needed her mother.

After she'd fixed a lock on her bedroom door, Mum became paranoid about me being in the house alone. She didn't finish work until 5.30 p.m., so she'd keep me locked out and refused to give me a key. With nowhere else to go to keep warm, I'd nip into town, where I'd trawl the make-up counters, trying on products to kill time. The first eye-shadow I stole was a breeze, so the next time I helped myself to a lip gloss. A small bottle of foundation followed until soon, nicking make-up from town had become my new hobby. Tall and skinny for my age, I could have passed for someone much older, so the shop assistants tended to leave me alone as I browsed the counters.

Unsurprisingly, I'd also started to rebel at school. Once, on a school trip, me and some other girls managed to get hold of some bottles of Hooch. I poured mine into an Evian water bottle and held it in my hand so that the teacher wouldn't get suspicious. But as soon as I stepped on the coach, my maths teacher stood in front of me, blocking my path.

'What's in the bottle, Gaia?'

I gulped. The guilt was written all over my face.

'Squash, sir.'

He nodded knowingly.

'Squash? Right, well, I don't suppose you'll mind me having a try of it then?'

As soon as he removed the bottle from my hands, I knew I was doomed. I looked to the others for back-up, but realised that no one was going to throw themselves under the bus for me. I immediately burst into tears. They streamed down my face as the teacher confiscated all the girls' 'squash' bottles. I'd just blown it. I also knew the others would kill me for being caught out. Although they didn't blame me, the school did, and I was suspended. My reputation had begun to precede me.

With both front and back doors locked at home, I'd often have to wait in the garden, starving hungry and desperate for food. Following my sanitary towel 'theft', Mum started to accuse me of stealing all her food.

'But I'm hungry!' I protested.

'Greedy, more like.'

The reality was I was a growing teenager and I needed to eat to fuel my rapid growth.

I'd feel hungry all the time, and I tried to eat whenever and wherever I could. As soon as I spotted an opportunity, I'd take it – not because I was naughty, but because I was starving.

Each day, Mum would make me take a packed lunch because it was cheaper than school dinners. To try and cut corners, she'd buy everything from everything from a supermarket basics range. Every lunchtime I would sit and watch as my friends opened their packed lunches – an array of thick, doorstep sandwiches, oozing with too much filling. They'd even have extra bags of crisps and posh chocolate bars too. Then I'd look down at my own packed lunch – a mixture of cheap, thin and unsatisfying food. My sandwiches would be a smear of sandwich spread on thin, white bread, and all my extra 'treats' were wrapped in tell-tale blue and white striped garish packets. I despised that packaging because it marked me out from my classmates. It reinforced the idea that I wasn't good enough and I didn't deserve to have anything nice to eat. The cheap blue stripes told me that Mum didn't care enough to pack me a decent lunch to eat. I longed to be normal and to eat normal food. Even a bag of supermarket crisps in a regular, brightly coloured packet would have felt like a special treat.

I was hungry all the time and I became so desperate that I'd jump the dinner queue so I could memorise the numbers of the kids who received free school meals.

One day, I took my place behind a girl who I knew came from a single-parent family. The dinner lady looked at her.

'Number?'

'132,' she replied.

The dinner lady noted it down and handed her a plate piled high with mashed potato, vegetables, meat and gravy as I slipped away. My mouth was still watering as I wandered off to find somewhere private to eat my depressing value meal. The following day I spotted the same girl as she headed towards the dining hall. I ran ahead to join the queue first. Looking over my shoulder,

I kept a check to make sure she was still behind me in the queue. Soon, I'd reached the front.

'Number?' the dinner lady asked, without looking up.

It was the same one from the day before. My stomach knotted with anxiety because I knew what I was doing was technically stealing. But I was so famished that my hunger pangs overruled any reservations I had.

'132,' I replied.

I waited for her to look up, narrow her eyes and call a teacher over, only she didn't. Instead, she jotted the number down and told me to move along to pick out my free school meal. It was so easy. I'd just left – a huge plate of fish and chips in my hands – and was looking for somewhere to sit when I heard a loud commotion coming from behind.

'No, you've already been,' the dinner lady said, as her voice rose above the general hum of chatter.

'I haven't. That's my number and I haven't had anything to eat.'

It was the girl – the one whose number I'd just stolen. I watched the dinner lady as she traced a finger down the list of numbers. Then she stopped and tapped a finger against her clipboard.

'No, look!' she said, turning the board to the girl. 'I've already ticked you off, so you must have been.'

The girl became upset and a pang of conscience shot through me. She was adamant she'd not yet eaten. I watched from a safe distance – tray in hand – as she folded both arms and refused to move. The dinner lady also refused to back down, so a teacher was called to sort it out.

I thought the guilt I felt might make the food stick inside my throat, but I was far too hungry for that. As I carried my plate back to the trolley, I spotted the girl. She was sitting alone at a table next to the kitchen with a plate of random food in front of her. I guessed she must have been given whatever was left. She was still upset because she stabbed an angry fork at her food. The girl must have sensed someone watching her because she glanced over in my direction. I turned away guiltily. Hunger had forced me to become devious in a way I'd never been before.

A couple of days later I came home from school to find the door locked as usual. I was standing there when Hendrix, our black and white cat, sashayed past me and went inside through the cat flap. The miniature plastic door rattled behind him, as he padded around the kitchen. A thin drizzle of rain had just begun to fall outside, soaking me to the skin. I dipped down and watched enviously as Hendrix tucked into his food.

She feeds him more than she feeds me.

I was still watching when an idea popped into my head. I removed my coat and, on my hands and knees, rolled up the sleeve of my school sweater. I threaded my bare arm inside the cat flap. Bending it at the elbow, I stretched my fingers out as far as they would go.

'Arrghh!' I shouted in frustration.

I tried a few more times but to no avail. Hunger rumbled inside, encouraging me to try again.

Wiping wet strands of hair from my face, I pushed my right shoulder up against the door to try and get more leverage. With the side of my head pressed against the door, I couldn't see a thing and would have to do it by touch alone. With my hand outstretched, I waved against nothingness until suddenly I felt something. A carrier bag rustled between my fingertips as I tried to grab it. It took me a few goes, but somehow I managed to pull and unhook it from the door handle. I tugged at it until something plopped against the kitchen floor. Hendrix came over to inspect the single bag of value crisps, but I grabbed it before he could and dragged it back through the cat flap.

'Bingo!'

As I hungrily tucked into the bag of crisps, I made a mental note to leave one of the carrier bag's handles unlooped next time to make things a little easier. As long as I didn't eat all the packs in one go, Mum would be none the wiser. However, food – or the lack of it – wasn't my only problem.

One afternoon, I returned home and settled down for my two-hour wait. I was sitting there when I realised that I desperately needed the loo. My bladder felt fit to burst as I scanned the back garden, looking for a place to pee. Our backyard was sparse; it had mostly been concreted over, but there were a few chipped pots dotted around with half-dead shrubs inside them. The shed was locked, and right next to it there was a smelly old fish tank that Mum had dumped. The garden was overlooked by neighbours on both sides, so there was no privacy and nowhere for me to pee. With no other choice, I decided to shin up onto the shed's flat roof. From there I shinned across the extension and in through Mum's half-open bedroom window. Once inside, I ran through and made it to the bathroom with seconds to spare. Mum usually kept her bedroom locked, but only when I was inside the house. With me waiting outside she'd left it open. A few hours later I was sat watching TV when I heard her come in. As soon as she saw me, her face dropped.

'How the hell did you get in?'

The keys rattled in her right hand as she perched it angrily against her hip.

I didn't know what else to say, so I told the truth.

'I was bursting for the loo. Your bedroom window was open, so I climbed up onto the shed and through it.'

Mum's eyes widened in surprise.

'You've been in my bedroom?' she shouted.

Her voice was so loud that it boomed across the front room, anger reverberating off the walls.

Clutching my legs, I pulled my knees up against my chest defensively.

'I was bursting for the loo. The window was open but the front door was locked and I ...'

But Mum's face had turned purple with rage.

'I don't give a shit! I keep that front door locked to keep you out of my bedroom.'

She turned to leave, but must have thought better of it because she spun back to face me, her finger still wagging.

'You'd better not have taken anything, because if you have ...'

I trembled against the sofa. I'd never seen her so angry.

'I didn't, I promise. I didn't touch anything. I just needed the loo.'

She grunted as though she didn't believe a word of it, turned and stormed out of the front room. Seconds later, I heard the click of the telephone receiver as she picked it up and dialled a number. The door to the front room had been left half-open so I tiptoed over to it to try and listen.

'Hello, yes. Could I have the police, please?'

I was confused.

Why was she ringing the police?

44

There was a slight pause as someone put her call through. Then she began to speak again.

'Hello, yes, my name is Tracey Cooper. I'd like to report a break-in at my house.'

My mouth went bone dry as I swallowed hard.

She was calling the police ... about me?

I decided it must be a wind-up.

She's not really calling them; she's just doing it to spook me out.

But this was Mum – anything was possible.

I continued to listen.

'What? No, they're still here, in the house. Yes, yes, I'm fine ... hmmm, that's right ... yes, through an open window ... my bedroom window. Yes, that's right. Yes, I do know them, it's my thirteen-year-old daughter.'

There was a slight pause as the police officer replied on the other end of the line. Undeterred, Mum pressed on.

'Yes, I understand that, but she broke in. She did it when I wasn't here. She climbed through an upstairs window into my bedroom.'

I imagined the officer shaking his head in disbelief as he listened to her. Mum became annoyed because it was obvious the officer wasn't taking her complaint seriously. Her voice grew louder as her patience ebbed away.

'Yes, she was locked out of the house. You don't under-stand. I have to lock her out of it because she steals from me. What? Food, she steals food. Anyway, she broke into the house after school.'

There was another pause and another question.

'Yes, of course she lives here, but I can't see what that has to do with anything. What do you mean? Why can't you do anything?'

She sounded beyond furious.

I couldn't help it – a smirk spread across my face. It was clear the police weren't going to do a single thing. I'd won, for now.

There was a short jingle as Mum slammed down the receiver in a temper. I backed away from the door and snuck back onto the sofa.

'Bloody useless!'

It had only been a small victory but a victory all the same. I was just thirteen. They must have thought she was completely mad.

In an act of revenge, a few days later I was hanging around the garden with time to kill when I spotted her dirty old fish tank over in the corner. Although the glass was cracked, it was Mum's pride and joy. The fish tank repulsed me; its sides were covered in a thick, green slime and it was half-full of stagnant water that stank to high heaven whenever the sun shone. Mum loved the tank and the frogs she was trying to incubate in it. I hated frogs – their slimy skin freaked me out and the thought of them hopping all over the garden filled me with dread. I despised the way the water's surface twitched with all the fledgling tadpoles living beneath. For once the shed door had been left unlocked so I wandered inside to look for something. My eyes scanned the shelves before they rested on a distinctive bottle. *FLASH* – the label's yellow letters read. Underneath there were more – *with bleach*.

'You'll do,' I decided, as I picked up the bottle and headed back to the fish tank.

I pumped the bottle's spray nozzle handle, until soon I'd emptied the entire contents in the tank. Then I hid it inside a thick privet hedge at the side of the garden.

On Saturday morning there was a loud scream from the bottom of the garden. Mum had gone to peg some clothes on the line, but as soon as she spotted the tank she froze. I wandered to the kitchen window to watch the drama unfold.

'Richard ... Richard ... come quickly!' she screamed.

Mum clutched a hand against her chest in shock as my stepdad dashed outside to find her hovering over the fish tank.

'Look,' she gasped, 'they're dead. All dead.'

I turned away and smirked. I'd never done anything cruel before in my life, but I was glad I'd done it. I'd hurt her, just as she'd hurt me. For the first time in my life, I'd won.

CHAPTER FOUR

CAR

I'd been at my new school for almost a year when I became friends with a girl called Scarlett. I'd first met her through Denise, although I was unsure how they knew each other. I think they might have both been at the same school before Scarlett was expelled for disruptive behaviour. As a result, she had to attend a pupil referral unit school in the centre of town. It wasn't that she was naughty – she'd never been in trouble with the police or anything like that – she was just a bit of a handful. She was also a real laugh and a fun person to hang out with.

At just sixteen years old, Scarlett was a couple of school years above me, so I really looked up to her. Unlike me, my new friend had a Saturday job in a local hair salon. Her dream was to become a hairdresser, so she swept the floors and washed hair to try and gain experience. With a part-time job and all the best clothes to wear, Scarlett seemed extremely sophisticated. She had her own money to spend and didn't have to answer to her mother, like I did.

When I first met Scarlett's mum Sandy, I realised why Scarlett and I had connected so quickly – Sandy was a hippy, just like my mum, both women were in their late thirties and she dressed in long, flowing skirts and kaftans. But that's where the similarities ended. Her hair was long and black, and unlike Mum she was kind, and it was obvious she adored her daughter.

'Gaia, your name is lovely,' she said as soon as Scarlett introduced us.

I couldn't stop smiling because it was the first time anyone had said anything nice about my stupid name. Most people would mispronounce it. They'd call me Gay-a, instead of Guy-a. Some kids at school teased me about it and asked if I'd been called it because I was a lesbian. It was puerile stuff, but then I'd heard far worse at home.

'Yes, I love that name,' Sandy said, lifting her face to smile.

'Thanks.'

I was unsure what else to say because I wasn't used to compliments.

Scarlett decided to make me her pet project and she soon took me under her wing. She became the older sister I'd never had, and I longed to be just like her. My new friend smoked, so I decided I would start. Sandy realised her daughter smoked and would allow her to do it at home. Meanwhile, I'd hide my roll ups in a medium-sized, lidded box that I stashed inside my bedroom cupboard. Once I'd smoked my illicit cigarettes, hanging out of my half-opened bedroom window, I'd stub the butts out on the brick window ledge before tossing them into the box to dispose of the evidence. I'd stash the box, which was the size of a small breakfast bowl, on a shelf, tucked in behind my jumpers.

Not long afterwards, I returned home to find Mum standing in the kitchen, waiting for me. As soon as I came through the door, she pulled my secret cigarette box out from behind her back.

'What's this?'

I couldn't look at her. Guilt was written all over my face as though someone had scribbled it in black marker pen.

'Gaia, are you listening to me? I said, what's this?' she asked, impatiently tapping her boot against the floor in annoyance.

I knew I'd just been caught bang to rights and there was no point in lying. Also, fearing she'd lose her shit, I decided to stay silent. But that only seemed to enrage her more.

Tap, tap, tap.

'Gaia, I'm going to ask you one more time, what is …?'

'It's a box – a jewellery box, okay!'

I knew what was coming, I could feel it building in the air – the mother of all tellings-off. Mum nodded knowingly.

'A jewellery box, you say. Well, if it's a jewellery box, then why does it have a half-smoked cigarette inside?'

She lifted the lid and pulled out the evidence. She held it between her fingers as though it was poison. I realised anything I said would just make things worse.

'Dunno,' I shrugged, as I averted my eyes to the floor.

'You don't know?'

Mum's temper began to boil.

'Well, I'll tell you what it is. It's disgusting, that's what it is! It's a disgusting habit and it stops right here, right now.'

I flinched as she threw the cigarette like a dart at my face, just missing me. Incensed, she then threw the box at me, which struck the side of my face. The lid came flying off on impact, and I was dusted in a shower of ash and cig butts. They landed in my hair and scattered all over my clothes. It was disgusting, and now I smelled disgusting.

'What the hell …!'

Mum pointed at me.

'I'll not have you smoking in this house. Do you hear me?'

She reached forward and grabbed me by the top of my arm to try and hold me still.

'And look at me when I'm speaking to you.'

I couldn't, I was too angry.

'I said, did you hear me?'

I nodded angrily, just so I could escape.

'Go!' she screamed, pointing at the door.

I ran up to my bedroom and slammed the door. I checked the side of my face where the edge of the box had struck me. It didn't hurt, but Mum's discovery had thoroughly pissed me off because I knew I'd never be able to smoke in secret again. Another freedom lost.

I wondered why she couldn't be more like Sandy, who was a hippy both by name and nature. Anything seemed to set Mum off these days. I decided to avoid her and spend as much time as I could at Scarlett's. Of course, she also had something to say about that.

'That Scarlett is a little slag. I don't know why you'd want to hang around with her.'

But I knew Scarlett wasn't a slag. In fact, she was still a virgin, unlike me. A few months previously I'd met a lad called Jack, just after my fourteenth birthday. Denise knew him and had introduced us, so when Jack made a move, I let things happen. At fifteen, Jack seemed to know way more about sex than I did, and when he pulled out a gold-coloured square packet from his back pocket, I didn't have a clue what it was.

'It's a johnnie,' he grinned, before ripping open the packet with his teeth.

I was so naive that I didn't understand what a johnnie was. It was only when he put it on himself that I realised what was about to happen, and I let it. Essentially, I craved love and affection – something I didn't get at home. Even the wrong sort of affection from a sex-mad teenage boy felt better than nothing. I didn't enjoy the sex, but at least it had been consensual. If Mum thought Scarlett was a slag, then God only knows what she'd have thought about me. Her dislike of Scarlett only pushed me towards her. In fact, I'd become such a regular visitor to their home that Sandy became a substitute mother.

A few weeks later I walked into town so I could meet Scarlett from the pupil referral unit. With little else to do, we headed back to her house, sat on the bed, and started to smoke. I'd only just lit up my first cigarette when Scarlett turned to look at me.

'Gaia, do you know a boy called Ali?'

I knew a few Muslim lads at my school but I hadn't heard of anyone with that name. I shook my head as I passed her the cigarette; she perched it between her lip-glossed mouth and took a long, slow drag.

'Why, which school does he go to?'

Scarlett began to laugh and blew the smoke out of her mouth. It caused her to choke and then begin to cough. She hammered a fist hard against her chest to try and stop.

'What is it? What's so funny?' I asked, feeling stupid.

It took her a while but eventually, Scarlett's cough began to subside. She stubbed out the remainder of the cigarette, rolled her eyes and smiled knowingly.

'Don't be stupid. Ali doesn't go to school. Not anymore, anyway. He's way older than me.'

'Older? Why, how old is he?'

She rolled her eyes again. It was obvious she was revelling in my shock.

'Oh, I dunno. He's twenty or something.'

I sat bolt upright on the bed and stared back at her in disbelief.

'Twenty? Christ, Scarlett, how do you know him? Where did you meet?'

She seemed a little coy and refused to be drawn further. She waved a hand in front of my face.

'Forget it, none of that matters … because you're going to meet him!' she said, excitement rising in her voice.

'We are …? When?'

Scarlett pushed up her sleeve and checked her watch.

'In about an hour. He's gonna pick us up.'

'What? From here?'

Scarlett nodded. I gasped and ran to check my reflection in her mirror. I needed time to fix my make-up and hair. The last thing I wanted to do was to show myself up. But Scarlett seemed unfazed. Instead, she picked up another cigarette and lifted the lighter to the end of it.

Click.

A bluish yellow flame danced in front of her face as she took one, then two puffs to try and get the tip of it to light.

'No, Gaia,' she said, blowing pale grey smoke out from the corner of her mouth. 'Mum would kill me. Not here, he's picking us up outside the shops.'

I looked back at my reflection and ran a hand through my long hair; it looked frizzy and had started to curl up at the ends like stale bread.

'God, look at the state of me, Scar. Can I borrow a lip gloss or something?'

The fag was still dangling from her mouth as Scarlett dipped to one side and picked up her make-up bag from the top of her bedside drawers.

'Knock yourself out,' she said, tossing it towards me.

I got to work, touching up my make-up. Once I was satisfied, I dragged a brush through my reddish blonde hair, twisting it this way and that, but no matter what I tried, nothing looked good enough.

'Could you blow-dry my hair, Scar? Please?'

'Okay.'

I beamed as she jumped off the bed, grabbed her hair-dryer and got to work. Ten minutes later I was done.

'There you go,' she said, standing back to admire her handiwork.

I looked in the mirror and pulled my fingers through my super-shiny locks.

'Thanks, Scar, it looks brilliant!'

'You're welcome. Shit!' she gasped, looking at her watch. 'Come on, Gaia, we gotta go!'

I picked up the lip gloss and Scarlett pulled on some clumpy black shoes.

'We can't be late, otherwise he'll leave without us.'

I grabbed what was left of our stash of cigarettes as we both ran downstairs.

'I'm just going out with Gaia, Mum. Won't be long,' Scarlett called, as we headed out through the front door.

'Okay, be good, and don't …' Sandy replied but we didn't hear the rest because we were already running along the street outside.

It was a hot summer's evening; the sky was light and the birds were still singing in the trees as we made our way through the housing estate. The shops were only a few streets away so we'd reached them minutes later. We waited outside a fast-food place selling mainly fried chicken, kebabs and pizzas, which was next door to a newsagent that doubled up as a local convenience store. The shop sold everyday goods at almost twice the price. Further along the row was a laundrette and a florist. The florist closed at 5 p.m., while the laundrette only seemed to cater for pensioners. They'd sit there for hours, watching their clothes tumble around large, battered machines as though they were TV sets. Apart from a stream of customers going into the fried chicken shop, the place was largely deserted.

Scarlett was determined that we didn't miss Ali. On the way over, she'd bored me senseless, telling me how good-looking he was and that he owned his own car. I was impressed. I'd never met a boy with his own car before. It soon became apparent Scarlett moved in very different circles to the ones I was used to.

Hoisting myself up onto a small brick wall that ran along the front of the shops, I perched myself next to my new friend. As we waited, I stole a quick glance; I couldn't believe Scarlett would want to be friends with someone like me. She was petite, with long, tumbling blonde hair that draped across both shoulders like a popstar. I was skinny and non-descript, but Scarlett was naturally curvy with big boobs that seemed to drive all the boys wild. I felt and looked positively dull sitting next to her.

I wish I looked more like you, I thought as the minutes ticked by. *You don't know how lucky you are.*

Scarlett twisted her head from side to side – her blonde hair falling to the left and then the right – as she scanned the road, looking out for Ali.

'What sort of car does he have?' I asked randomly.

It was a stupid thing to say and, as soon as it left my mouth, I realised that I didn't know the first thing about cars anyway.

But Scarlett hadn't heard me because she was too distracted. She checked her watch constantly and jiggled her legs. Impatiently, she drummed the thick heels of her chunky Spice Girl shoes against the wall.

'Where is he? He should be here by now,' she complained beneath her breath.

It was late June, so it was boiling hot, even at teatime. I ran my fingers through my hair to try and straighten it. The heat and sweat had made it go all frizzy again, and Scarlett's hard work had become undone.

'Where is he?'

My black flared trousers stuck to my legs in the stifling heat. I pulled at them, trying to peel them from the backs of my thighs as I shifted around uncomfortably.

'Are you sure he said the shops?'

Scarlett shot me a glance, a flicker of annoyance flashing across her face.

'Yeah, of course I am.'

Her voice trailed off as she checked the road again, twisting in both directions.

In the end, we waited for almost two hours before the spluttering sounds of a souped-up car engine broke the silence. Scarlett's face lit up with delight as she jumped down off the wall. She ran both hands down the legs of her trousers to try and straighten them out before hoisting them back up by the waistband.

'Here he is, here's Ali!' she beamed.

Scarlett stepped forward and began waving as a knackered old car chugged into view. She was still smiling as she dashed over to the kerbside to greet him. The clapped-out brown Renault had seen better days. It creaked as it pulled up along the kerb and came to an abrupt halt in front of us. There was music playing inside the car. It was so loud that I heard it even before Ali had wound down his window.

Thud, thud, thud.

I vaguely recognised the garage track as it blasted out from the car's tinny stereo. Although Scarlett had gone over to speak to him, Ali didn't turn the music off or even attempt to turn it down. It was so loud that she had to shout above it just to be heard.

Thud, thud, thud.

I wondered if she might say something to Ali about being late, but she didn't.

'It's good to see you!'

Ali, who looked in his twenties, nodded. Then he smirked as he took in my friend from her head to her toes. She was right, he was absolutely gorgeous, with hair that flopped playfully across his eyes as though he'd just stepped out of a boyband video. Something unnerved me, however. I couldn't place it, and I wondered if it had just been the way he'd looked her up and down. Although she'd mentioned Ali's age, I was surprised by how much younger she looked than him. Scarlett was only sixteen, but this lad was clearly six or seven years her senior. Pretty or not, I wondered why an older boy would want to hang around with a couple of schoolgirls like us.

'You been waiting long?' Ali shouted over the pounding music.

'Nah, we've only just got here,' Scarlett lied.

She played with a strand of her hair, twirling it around her finger as she spoke and I could tell she really fancied him. She leaned into the car, trying to get her face as close as possible to his. Ali dipped forward in the driver's seat as though trying to look past her.

'Who's your friend?' he asked, pointing over to me.

My stomach flipped, and suddenly I felt young and self-conscious. I knew I was way out of my comfort zone.

'Oh, that's Gaia,' Scarlett said, nodding over in my general direction.

Then she turned her attention back to Ali as I sat on the wall, feeling like a spare part. I hated being the odd one out – I'd had a lifetime of it. I was just wondering what excuse I could make to get up and leave when Ali shouted something.

'Oh, this is my mate, Salim.'

My stomach somersaulted because I knew Salim – or Sal, as everyone called him. I'd seen him hanging around town. In fact, his sister had gone to my old school, and I'd once stupidly revealed that I had a crush on her brother.

'Really?' she'd gasped, wrinkling her nose at the thought.

Now he was here. My heart sank.

What if she'd told him?

I cringed at the thought.

Ali gestured towards Sal, who was sitting in the passenger seat. I dipped down to try and see, but he was hidden by Ali's shadow and the darkness of the car. My stomach fluttered because I knew what this meant – it was going to be a double-date.

The car roared as Ali pressed an impatient foot against the accelerator. A thick cloud of black smoke flew out of the exhaust pipe and rose up into the air.

'Well, are you girls gonna get in the car, or what?'

He didn't need to ask Scarlett twice because she almost squealed with delight. There was a sudden movement in the shadows. The passenger door opened and out climbed Sal. He was Moroccan, with a box-style haircut and tramlines cut into both sides. He was wearing his trademark bomber jacket, trackie bottoms and Nike trainers. I watched in silence as he dipped down, clicked the passenger seat forward and held the door open for Scarlett. She walked around to his side and began to climb into the back. As she did, she stopped for a moment and straightened up.

'Come on, Gaia,' she shouted.

Scarlett lifted her hand and beckoned me over. I couldn't explain it, but something told me not to get into that car. The instinct was so overwhelming that I could almost taste it on the tip of my tongue, but although my brain screamed at me to stay exactly where I was, I ignored it. I jumped down off the wall and approached the car. My friend seemed so happy, and I didn't want to be the one to burst her bubble.

I'm with Scarlett. I'll be fine. We'll be fine.

Stepping across the grass verge, I looked over at Sal, who was standing there, holding the car door open. As I went to climb inside the vehicle, I raised my face to say thanks, and that's when I saw it. It had only been fleeting but I knew what I'd seen. Sal sneered at Ali, as though the two were sharing a secret joke that we weren't privy to. Needles of anxiety stabbed inside my stomach.

The car ... don't get in the car, a voice inside me warned.

But I did. And that's when I knew – I knew without a doubt – that as soon as I climbed into the back of that car, my life would change forever. And I was right: it did.

CHAPTER FIVE

THE SHOP

The car stank of dope. At first, I wasn't sure what the odd smell was, but then I watched from the back seat as Ali passed Sal a long joint. Hot rocks of hash spilled from the end of it, making Ali hop around behind the wheel. He brushed his hand against his joggers as the car swerved and veered over to the wrong side of the road.

'Watch out!'

It was Scarlett. She'd seen what had happened before anyone else did. Ali glanced up and grabbed the wheel as the car careered sharply back to the right side of the road.

'Shit, man!' Ali complained, still brushing a hand against his trackie bottoms. 'You almost burnt a hole in me, didn't you, bruv.'

His remark made Sal cackle with laughter, and soon Ali joined in. He took a long drag on the joint before passing it back to his mate. Sal pulled up his feet and rested both trainers on the car's dashboard.

'Want some?' Sal asked.

He held his right arm behind his head. It dangled there, swinging in time with the car's movements as he held the spliff precariously between two fingers.

A plume of blueish-grey smoke rose above his head as he exhaled.

Scarlett was older and wiser than me, so I looked to her for guidance. She dipped forward and plucked the spliff from Sal's fingers. He grinned and nodded approvingly. I knew it would soon be my turn, but I felt too unsure. I'd only just started smoking but drugs were a whole new world. As the distinctive, sweet aroma filled the car, I closed my eyes for a moment as I tried to recall where I'd smelled it before. Suddenly, I was transported right back to a stranger's flat. The place had been poky and dark. Mum and I had to climb two flights of concrete steps just to reach the front door, which was painted red. The stairwell smelled of wee and I'd held my nose so I didn't have to breathe it in.

I opened my eyes.

What the hell had we been doing there?

I closed them again as I tried to scour my memory for more details.

A Formica table in the middle of the room, with a man standing next to it. A dark flat … curtains drawn, even though it was the middle of the day.

I tried to think. Tried to remember.

A large, brown slab in the middle of the table … Mum looked on, watching as he cut into it. His birthday? No, it wasn't cake, it smelled of herbs. A dirty table. A full ashtray spilling grey ash … a tiny piece of cardboard that had been ripped.

The smell, that smell. My nostrils flared with the memory.

The man had a knife. He'd cut a piece off the cake. Not a slice, a chunk. Small weighing scales that rattled as he placed the brown chunk onto it. Money. A long, white cigarette, still burning in the ashtray. Smoke curling up into the air. Drugs?

I shook my head. I couldn't be certain, but the smell transported me right back there.

The man lifting the cigarette … blueish-grey smoke.

Think. Try to remember.

'What's wrong with this one, Scar?'

It was Sal. The sound of his voice jolted me back into the moment. I opened both eyes with a jolt.

'Is she already stoned, or what?' he laughed, as he directed the question to my friend.

Scarlett shot me a look with widened eyes, as if to say, 'Don't show me up.'

Smoke from the spliff rose upwards and into my face. I glanced down at it, wedged between her fingers. It burned away between us as she waited for me to take it from her.

'Er, I … I …' I stammered.

I racked my brain, trying to think of an excuse not to take it.

'Go on, Gaia.'

It was Scarlett. She nudged her hand against mine as she shoved the spliff in my direction. With one eyebrow arched, she waited for me to take it. I became conscious of Sal staring at me. He'd twisted in his seat to get a good look.

'No, I'm not bothered.'

Sal threw his head back and snorted as though he was in shock. But I didn't want the spliff. I didn't even want to be inside the car – a car travelling too fast with Sal and a man I'd never met before.

What the hell am I doing?

'Come on, Gaia.'

It was Scarlett again.

I was worried she'd think I was pathetic, but I didn't want to smoke the joint. I was fourteen years old and felt way out of my depth.

'Ha, cuz, she's just dipped out,' Sal said, still smirking.

He nudged Ali's shoulder and began to take the piss out of me. I withered with embarrassment and shrank down into my seat, trying to make myself small. However, when I looked up, Ali was staring at me in the windscreen mirror.

'Aww, what's wrong? Is it past your bedtime?' he whined.

Sal burst out laughing as my face burned.

'Come on, it's only a bit of solid,' Sal teased.

He leered at me.

'You should have some, it might loosen you up and make you feel reaaaal niiiice,' he said, stretching the last two words out.

I couldn't look at Scarlett, but I didn't have to. Her stiffened body language told me all I needed to know. I'd shown her up.

'It's okay,' she said breezily. 'It'll just leave more for me.'

Sal punched the air with his fist and cheered.

The Rizla paper crackled and burned as she took another long drag, pulling the smoke into both lungs. I watched in awe, feeling foolish.

I wish I was more like Scarlett.

We drove around the streets for a bit before Ali parked up in the middle of nowhere – a place without street lights or CCTV cameras. The men sparked up a couple more spliffs and smoked them, before beginning to rip the piss out of each other. It was just banter – the kind of things young boys do when they're trying to impress a couple of girls. But these weren't boys, these were grown men in their twenties. As I stared out into the darkened night, I fretted something bad might happen. Thankfully, nothing did. A couple of hours later Ali drove us back to Scarlett's estate, where we were unceremoniously dumped back by the shops. I was relieved we were both still in one piece, and I questioned my earlier uneasiness.

Maybe I'd been wrong?

'That wasn't so bad, was it?' Scarlett said.

She linked her arm through mine as we headed back to her house.

'No, it was fun,' I lied.

But it hadn't been fun. It had felt weird and way too grown up. I'd been way out of my depth, even though nothing had happened.

Maybe Sal's right. Maybe I need to chill out more?

The second time Ali and Sal picked me up I was alone. Scarlett had arranged it, but then she'd been called into work at the last minute. Sadly, I didn't have the same excuse when Ali texted me. I stared down at the screen of my new Nokia mobile phone.

See u outside shops. Don't be late.

I'd taken a seat on the wall and prepared myself for a long wait when Ali's car zoomed into view. It was going too fast and he had to brake sharply. This caused the car to splutter as it came to a sudden halt right in front of me. Although I felt nervous, I was secretly delighted to see Sal, who I'd decided I had a crush on.

'Hiya,' I smiled.

Sal climbed out of the car to let me get in the back. I wasn't sure where we'd be going but I didn't care. I also decided that if they did offer me a spliff, this time I'd try it. I was sick of being different. I wanted to be older and more sophisticated, like Scarlett. I wanted Sal to think I could handle it – that I'd be perfect girlfriend material. *His* girlfriend.

We'd been driving less than half an hour when Ali indicated and pulled the car over. I stared out of the back window; we'd stopped right outside a newsagent. Ali turned and then nodded to Sal.

'Go on, bruv. Give it to her then.'

I wasn't sure what Sal was going to give me – alcohol or drugs – but I sat there waiting. He dipped a hand deep inside his jacket pocket and, moments later, pulled out a card.

'Ooh, look!' he grinned, waving it in front of me.

I was confused. Back then, I didn't know the difference between a credit card and a regular cash card because I wasn't old enough to have my own bank account. The men began to speak to one another, although I didn't have a clue what they were saying because they both spoke in Arabic. I wasn't sure if they were doing this on purpose so I wouldn't understand what they were saying.

Scarlett had already told me that Ali was Moroccan, and I knew Sal was because I'd gone to the same school as his younger sister. However, this was the first time I'd heard either of them speak in their native tongue. The men continued to discuss something, and at one point the debate became heated. Sal appeared to disagree with something Ali had said, but Ali didn't seem to want to back down. Instead, he sighed heavily and twisted in his seat to face me.

'Go on, Sal, go on, cuz, give her the card,' Ali urged, this time in English.

Why does he keep calling him 'cuz'? Are they cousins?

Sal stared at his friend.

'You trust her? You think she's up to it?'

He'd said it in a voice that suggested he didn't. I felt insulted, even though I didn't know what it was about. It was obvious that I had a schoolgirl crush on Sal. However, he thought this gave him licence to speak to me – and about me – like I was a piece of shit. But I was also desperate to try and impress him.

'I can do it,' I blurted, butting into the conversation. 'Whatever it is, I'll do it.'

'You sure?' Sal asked.

I knew he didn't think I was up to whatever it was they wanted me to do, which made me even more determined to prove him wrong.

'Yes.'

Sal exchanged a knowing glance with Ali, then he turned to speak to me.

'Do you really know what to do with it?'

'Yeah, of course I do!'

However, my bravado was just that. I shifted uneasily in my seat. I must have looked a bit blank because Ali decided to elaborate.

'You go into the shop,' he said, pointing at it through the car window, 'and ask for forty Benson & Hedges, two £15 mobile phone top-up vouchers and some cash. But it must be under £50 in cash, so don't get too greedy now, will ya?'

Greedy? What the hell was he talking about?

It took me a moment before I realised what it was they were asking me to do.

'What, you want me to go in there and buy things with that card?'

Ali nodded.

'Yeah, that's why we brought you here. That's why we wanted to meet you today.'

My eyes darted between the pair. I felt deflated because I realised why I was there, sitting inside his car. They didn't want to see me because they liked spending time with me, they wanted me to go into a shop with a card that wasn't mine and buy all these things.

'But it's not my card,' I replied quietly.

Sal began to snigger, which made me feel even more stupid. Ali joined in. He tapped his hand against the steering wheel, then shrugged his shoulders as though it was no big deal.

'Yeah, well, it's not our card either, that's why we're asking you. I mean, the shopkeeper isn't going to stop a girl, is he? Especially not a pretty-looking one like you.'

My heart swelled with joy.

Pretty? Did he actually just say that?

I glanced at Sal to see if he thought the same, but his face was deadly serious.

'Yeah,' Ali continued, warming to the theme. 'I mean, he'd stop us, wouldn't he, because like me and my bruv, well, we're not white, like you, are we?'

'Yeah,' Sal agreed. 'We're not a good girl, like you … and no one's going to ask questions when a good girl goes in a shop to buy something, now are they?'

I felt torn but I also felt very important. Ali and Sal had trusted me with their secret. More importantly, they'd trusted me, not Scarlett.

Looking back, I was so naive but because they'd explained it in such a casual way I didn't think about the consequences. They'd both made it sound easy, as though all these things I couldn't usually afford were just waiting there, ripe for the picking. They made it sound as if I couldn't lose and that this card gave me licence to spend. In short, they'd made it sound like a fun challenge.

How hard could it be?

'Here,' Sal said, handing me the blue bank card. 'Memorise the signature on the back.'

He pointed at it with his finger.

'You need to know it because you'll have to sign a piece of paper just like that before they'll let you take the stuff.'

I held the card in my hand and traced my index finger along the blue ink.

Miss M. Smith

I took in all the details, the looping signature and slant of the letters as they leaned over towards the left. The 'S' had been written in a fancy swirl. As signatures went, it looked easy enough to copy. I flipped the plastic over in my hand to check for more clues but there were none, just the same name on the front stamped in embossed silver letters. Above that was a long row of numbers.

M. Smith, M. Smith, M. Smith, I chanted over and over inside my head.

I studied the signature again. I couldn't afford to slip up and I certainly didn't want to show myself up, not in front of Sal. My fingertip rested against the first letter 'M'. I wondered what the 'M' stood for and what my new, imaginary name could be.

Michelle? I shook my head; it was too old-fashioned.

Marcia? No, too unusual.

Mandy? I decided that Mandy suited me best.

'Come on,' Sal said, as he tried to hurry me along. He climbed out and pulled the seat lever forward to let me out. As I did, Ali grabbed the top of my arm.

'Remember, forty Benson & Hedges, top-up vouchers and cashback. But nothing over £50, all right?'

I gulped down my fear. It had unexpectedly risen at the back of my throat, taking me by surprise.

What the hell have I got myself into?

By now, adrenaline was pumping through my body, spurring me on. For a split second I wondered if I should make a break, but then I thought better of it. The thought of letting Sal down seemed too horrible to contemplate. Then there was Scarlett. She would be mortified if I showed her up. Scarlett and Sandy had both been so good to me – I couldn't let them down. I had to do this because it was the least I could do. Swallowing down any misgivings, I tucked the card inside my jacket pocket.

'It'll be fine,' Sal said encouragingly.

He gave me a reassuring tap on my back as I squeezed past him.

'We do this all the time. No sweat.'

Both men seemed so utterly calm that I wondered what I'd even been worried about.

I'm overreacting. They do this all the time.

I was at a crucial time in my life and I craved affection. Mum had starved me of it, so it was something I actively tried to seek out. I'd done the same with Jack – the boy I'd had sex with. Now I was doing the same with Ali and Sal. I also craved approval. It was like an addiction, and I'd do whatever it took to be on the receiving end of it.

Although I was barely into my teenage years, I was tall for my age. With my long hair and glasses, I was certain I could pass for a girl much older. Thanks to Scarlett, I now dressed smartly too. My friend would lend me clothes and she was obsessed with labels, so I always had something cool to wear. My days of jumble sales were long gone. I dressed myself now, and I'd use Christmas and birthday money to choose the things I wanted to wear.

Flicking my long hair over my shoulders, I pushed open the door to the newsagent. A loud beeping noise sounded. It made an old guy, who was sitting behind the counter, glance up as I stepped inside. I didn't look his way because I didn't want him to see how nervous I was. With my eyes focused straight ahead, I walked over towards the newspaper and magazine rack. I'd already decided it would make me seem older than I was – the sort of woman who'd go into a shop to buy a glossy magazine. Lifting a couple off the shelf, I went through the motions and flicked through them nonchalantly before putting them back. Taking a deep breath, I approached the counter. Standing before it, I looked up at the different brands of cigarette lined up behind the man, my eyes searching for the distinctive gold packet.

'Forty Benson & Hedges, please,' I said, pointing at them.

I held my breath and waited for the man to ask me for ID. I'd expected him to call the police or throw me out of the shop, only nothing happened. He turned and took a packet off the shelf and put it down in front of me.

Wow. That was easy.

'Is that all?'

Spurred on, I shook my head.

'No, could I also have two £15 top-up vouchers, please.'

My confidence grew with every second.

He rung them through the till along with the price of the cigarettes.

'Any cashback?' he asked, as though he was on autopilot.

I nodded with relief. I'd been so busy trying to concentrate on the cigarettes and vouchers that I'd almost forgotten.

'Yes, could I have £50?'

The newsagent inputted the total sale into the till as I handed the credit card over. My hand trembled slightly so I withdrew it quickly. Thankfully, the man hadn't noticed because he was too busy looking for something underneath the counter. I watched as he pulled out a plastic machine and put it down in front of me. He placed a slip of paper on the top of the card and dragged the plastic across it, making an exact copy underneath. Then he handed me a pen.

M. Smith, I wrote.

I slanted the signature over to the left and gave the 'S' a flourishing swirl. I waited for him to scrutinise it but he didn't give it a second glance. Moments later the packet of fags, top-up vouchers and money were in my hand. I tried not to stare at the bundle of notes because I'd never seen so much cash.

'Have a nice day,' the newsagent added.

He pushed the slip of signed paper flat inside the till and snapped it shut.

Was that it? Was that all I needed to do?

'Thanks!'

I left the shop smiling. I couldn't help myself because I realised just how happy Ali and Sal would be with me.

'Did I do okay?' I asked, desperate for approval as I handed everything over.

Ali's eyes widened. He seemed delighted as he counted out the £10 and £5 notes and gave Sal half.

'You did well, Gaia. You did really well, didn't she, Sal?'

He nodded and tucked the notes into the side pocket of his trackie bottoms.

'Yeah, you can come again.'

'Really?'

My heart soared. Ali smirked and turned the key in the ignition as the car fired back into life.

'Yeah, we might even give you some fags on the next one.'

Resting back in my seat, I couldn't stop smiling. I'd finally found something I was good at. It didn't even matter if it was wrong, because everything about it had felt so right.

CHAPTER SIX

CIGARETTES

The next time the men picked me up outside the shops I was ready and waiting.

A few days earlier, I'd confessed to Scarlett about the credit card and buying fags and top-up vouchers at the shop. Her eyes widened with horror as I recalled each detail. I thought she'd be impressed or even proud, but instead she went crackers.

'What the hell, Gaia? Please don't do it again. If you get caught, you'll get into a shitload of trouble.'

I reached for a cigarette and batted away her concerns with a wave of my hand.

'That's it, don't you see? I'm not going to get caught. Ali knows what he's doing and he wouldn't let me get into trouble. They've got my back, Scar. I'll be fine.'

She didn't seem convinced. Even though she seemed to worship the ground that Ali walked on, she made it clear she'd never get involved with something like that.

'Imagine what your mum would do to you if you got caught? She'd kill you! It's serious shit.'

But I'd already switched off. The thrill of being part of the gang had opened my eyes. All my life I'd been desperate to fit in and, for once, I had. Scarlett didn't understand how it felt to be the plain girl with the glasses. It was okay for her because she was pretty and had everything going for her. Unlike me, she'd stand up for herself. That was part of the reason she went to a pupil referral unit. My friend had balls, whereas I'd always been quiet and non-confrontational. I secretly hoped Ali and Sal had chosen me over her.

They trust me. They think I'm up to the job.

I paused, lit a cigarette and pulled the smoke inside both lungs.

'Promise me you won't do it again, Gaia,' my friend nagged.

I shrugged.

'I'll think about it.'

Scarlett rolled her eyes in exasperation.

'Well, don't say I didn't warn you.'

So, when Ali texted me a few days later, I was back there, outside the shops, waiting on the usual wall. Ali drove us around for a while before he pulled to a halt outside a small supermarket. This time, he jumped out of the car to let me out.

'Thanks,' I grinned, feeling a little honoured.

Ali had already given me the same instructions as last time – forty Benson & Hedges, two £15 Vodafone top-up cards and £50 cashback. Not a penny more, otherwise the shopkeeper would have to ring for authorisation. He'd even smiled at me as he ran through the list. However, as I pushed past, his initial charm seemed to evaporate.

'Don't get the card taken off you, do you understand?'

His voice was low and the words came out as a snarl.

Why would I get it taken off me? I was fine last time.

Suddenly, Scarlett's voice rang inside my head: '*If you get caught, you'll get into a shitload of trouble.*'

My heart began to pound.

I wonder where they get these cards from? I thought, as I glanced down at it in my hand.

It sounds naive but not for a single minute did I think that they were stolen. Credit cards belonged to the adult world – one I knew nothing about. Besides, I trusted the men and I wanted to impress Sal. I wanted to impress him so much.

Ali was staring straight at me, waiting, as I uncurled my fingers and studied the card's signature strip:

Miss Jenny Woodthorpe

I memorised the loops of the two 'N's and the upturn of the 'W'. The surname was much longer and more complicated than last time, although I was certain I'd be fine. Ali, on the other hand, seemed edgy.

'You should have practised the signature.'

He bent down, stretched a hand across Sal and patted it around inside the glove compartment. Leaning further across, he checked the shallow pocket in the passenger front door, then on his own side.

'What are you looking for, bruv?'

'A pen,' Ali said. 'She needs to practise.'

Between them the men found one, but then there wasn't any paper. Ali huffed in annoyance.

'We shoulda thought this one through more, cuz.'

Sal held both hands up in dismay.

'Listen, I'll be fine,' I said, butting in.

And I honestly believed I would.

It was the new millennium – the dawn of a new century and there was no such thing as chip and pin – that was still four years in the future. I'd signed for goods before and everything had gone to plan, so I wasn't worried. After the first time, I started to watch Mum and my stepdad whenever they paid for things in shops. I noticed some shops would swipe the card through the till and ask you to sign a receipt, while others – usually smaller shops – used the older, plastic imprinter machine that took a carbon copy of your details. Still, a simple signature was all you needed to buy anything.

Although Ali seemed worried, he was also aware that the majority of shopkeepers barely checked the signature. As long as the person presenting the card looked honest and trustworthy, which I did, then everything would be fine. He also realised that small shops made for easier targets.

I glanced up at the small supermarket. It looked more modern than the newsagent's we'd previously targeted. I wasn't too worried because I had a talent for forgery and I was adept at copying signatures. I'd regularly sign Mum's name in my school planner and, so far, there had been no questions asked. Mum also had a distinctive signature, much like her dress sense and personality, so it was much harder to fake than … I uncurled my fingers and checked the card again.

Jenny Woodthorpe, whoever she was.

'Right. Here goes.'

The men's eyes followed me as I strolled over towards the supermarket door. It made a loud whooshing sound as it slid open. Once inside, I craned my head to check out the layout of the shop. The main till was to my right and

it had four long aisles leading off it. But I wasn't interested in booze or food; I was here for cigarettes, vouchers
and hard cash. I twisted my head and checked over
towards the till – no queue. Realising I'd be served
straight away, I made my way over to it.

'Hello, and what can I get you?' a friendly middle-
aged woman asked as I approached.

The shop worker had a kind face and was wearing a
green tabard with the shop's logo on the front. Her once-
dark hair, scraped high behind her head with a brown
plastic clip, was peppered grey at the temples. I tried my
best to avoid her gaze and stood to the side so I could scan
the cigarettes neatly stacked on the shelves behind her.

'Forty Benson & Hedges, please.'

I pointed up to the gold packets as they shimmered
beneath the intense strip lighting.

'Right you are.'

She turned but, as she was short, she had to lift onto
her tiptoes to grab two packets of twenty. She placed
them on the counter between us and a pang of guilt
twisted inside my gut.

Don't lose your nerve. Not now.

'And two Vodafone top-up vouchers, please.'

'Okay. How much?'

'Fifteen pounds each, oh, and some cashback – fifty
pounds.'

I figured the more she had to remember, the less time
she had to look at me. Once she'd rung it all in, she
swiped the card through the till, which triggered a
receipt. She handed me a pen to sign it as I tried to visual-
ise my new name – Jenny Woodthorpe. I signed
confidently and in a flourish of swirls.

Perfect.

I handed it over and, as the woman inspected it, I felt the muscles in my stomach tighten.

This is it … this is where she notices it's a fake and I'm not Jenny Woodthorpe …

I turned my head and glanced over my shoulder towards the exit. There seemed to be no sign of a security guard and I was certain I'd be able to outrun the shop worker. The next few seconds seemed to stretch out forever as I waited for her to scrutinise my features, question my age or press the bell to call the manager. But she didn't do any of those things. In fact, she barely gave me a second glance. The till bleeped as it sprung open towards her stomach. She lifted a black plastic arm and placed the receipt beneath it, snapping it shut. Then she counted two, crisp £20 notes out into my hand.

'And that's fifty,' she smiled, adding a final £10 to the pile. 'Have a good day.'

'You, too.'

I quickly gathered the packets of cigarettes and phone vouchers as she beckoned the next customer forward.

'Can I help?' I heard her voice call out behind me, as I quickly made my way over to the door.

Outside, I took a deep breath of air. Then I began to grin until soon I couldn't wipe the smile from my face. Sign, sealed and delivered. It really was that simple. I felt absolutely fearless; it had been the easiest thing in the world and one that carried a great reward. Only that reward would be for Ali and Sal, not me.

It felt like playing a game of shops, only a grown-up version. I was still acting out a part, only this time I was someone else and I was playing with their money.

Ali and Sal turned in their seats as I approached. I couldn't stop grinning as Ali wound down his window.

'Yeah, cuz, told ya she was good,' he said, flicking his fingers before he high-fived Sal.

Ali hopped out to let me climb onto the back seat. I grinned, delighted I'd won their approval as they divided the spoils between them. I watched as Ali laid a £20 note in Sal's palm.

'I'll get change for the tenner, bruv, and give you half.'

Sal seemed slightly suspicious.

'Just make sure you do, cuz.'

Ali nodded sharply. As he did, he noticed me looking at them and the money.

'You can have some from the next one.'

You said that last time, and this is the next time.

Annoyed, I stared out of the window as a feeling of guilt started eating me up. I lifted a hand and used my sleeve to wipe away some condensation that had formed on the back window. With the glass now clear, I glanced through it and over at the supermarket.

I hope she doesn't get into any trouble.

The woman was so lovely.

I hope she doesn't get the sack. I wonder if it's her only job.

I shuddered.

It's too late now.

'Come on!' Ali cheered, punching the air.

His voice broke my thoughts. With his foot revving against the accelerator, he turned to Sal and grinned.

'Come on, let's do the next one.'

I assumed that we'd drive miles away to somewhere else, so I was shocked when we parked up outside a second shop just around the corner.

'Ready?'

I nodded, climbed out and repeated the same thing. Only this time when I returned, Ali gave me a packet of cigarettes. It was only a pack of twenty, but it felt as though I'd just won the lottery.

'Really?' I gasped, thrilled he'd remembered.

He nodded abruptly.

'Thanks.'

I looked down at the pack, knowing just how long it would take me and Scarlett to save up for one. Usually, we'd just about scrape enough together for a ten-pack of Sovereign, the only fags you could buy for under £2. But now I had twenty Bensons, and I couldn't wait to share them with Scarlett. Thanks to my new 'job', there'd be no more standing out in the freezing cold, begging strangers for spare fags. I was starting to realise that credit cards gave me new superpowers. Shopkeepers wouldn't even question my age, not any more, because once I'd put a credit card down on the counter that was proof enough.

I was still staring at the gold pack of fags when a hand reached over and snatched them away: Sal. I looked across to Ali for back-up.

'Give her the fags back now, bruv,' he insisted.

But Sal refused.

'Nah, I ain't gonna do that, cuz.'

Ali's eyes darted between the pair of us.

'I said, give her them back.'

Sal shook his head and Ali began to lose his temper.

'You're fucking tight, bruv. I just said she could have them, didn't I?'

I was grateful to Ali, thankful that he was on my side.

There was a short silence as the two men stared at one another. Ali's eyes bored into Sal as he waited for him to do the right thing. A kind of honour among thieves.

'Look, bruv, I'm not moving this car until you give 'em back to her, understand?'

Ali was adamant and he refused to back down. Tension rose inside the car as the stand-off continued for a few minutes more. Neither man wanted to lose face or be seen to do so. Eventually, and only because he realised that he'd have to walk, Sal cracked. Humiliated, he could barely contain his anger as he threw the half-crushed packet back at me.

'Here you go, Four Eyes.'

Blood rushed to my face. I was mortified.

Four Eyes? Had he just called me that?

Sal's words cut me because I'd only done it in the first place to try and impress him, but it was clear he had zero respect for me. Angry and upset, I grabbed the fag packet and pushed it inside my jacket pocket. His insult stung me. He knew how much I fancied him – everyone did – yet he seemed hell-bent on trying to humiliate me. He loved the power it gave him.

It had started to rain outside. Raindrops gently pitter-pattered against the glass as rivulets streamed down the window. The weather mirrored how I felt inside – miserable. Nothing more was said as Ali turned the key and started the engine. The car shuddered and spluttered as it roared into life, and we moved on – on to the next place. We 'did' two more shops that day. Packets of fags and phone vouchers accumulated in neat piles inside the glove compartment. The previous argument seemed to have been forgotten, although I noticed there was no banter to fill the empty space. Eventually, Ali muttered something about getting me home, and we wound our way along roads and back towards the row of shops near Scarlett's house.

'Bye, Four Eyes,' Sal said cruelly, as I climbed out of the car.

He sneered and waved his fingers sarcastically.

'Don't be such a bastard, bruv,' Ali said, trying to hush him.

But it was too late – I'd heard. If anything, it made me even more determined to try and win him over. Sal was a complete bastard, but it almost didn't matter because I'd fallen in love with him. I was a teenager with a schoolgirl crush on a bad boy. I didn't realise at the time that I was already fighting a losing battle. Sal held all the power. I held none.

* * *

'Where did you get those?' Scarlett shrieked, as I dangled the gold packet of twenty Benson & Hedges in front of her.

'Here,' I said, tossing them over.

She raised a hand and caught them mid-air.

'I bought them.'

Scarlett arched an eyebrow.

'You didn't go out with Ali and Sal again, did you?'

I smirked and shrugged.

'Gaia! I told you not to do it. I thought you promised me …'

I held up my hand to stop her.

'No, I didn't promise. I said, "I'd think about it," and I have.'

Scarlett shook her head.

'Well, I wouldn't take the risk. They're making you take all the risks. You do know that, don't you?'

I leaned forward and grabbed the packet off her. Pulling at the seal, I ripped it around the packet as it cut through the polythene wrapper like a knife through butter.

'Well, you won't be wanting one of these then,' I sniffed haughtily.

I shook a cigarette out of the box as Scarlett pulled a face. It was obvious she felt torn. She clearly wanted to enjoy the spoils, but she couldn't and wouldn't condone it.

'Go on …' I said, as I continued to taunt her.

I waved a solitary cigarette side to side in front of her face. She paused and thought for a moment.

'Okay, but it doesn't mean I agree with it – with any of it.'

I smiled and plonked myself happily down on the bed next to her.

'I know, Scar, and you're a good friend. I know you're only trying to look out for me but I'm fine. Honestly!'

She reluctantly took the cigarette, rolling her eyes as she did.

'Atta girl!'

A few hours later we'd managed to smoke nearly all the packet. Scarlett's face fell as she shook the almost-empty box.

'I'll get the next ones,' she insisted.

'Nah, we're all good.'

I was delighted that I could finally repay her for her friendship, although I still didn't understand why Ali and Sal had chosen me instead of her. I wondered if she'd already refused. It made more sense to use her instead of me, after all, as she was older. But then, I was younger and more pliable.

Later, I discovered that before they'd found me, Ali and Sal had used drug addicts to do their bidding. However, their emaciated appearance often provoked suspicion, so they needed to find another girl quickly. They needed someone who looked presentable, ordinary but old enough, and I ticked all the boxes: I was easy pickings.

Soon, I'd begun to bunk off school so I could meet Ali and Sal and spend the day stealing for them. They'd pick me up from shops close to my secondary school. The school knew I was bunking off and my head of year would follow me in despair as she tried her best to keep me inside school. In a way I felt sorry for her. I was never rude or nasty, I'd just decided that I didn't want to be there anymore. My 'new life' was way more exciting.

I didn't realise it then, but I'd walked straight into their trap.

████████████████████ **Social Services**

Initial Assessment
Gaia Cooper, D.O.B: ████████

████████ made initial referral by phone as very concerned re: her daughter's recent offending behaviour. ████████ came in for a duty appointment Wednesday 24.5.00.

████████ has been having considerable problems with Gaia for some years. She describes her daughter as being out of control and comes and goes when she pleases. We talked about installing boundaries and that as Gaia's responsible parent she should be reporting her missing when she is late in. ████████ said she had done this, but I told ████████ she has to gain back control and not let Gaia win.

Analysis: Gaia seems to have her mother exactly where she wants her and her mother feels she is powerless. I am concerned that Gaia is leading an offending lifestyle, which may be beyond her own control. ████████████████████████████████████
Will try to check this out.

I honestly accept that if this young girl doesn't engage then, as a department, we are powerless to do anything but, due to her age, I feel she needs immediate interaction. I would like to explore Protective Behaviours with her.

Signed,
████████████████ Social Worker

CHAPTER SEVEN

THE HOUSE

A couple of weeks after I'd first met them, Ali and Sal arranged to pick up both me and Scarlett from our usual meeting point. My friend drummed her fingers impatiently against the brick wall as we sat on top of it, waiting for them to arrive.

'Ali is just so …' Scarlett gushed. Her voice trailed off and her eyes misted over as she tried to sum him and his fabulousness up in a single word.

'Great … you know, he's just so great. He's older and good-looking, and he's done things … lots of things. He's not boring, and being with him … well, it's just so exciting, isn't it?'

She turned as I nodded along in agreement. Spurred on, she added, 'He's got his own car and, well, we're always doing exciting stuff, like this.'

She held out her hands to emphasise the last part, but I wasn't entirely sure what 'this' was. When Scarlett was there, all we seemed to do was drive around while they slowly got stoned. I'd sit there, quiet and passive, on the back seat, while Sal treated me like a piece of shit. It was as though I'd become his new hobby.

Ali was late, as usual, so I had to sit and listen to Scarlett rabbiting on. However, unlike my friend, I'd seen the real Ali – the one who routinely sent her fourteen-year-old friend into various shops with different credit cards. I hoped that, because I was the one taking all the risks, Sal might start to see me in a different light and I'd manage to win his respect. I was certain that Ali respected me, but Sal was an entirely different matter.

We were still waiting on the wall when the silent night-time air was broken by the telltale chug of the Renault. As it limped into view, a thick plume of black smoke belched up from the exhaust. Scarlett excitedly hopped down onto both feet.

'Here's Ali!'

She ran a finger around her lips to try and perfect her heavily lip-glossed mouth. Then she smoothed her hands down the legs of her flared jeans.

'How do I look?'

I took her in.

'Stunning.'

The spaghetti-strap top she was wearing skimmed her curves in all the right places. The baby-blue satin fabric clung to her and the pale jeans she was wearing fitted her like a glove. I looked positively dreary next to her. A pang of jealousy ripped through me.

She makes me sick; why don't I look like that?

Although I wasn't exactly plain, my frizzy, reddish-blonde hair and glasses made me appear studious and boring. Unlike me, Scarlett stood out from the crowd, and in a good way.

'Hiya girls,' Ali shouted out, as he pulled the car up alongside the kerb.

His arm dangled outside the open car window as he drummed a flat hand against the metal door in time with the music.

Thud, thud, thud.

His eyes flitted from me and over towards Scarlett. That's when his face changed. He almost salivated as she swayed and walked over towards him.

'Good to see ya!' he grinned, clearly unable to stop himself.

Something flashed across his face.

What was it?

I couldn't be sure, although it was clear he only had eyes for my friend. I followed Scarlett and wandered over towards the car. As I grew close, I dipped down and looked through the open window.

'Hi Sal!'

I gave him a friendly wave, but he didn't return it. In fact, he could barely look at me. Instead, he stared straight ahead as though I wasn't even there.

'Don't mind him, he's sulking,' Ali laughed.

He jabbed a thumb over towards his mate. I wanted to ask why and find out what was wrong with Sal, but thought better of it. Unsure what to say, I nodded as though I understood. Only I didn't. I didn't understand a single thing about either of them. For starters, they constantly called each other 'cuz' and 'bruv', yet, according to Scarlett, they weren't even related.

'Come on, Gaia,' she said, urging me to follow her and get into the car.

Sal climbed out and pulled a lever, flipping his seat forward to let us in. Scarlett went first, but as I followed, Sal dipped down to whisper something in my ear.

'Come on, Four Eyes.'

My heart plummeted as tears pricked at the backs of my eyes. But I refused to let them fall. As I passed, I even mouthed a silent 'Sorry'. Then I hated myself for doing so. I squashed myself next to Scarlett and the car roared off into the night. Neither of us had bothered to fasten our seatbelts; we were young and so, by default, felt invincible. Scarlett was giddy with excitement – more than usual – as the car picked up speed and flung us both around in the back as though we were on a fairground ride. Ali slammed his foot down and we began to take corners and bends in the road far too fast as he showed off.

'Where are we going?' my friend shrieked.

Sal held his hand over his head and passed her a spliff.

Scarlett smoked it happily and we continued to tear through the estate and towards the other side of town.

'Where are we going?' she repeated.

She blew out a lungful of smoke and waited for one of them to answer. But Ali ignored her. He dipped forward and cranked the music up a little.

Thud, thud, thud.

He turned and grinned at Sal, as though the two were sharing a secret joke.

'Off to a house, ain't we?' Ali shouted over the din.

I spotted his reflection in the windscreen mirror – he was grinning, although I didn't understand what was so funny.

Thud, thud, thud.

'A house? Which house?' Scarlett hollered back.

She passed the joint back to Sal, who snatched it from her greedily.

'Sam's house.'

'Who's Sam?'

Ali rolled his eyes. His knuckles flashed white as he gripped the steering wheel. It was clear from where I was sitting that Scarlett's constant questions were doing his head in.

'What is this, man? A million questions or summat?'

But she didn't care. Fuelled up on hash, she just grew more determined to find out.

Ali took his frustration out on the car. I watched as the speedometer needle flickered against 60mph on the dial. Houses, trees and street lights whipped past in a blur outside. Ali took the spliff from Sal and had a drag before passing it back. Then he replied to Scarlett's earlier question.

'Sam. Sam Green. We're going to her house.'

My friend turned and stared at me with a look of confusion. I didn't know Sam Green and it was clear that neither did she. Scarlett shrugged as I shook my head to indicate I didn't have a clue either. Ali noticed and glared at me in the windscreen mirror. He turned down the music for a moment.

'Sam. Come on, you both know Sam. It's Heidi's mum, innit?'

And that's when the penny dropped. Heidi Green lived on the other side of town. I vaguely knew her through Denise, but not well enough to call her a friend. Heidi came from a rough family, that much I did know. Although her mum had six kids, she was a single parent and hardly ever at home. Rumour had it that she would save up her benefits and travel to Egypt, where she'd meet up with much younger men. The family was notorious and were known to be 'dodgy'. I guessed Heidi's mum must have gone away again. Every time she left the country she'd leave her oldest son in charge, but he didn't give a shit. As a result, her home would turn into a doss house.

'Ah, is that her name? I didn't know what she was called,' Scarlett replied, sounding a little vacant.

It was clear she felt stupid, and was now trying to backtrack to cover her embarrassment. She hated looking stupid in front of Ali.

'No sweat.'

Scarlett smiled with relief as Ali dipped forward in his seat and cranked up the stereo once more. The car began to pulsate as a garage tune blasted out. The music was so loud that I thought my ears might bleed. 'Masterblaster 2000' continued to thump behind me, each note punching its way through the speakers, as my head throbbed in time to the beat.

Ali and Sal both began to nod along in the front of the car. Scarlett grinned, grabbed hold of my hand and gave it a squeeze as though this was the best day ever. I smiled back at her. I wanted her to believe I was as happy as she was, but I felt young and out of my depth. Sal turned with the spliff in his hand and tried to pass it to her, but I intercepted. Grabbing the smouldering joint, I put it between my lips and took a confident drag, as though it was something I'd done a million times before. Secretly, I was absolutely shitting myself. I hated the feeling of losing control, especially now with Ali and Sal, on our way to a doss house in the roughest part of town. Sal watched in admiration, so I took another drag and then another.

'Whoah!' he screamed.

I could tell he was impressed, so I took another long drag and then another.

'Shit! Yeah, bruv!' he cried, giving Ali a nudge.

His approval thrilled me. Ali swivelled around in his seat to stare at me.

'She's finally doing it? Yeaaahh!'

Their howls filled the air as Scarlett beamed. I felt good and glad – glad I'd finally done it.

'Hey, cuz. Old Four Eyes isn't such a shitter, is she?'

I flinched.

Four Eyes, that name again.

I chose to ignore it – and him – and passed the spliff to Scarlett, as smoke filled the car. Up until then I felt like I'd been smoking a normal cigarette until …

BOOM!

A weird calm washed over me and my body began to relax, as if something soft had brushed against my skin. Every sensation felt heightened as I sank down in my seat and closed my eyes. My body felt liquid, like it had just melted into a puddle. I allowed myself to drift off.

A few minutes later I felt the weight of a hand resting on top of mine. It belonged to Scarlett.

'You okay, Gaia?'

It took all my strength to open my eyes. Scarlett's face zoomed into view so sharply and vividly that I began to laugh until soon I couldn't stop. I was sitting there, grinning like an idiot but I couldn't explain or answer why. Instead, I continued to giggle.

'She's stoned, bruv,' Sal remarked.

I saw Ali's dark eyes as he stole a glance at me through the mirror.

'Sweet.'

I couldn't place it, but he seemed to sound oddly pleased about something. Then he indicated and the moment had gone. The car turned into another street before it parked up outside Heidi's house. The place looked deathly quiet. In fact, it seemed so quiet that I wondered if anyone was in.

'Come on,' Ali said, as he climbed out and we followed.

Scarlett looked as puzzled as I felt as we approached the front door. Although the light of the day had faded, I could just make out a large pile of rubbish in the shadows. Someone had dumped the lot in the front garden. There was a series of broken paving slabs leading to the front door. Moments later I heard a loud scream as Scarlett went over on her ankle and fell to the floor with a thud.

'Owww!'

I ran over to help her as she clutched at her leg.

'Oh my God, Scar, are you okay?'

I tried to help prop her up but, as soon as I did, she pushed my hands away in embarrassment.

'Yeah, it's just these stupid shoes.'

But it wasn't her shoes, it was this place. It was an absolute dump and a death-trap.

With me helping my friend, Ali reached the front door first. I'd expected him to knock and wait, so I was astonished when he pushed down the handle and let himself in. Sal followed, then Scarlett and me.

Although the house had looked deserted from the outside, the front room was heaving. It was full of Arab men I'd never seen before. A cheer rang out as soon as Ali entered the room. The main light was off and all the curtains were drawn, but low-level lighting from a TV illuminated the many faces in a weird blueish artificial light. The TV was playing away to itself in a corner, and the low glow emitting from it masked the general squalor of the room. Ali went over to a leather sofa at the side of the room and took a seat. Another man, whose name I later discovered was Bilal, looked up as he passed by. He was sitting on the floor next to the coffee table, smoking a bright green and gold contraption called a bong. I'd seen them before, displayed in the windows of a few tacky local corner shops, although I hadn't realised what they were until then. The smell of dope was overwhelming. Bilal's fingers tapped against the bong as he inhaled the smoke, then spent the next few moments coughing it all back out again.

'Yo, Bil,' Ali called over to him.

He bent forward and clasped Bilal's hand in the air in a makeshift high five.

I felt awkward, standing there. My eyes scanned the room, searching for a spare seat. I was grateful for the low lighting because it helped hide the shock on my face. I couldn't believe people lived like this. Bilal noticed me but gave no reaction as I passed by and took my place next to Ali. However, as soon as Scarlett entered, his eyes stalked her as she crossed the room and perched herself on the arm of the sofa. With nowhere else to sit, Sal took a seat opposite.

'Yo, cuz,' he said, grasping Bilal's hand.

'My man,' he replied, clearly delighted to see him.

Ali dipped a hand inside his tracksuit bottoms and pulled out some hash. As soon as he spotted it, Bilal passed him the bong and the two of them began to smoke it together. Conversation flowed, but I couldn't understand a word of it because the men spoke in Arabic. Neither Scarlett nor I could follow the conversation and we soon grew bored. To try and pass the time, we began to take the piss out of them all behind their backs. The language had a very guttural sound. Scarlett turned to me and did a brilliant impression, as though clearing phlegm from the back of her throat and we both dissolved with laughter as the men watched in confusion. Suddenly Sal stopped us.

'Hey, Four Eyes!'

I glared at him.

'What's so funny?'

Sal was a total bastard. He loved it because he had an audience. Bilal overheard Sal's cruel nickname for me and began to laugh.

'Oh man, Four Eyes, that's good!' he said, pissing himself laughing.

I wanted to stand up and leave the room right then, to get as far away as I could from Sal. But I was stuck. I had no money and no way of getting home. Besides, I couldn't leave Scarlett alone with all these men. In the end, I did what I always did: I kept quiet and prayed the conversation would move on.

Smoke continued to cloud the room until soon, I could barely see Sal at all. The bong was passed around from man to man. I decided that, if I was offered it, I'd refuse. Bilal's constant coughing was enough to put anyone off. Moments later I was passed a joint and I gladly took it. I figured the hash would relax me and help me to blend in. But just after I'd taken a drag, I felt myself choking. The spliff was so strong that it was as though my insides had been scorched with a blowtorch; I coughed and spluttered, drawing attention to myself. I'd naively thought it would be just like the one I'd smoked in the car, but this was something else entirely. I didn't want to show myself up, but I couldn't stop coughing. I gasped like a fish out of water as I struggled to breathe. Scarlett's face loomed towards me and I felt her hand slapping my back hard. Still, I continued to cough and I was convinced I was going to die. My mouth felt as dry as scorched earth and my heart raced. After a while, the coughing began to subside but it was soon overtaken by paranoia washing over me.

What the fuck am I doing here?

I scanned the room. It was hard to make out any faces through the thick, grey smog. I tried to retrace my steps inside my head in case I needed to make a quick escape, but my mind seemed to slip, and I began to lose control and all sense of time. At one point, a man placed food and drink on the coffee table in front of me. My paranoia returned and I refused to touch it in case it had been laced with something. I felt small and insignificant, even inside such a tiny, crowded front room. I was a child playing at being a grown-up. A child smoking drugs in a doss house with adult men.

What the hell am I doing here?

My stomach ached as the night wore on. I desperately needed a pee, but I didn't dare move. I knew Ali and Sal, but I didn't know anyone else or my way around the strange house. My gut instinct told me to stay put, so I did. I was scared someone might follow me up to the bathroom, especially when I felt so wasted. I knew if they did, I wouldn't be able to fight them off. Desperate for the loo, I sat and held it in as my bladder ached with pain.

The next few hours crawled along as the men smoked and chatted away to each other. The smoke didn't bother me; in fact, it allowed me to hide in its folds as it clouded the room.

If I'm invisible then they won't touch me.

But every time the spliff passed my way, I took my turn. I wanted to forget that I needed to pee. I desperately wanted to leave but I couldn't without Scarlett.

Scarlett.

I twisted my head to look for my friend and became acutely aware that I couldn't see or hear her voice anymore. I felt along the arm of the sofa: empty.

Where is she?

Sitting upright, I looked for Ali but there was no sign of either of them. I twisted to look for Sal, but as I did, the walls seemed to bend in towards me.

Whoah!

I blinked once, twice, as the off-white woodchip wallpaper rushed towards me. I ducked and blinked again.

Christ! What had been in that last joint?

Closing my eyes, I tried to make the world stand still again. It didn't. Instead, it swam all around me as men and objects zoomed in and out of focus. Voices grew loud as they pierced through the fog. Laughter and banter.

Scarlett?

Still no sign of her. I gagged on the smoke as it choked at the back of my throat. The room felt hot and claustrophobic – too many bodies crammed into too small a space. I wanted to claw open the windows and let the fresh air come flooding in. I wanted to breathe clean air again. I patted the sofa to my left and right. Still empty.

'Wheeeerrrre iiiiis ssssssshe?' I cried, unable to stop myself.

It was the first time I'd spoken, and the sound of my slurred speech took me by surprise.

Bilal landed next to me on the sofa with a soft thump.

'Wherrre issss sssheee? Wherrre's S … S … Scarlett?' I begged.

I felt mortified by my own voice. Mortified by how I sounded.

Bilal pulled the bong from his mouth. He blew out a greyish-blue cloud of smoke into my face. It momentarily obscured him but, as it cleared, he came back into sharp focus. To my horror, I realised he was leering and trying to look down my top. I self-consciously pulled it back up.

'Chill. She's with Ali. She's outside with Ali.'

My stomach flipped.

'Arrre yooou shhhure?'

Are they even still here?

Scarlett's sudden absence somehow shocked me back into the moment. It felt as though someone had just thrown a bucket of ice-cold water over the top of me. Panicking, I grabbed the top of Bilal's arm and gave it a shake.

'Howww l … long? How l … long has she been gone?'

He shrugged my hands away in annoyance.

'Chill, bitch. I just told you. They'll be back soon.'

I didn't believe him. I scoured the room as I tried to take in all the faces. I didn't know any of them. That's when I realised. I was trapped inside a doss house with a bunch of men I'd never met before, on the other side of town, miles from home. I had no way of getting back and now my best friend was missing. Fear took hold and I began to shiver.

Get out ... I need to get out of here.

I tried to stand up, but my limbs felt loose and disjointed, and I fell back onto the sofa. A cheer rose inside the room as the men laughed at my pathetic attempts.

Stupid ... so stupid. I'm alone ... all alone with these men.

I was just wondering what to do when I heard a familiar voice – Scarlett.

Relief flooded through me.

She's okay.

I wanted to run over to her and hug her for all I was worth, but I couldn't move.

'Guy ... ya ... Guuuuy-yaaaa,' Scarlett said, as she began to slur.

My friend staggered across the room like an alcoholic and landed heavily on the arm of the sofa, almost losing her balance. Bilal cheered. Then he laughed as she blinked repeatedly, trying to focus.

'Yoou o ... okay?' I slurred.

I tried to think and talk normally, but it felt impossible as my thoughts skittered like marbles in a crystal bowl. Scarlett nodded clumsily. It was clear she was either drunk, stoned or both.

'I'm fiiiiiine, aren't I, Ali?'

Her voice sounded odd. I looked up to find Ali standing there right in front of me. I wasn't sure how long he'd been there or if he'd just returned.

He smirked and nodded with a look that said, *Don't ask any questions.*

'We're good.'

Thankfully, nothing else happened that evening. Instead, Ali dropped us off, as promised, by the shops. Although my head had cleared, Scarlett still seemed a little worse for wear.

'Come on,' I said, hooking her arm around my shoulder. 'We need to walk around the block a few times. We can't let your mum see you like this.'

As laid-back as Sandy was, I knew she'd be horrified if she saw her daughter in such a state. Also, I didn't want her to ask me questions I couldn't answer. She'd want to know where we'd been and who'd given Scarlett so much booze that she could barely stand.

I couldn't – and wouldn't – tell her.

CHAPTER EIGHT

BLUE LIGHTS

The men's grooming had been insidious. Despite what had happened, I still viewed them as friends. But friends didn't give you a credit card in someone else's name. These men weren't my friends, they were my abusers, with Sal my tormentor-in-chief. Only, I didn't see it like that. If anything, I began to hang around with them even more, desperately waiting for them to throw me a crumb of affection. I'd decided that any affection was better than none.

One day, Scarlett and I met up with two other guys, called Zain and Waleed. They were friends of Sal's.

'Wanna get the train into town?' Zain asked, as they passed us in the street one afternoon.

'Sure,' Scarlett grinned.

We caught the train and began to chat. Zain had just started to flirt with Scarlett when the train pulled into the next station. I glanced through the oblong window and a line of people whipped by as we came to a slow halt. I spotted two telltale yellow high-vis vests waiting on the platform: police.

'Shit, bruv,' Waleed cursed.

Panicking, he glanced across at Zain, who seemed equally shaken.

I wasn't sure what was wrong, but I could tell from the look on Zain's face that whatever it was, it wasn't good.

'What's wrong?' Scarlett said.

'Nothing, it's cool,' Zain insisted.

However, as soon as the door opened, he began to run, followed by Waleed. The two of them bolted along the platform, pushing shocked commuters out of the way as they went. But more police were standing by the exit, waiting for them. The other two officers left the platform and climbed onto the train. The rest of the carriage turned to look as Scarlett and I were read our rights, cuffed and taken to the police station.

'But we haven't done anything,' my mate began to cry.

We were terrified, and neither of us had a clue what it was all about. But once we'd reached the station, everything became clear. Unbeknown to us, Zain and Waleed had stolen a mobile phone from a hairdresser. They'd been caught on CCTV and the police were out looking for them.

Scarlett and I were held and questioned separately, and it soon became apparent that we didn't know a thing. The police contacted Mum and Sandy to come and sit with us as we were both underage. Of course, Sandy arrived within the hour, panicked and upset. But when the police contacted Mum, she refused to come. Eventually, I was chaperoned by an on-duty social worker. Although we had absolutely nothing to do with the theft, we were bailed, pending further investigation. Eventually, the police dropped the charge against us with 'no further action'. However, despite my innocence, Mum used it as a weapon to beat me with.

'You're out at all hours with that little tramp, and now you've brought the police to our door.'

I turned and rolled my eyes.

'Scarlett isn't a tramp, and the police didn't come to our door. We had nothing to do with it. I've done nothing wrong.'

But she refused to listen.

'And those men, who are they anyway, and what does a young girl like you want to hang about with two older men for?'

I knew anything I did say would only infuriate her even further, so I decided to keep quiet.

'You're disgusting – I'm disgusted you're my daughter.'

I sighed and made my way upstairs because I'd heard it all before. I thought it ironic that I'd been arrested for a crime I hadn't committed when I'd already made so many dodgy purchases with credit cards that didn't belong to me. However, Mum was right about one thing – I was out all the time. But it was only to try and escape her.

As shit as Sal was towards me, he was nothing compared with Mum, or that's how it felt. A small part of me even wondered if I'd sought him out. After all, being treated like dirt was all I'd ever known.

██████████████ Social Services

Initial Assessment Form
Date: 9 June 2000

Concerns: Gaia arrested two weeks ago. Out of control. ██████████ wanted help. She punched mum in the eye.

Problems at ████████ school bullying. Mixing with gangs at ██████. Out of school for three months. Has only been to school in a short time and refuses to go. Gaia very jealous of step-siblings who visit. Told school she had some family illness (untrue).

Gaia: Gaia missing since yesterday morning. Gaia was abusive to her mother and steals. She's a bright girl who may be having unprotected sex. Visiting with men in their 30s, smokes dope. Problems started approximately two years ago.

Police: ████████ aware of Gaia's associates. Gaia doesn't tell her mother where she's going and is not on time. Doesn't eat meals, raids the fridge at night.

Natural father: Natural father Gaia has never had any contact. ████████ told her that she saw her father recently and he doesn't want to know.

Yesterday: Gaia rang when police visited as she was reported missing, abusive on the phone.

Advised: We have a duty to work with family that Gaia may be subject of a police protection order and if they refuse to have Gaia back, she could be accommodated. Girls involved with gangs did not always make complaints because of threats.

Analysis: Mother unable to cope.

Name: Gaia Cooper
D.O.B: ▮▮▮▮▮▮▮
Address: ▮▮▮▮▮▮
▮▮▮▮▮▮
▮▮▮▮▮▮

▮▮▮▮▮▮▮▮▮▮ **County Council**

Emergency Duty Team

Detailed Contact Sheet
Date: 11 June 2000

Telephone call from ▮▮▮▮▮▮ demanding DSW come immediately to remove Gaia from her care or she would call police or put her out on the street.
   ... went over same ground as recorded by ▮▮▮▮▮▮ in EDT (Emergency Duty Team) dated 10 June. Apparently since then Gaia has run away and just returned.

Signed: ▮▮▮▮▮▮▮▮▮

Thankfully, the phone thing soon blew over and life returned to normal, whatever that was. My new 'normal' was bunking off school and spending money on credit cards that didn't belong to me (or them). Bilal had told me he was Sal's cousin, but I wasn't sure I believed him or anything he said. Sal called all his friends 'cuz' or 'bruv', so it was hard to tell.

Not long afterwards, Ali and Sal drove me to another small supermarket on the outskirts of town. By now I was full of confidence and knew exactly what to do. Even Ali had stopped reminding me of the £50 cashback rule. Only this time, when the cashier swiped the card, something must have popped up on the till.

'I'm sorry, but your card has been declined,' the woman said, eyeing me coolly. 'Do you have another card you'd like to pay with?'

Up until that point I'd become so blasé about the whole process that I was stunned when my card was rejected.

'I … erm …' I stammered, trying to find the right words.

The lights felt too hot as the cashier stared at me, waiting for my response. I glanced down at my watch.

'Erm, it's okay. I'm running a bit late, so I'll just leave it for now.'

I waited for her to hand my card back, only she didn't. She glanced down at it and then at me.

'I'm sorry, Miss Johnson, but I've been told the card has been retained.'

I gasped.

'Retained? What does that even mean?'

The cashier narrowed her eyes suspiciously.

'It means I can't give it back.'

I was lost for words.

This never happens.

'Right, I see. But it's my card. You can't hang onto my card. It's my property.'

The woman smirked.

'Is it?'

And that's when I knew I'd been rumbled. Blood whooshed inside my ears, and I started to panic. I glanced over my shoulder towards the door.

'I … erm … I …'

I knew that Ali would go mental if I left without the card, but I didn't want to push my luck. There was nothing else I could think of to say.

'I could always ring the bank for you?' the woman suggested.

She signalled to a phone fixed on the wall behind her.

'No, it's fine. I'll just, erm, I'll just sort it out when I get home. I'll give them a call. Thank you.'

With that I bolted for the door.

Ali glanced up eagerly as I ran towards the car. When he realised that I was empty-handed, his face fell.

'Hey,' he cried. 'Where's the stuff?'

But I didn't have time to explain.

'Go! We need to go!'

I pulled at the door handle repeatedly, so Sal jumped out to let me in. Then Ali started up the engine.

'Drive … just drive!' I gasped.

I turned and checked through the back window to make sure I hadn't been followed.

'Fuck, man, what happened?' Ali said, bashing his hand against the steering wheel in annoyance.

I took a deep breath to try and calm my heart as it rattled inside.

'The card, they kept the card. She took it off me. Said it had to be retained, whatever that means.'

'Fuck!' Ali cursed. 'Fuck's sake, Gaia!'

By now I was trembling and felt close to tears.

'Shut up, Four Eyes!'

It was Sal. He lifted both hands and put them against his eyes.

'Boo, boo …'

Ali sniggered, encouraging Sal.

Bastard.

I felt utterly miserable.

'I'm sorry,' I whispered. 'I'm sorry I fucked it up. I tried to get the card back, but she wouldn't give it to me.'

Ali sniffed and rubbed the back of his hand against his nose. I noticed he did this every time he was annoyed, a tick that came and went.

'It's fine. But we'll have to go and get another card.'

'Another one?'

Ali nodded.

'Yeah. It's your turn, Sal. I did the last one.'

My mind whirred.

What the hell were they talking about, and where did they get all these cards?

My answer came a short while later when Ali parked up outside a building I'd never seen before.

Claremont Medical Centre, the chrome sign fixed on a wall at the side of the door read. The place was busy. People seemed to be coming and going through the main doors every few minutes.

Why have we parked up outside a doctor's office? None of us are sick.

Ali's voice broke my thoughts.

'Go on then, bruv,' he said, pushing Sal out of the car.

I wanted to ask why we were there, but Ali seemed agitated. I'd already messed up today, so I decided to keep quiet.

Five minutes later Sal reappeared. He was grinning widely as he came towards the car, waving a credit card around triumphantly in Ali's face.

'Sweet!' Ali called out.

As he started the engine and we drove away, Sal began to laugh. Ali turned sideways, waiting for him to share the joke.

'What's up, cuz?'

Sal slapped a hand against his knee, still laughing out loud. Something had clearly tickled him.

'Oh man, you should have seen it. I was in the back rooms, you know, going through a handbag when this nurse walked in.'

Ali's eyes widened.

'Wha?'

Sal shook his head.

'No, no. It's fine, bruv. This bitch asked me what I was doing, so I told her I was looking for someone.'

Ali's mouth hung open as he waited for the rest of the story.

'Anyway, I was gonna say the doctor, but I couldn't remember any of their names on the board.'

'Fuck, bruv, so what did you say?'

Sal began to piss himself so much that he could barely get the words out.

'I said ... I said, I was looking for Dr Shipman.'

Ali screamed so loud that I almost jumped out of my skin.

'Bruv, you didn't!'

Sal wiped tears of mirth from his eyes.

'I did. It was the first fucking name that came into my head.'

The two men continued to crack up, but I didn't understand. I did, however, now realise where all the cards came from. Handbags. They'd stolen each and every one of them.

Fuck!

I recalled the dozen or so cards that had already passed through my hands.

'You cracked cunt!' Ali cried out to Sal.

But it wasn't funny. None of it. It wasn't even exciting – not anymore. However, I was already in too deep, and I couldn't see a way out. Scarlett had been right – Mum would kill me if she knew.

One day we'd visited a few shops using stolen cards to pick up the usual stuff only this time Bilal, the guy I'd met – the one smoking the bong at the house – was with us. He sat alongside me in the back seat. He didn't seem fazed by what was happening. If anything, he seemed just as involved as the other two. Afterwards, Ali parked up in a quiet side street so that he could count the day's takings. As he shuffled the notes in his hands, he turned and looked over at me.

'You're gonna do this in the sports shop in town, yeah?'

Although it had been said as a question, the inflection in his voice told me that I didn't really have a choice. Ali had made it clear that I worked for him and Sal now, and I'd do whatever I was told. But the sports shop was a big chain, not a corner shop. My brain began to splinter with fear. Little supermarkets where there was zero security and a bored shop assistant were one thing, but it was quite another to try and rip off a major retailer.

I stared back at Ali in disbelief.

'But where will you be? I mean, you can't park outside because it's in the middle of the shopping centre.'

He waved his hand away as though it was nothing.

It's okay for you, I thought bitterly. *I'm the one taking all the risk.*

It didn't matter how much Ali tried to sugarcoat it, this would be a hundred times harder.

'Chill, it'll be fine. Besides, I'm going to go in with you, aren't I?'

Go in with me?

Now he had my attention.

'You are?'

I felt a faint sliver of hope inside.

'Yeah, course I am. I need to go in and show you which trainers I want, don't I?'

Bilal snorted with laughter and slapped his mate on the back as though the whole thing was a joke. The car started up, Ali indicated and we pulled away, heading to the centre of town. He parked up in a road adjacent to the shopping centre and climbed out. My legs trembled as he signalled for me to follow him. But I didn't want to do it. This wasn't fun anymore. It had stopped being fun weeks earlier, when I realised where the cards came from – the back rooms of doctors' waiting rooms. Sick people and nurses – vulnerable and kind people – people who didn't deserve it.

'Come on.'

It was Ali. His hand was against my shoulder as he gave me a slight push towards the shopping centre. Just then, Sal wound down his window and called out.

'Don't forget to get a size eight for me.'

I spotted Bilal laughing along with him from the back seat.

Ali had parked in a loading bay, next to a side entrance to the shopping centre. It was busy – drivers were making deliveries and other people were milling around. Ali spun round to try and shut his mate up. He looked livid as he marched over to the car to speak to Sal.

'Nah, bruv, it's not happening.'

Sal raised his hands in protest, but Ali was having none of it.

'I said, you can wait.'

Sal immediately backed down. He pulled out a spliff and lit it, taking short, angry drags. Ali came back over to me and nothing else was said as we walked the rest of the way in silence.

The lights in the shopping centre were blinding. I'd never noticed before but now, standing there beneath them, I felt they were all focused on me, making it very obvious what I was about to do. Outside, it was a warm summer's day. Even though the shopping centre was vast, the inside felt hot and claustrophobic. I anxiously fanned a hand against my face to try and cool myself down.

Nerves, it's just nerves. I'll be fine.

'You okay?' Ali asked.

He was standing there, staring at me. I forced a weak smile because I didn't want to make him angry.

'Yeah, I'm good. I'm just a bit … God, it's so hot in here.'

Ali placed his mouth against my ear and I flinched as the skin of his lips brushed against my earlobe.

'Don't fuck this up. Keep your shit together, understand?'

'Yeah, I'm good.'

It was a lie. Inside I was a trembling wreck. I'd never felt so scared in my life. I knew the shopping centre well, as Mum popped in to window shop, dragging me along with her when I was younger. Of course, she'd never buy anything – everything was far too expensive. Yet, there I was, about to 'buy' trainers from one of the biggest stores in the entire complex.

We made our way through the throngs of people – families on weekend shopping trips and friends killing time – when something occurred to me. In fact, it almost made me stop dead in my tracks. Scarlett was good friends with a couple of guys who worked there. She'd even introduced me to them months before when we'd browsed the trainers.

What if they recognise me?

But I looked different now. Back then, my clothes and hair had been awful. Scarlett had helped me sort myself out. I'd reinvented myself.

No, they'll never recognise me.

I needed to be confident because if I acted it, then I'd look it. Then I remembered Barry – the security guard who fancied Scarlett. She'd flirt with him every time we went into the store. We'd laugh about it afterwards because Barry was tall, skinny and ginger – he didn't stand a chance, and everyone knew, everyone apart from Barry.

What if he's there? What if he sees me?

Just then, the illuminated logo flashed into sight.

'Right,' Ali said, stopping for a moment. 'I'll show you the trainers I want you to buy. Then I'll leave the shop, and then – only then – do you go up and take them to the counter. Do you understand?'

I nodded.

Ali stared as though he didn't believe me.

'Gaia, don't fuck this up.'

'I won't, I promise.'

He rested both hands on my shoulders and gripped them tight.

'Stay chilled. Okay?'

'Okay.'

With that we walked over and into the store. It was bright and busy with shoppers looking at sportswear or sitting down on seated cubes to try on trainers. There were so many people – bodies everywhere. As we made our way through the crowd, I craned my head to look for Barry, the security guard. Thankfully, there was no sign of him.

I followed Ali as he wound his way over towards the trainers, which were stacked high on shelves that ran the entire length of the wall. Ali made his way over to a pair of Reebok Classics. The trainers were loud and ugly, with a gold bar emblazoned with a logo on the side. A brightly coloured tag dangled from them as Ali held one up in his hand. I twisted it to try and read. The tag stated that the trainers were exclusive to the shop.

'Hey mate,' Ali said, signalling over to one of the young shop assistants.

The lad stopped what he was doing and came over.

'You got these in a nine?'

The assistant took the trainer from him and checked the sticker on the sole.

'I'll go and check.'

'Thanks, mate.'

I tried not to react. Ali wasn't his mate – he wasn't anyone's mate. He certainly wasn't mine, and yet here I was. The assistant disappeared through a side door to go and look for Ali's size. As I turned back, Ali had gone.

Has he left already?

I began to panic.

What do I tell the assistant? Should I buy the trainers when he brings them back?

I tried to stay calm, but the fact that Ali had walked off without any warning freaked me out. Just then, I spotted a familiar head bobbing around in the distance – Ali. His floppy fringe marked him out as I walked over to him. That's when I realised he was still shopping. He already had a few things piled up in his hands and it was clear he was far from finished.

I gulped.

I thought you just wanted a pair of trainers.

The assistant was standing over by the trainer wall, craning his head to look for us. I nudged Ali and gestured to the lad.

'Do you want to try them on?' the assistant asked Ali as we went back over there.

'Nah, mate. Just give 'em to her.'

The assistant seemed a little bemused.

'Is it his birthday?'

I smiled politely.

'Yeah, something like that.'

Only it wasn't. They weren't gifts, they were things I was about to steal for a man who didn't give two shits about me.

As well as the Reeboks, Ali picked out a pair of Nike TNs. They were covered in garish blue swirls and were expensive at £110 for the pair.

'Sick!' he exclaimed, handing them to me.

My stomach churned with dread. But Ali wasn't finished. He crossed the store to rifle through a rail of tracksuits, checking each one for its size as he swiped them by. Finally, he stopped, lifted one up and plonked it on top of the Nike and Reebok trainers I already had in my hands.

'Well, don't just stand there, go and pay for 'em. But wait until I've gone. You understand?'

'Yeah.'

He strolled casually out of the store, pushing his way through a crowd of people before leaving by the main entrance. This was it. I was on my own. With both my arms full, I walked over to the counter. It was a Saturday afternoon – the busiest day – and a small queue had already started to form. I took my place at the back and glanced around.

No Barry, I mouthed silently inside my head.

The waiting seemed to make my anxiety worse. Although no one had batted an eyelid, I felt as though all eyes were on me. Biting my bottom lip, I waited, my stomach churning, as I neared the front of the queue.

Calm, keep calm.

A man approached the counter in front of me. His young son was with him. The boy grinned as his dad paid for some trainers and the sales assistant smiled sweetly as she handed the young boy his bag. His eyes lit up as he peered inside.

'Can I wear them now?' he asked his dad.

'Yeah, of course you can.'

Mum flashed across my mind.

She'd never do anything like that for me.

'Next,' a young shop assistant shouted, calling me forward.

But my thoughts were still full of Mum.

'Can I help you?' the girl called out again.

A woman standing behind me tapped me on the shoulder. It made me jump.

'I think you're next.'

'Oh, yes, sorry.' I replied, feeling flustered.

I went over to the till and rested both sets of trainers on top of the counter. Although she'd smiled, I noticed it didn't reach the shop assistant's eyes. It didn't matter. I was grateful I'd got her and not her older colleague. A long blonde ponytail swished at the back of her head as she lifted each trainer out of their boxes to check they were the same size.

'Did you find everything you were looking for today?' she asked.

'Um, yeah, thank you.'

I prayed that I sounded much more confident than I felt. The girl turned both boxes around, looking for the price. I studied her while she was distracted. She looked young – possibly a school leaver. The till beeped as she scanned and inputted the prices of the trainers and tracksuit. I was almost home and dry.

'Card or cash?' she said, looking up at me properly for the very first time.

'Card,' I replied, as I pulled it out from inside my jacket pocket.

She seemed surprised and gazed at me quizzically as though trying to weigh me up. As she took the card from me, my stomach knotted.

She knows. She's a similar age; she knows I'm not old enough to have a card.

I knew it and so did she. It was written all over her

face. I thought I might be safer with a younger assistant, but I was wrong. She could see I was a fraud. She realised I was younger than she was. But the card was already in her hand and I didn't know what to do.

Think, think …

My mind scrambled as I tried to hold it together. I rearranged my face and tried to look nonplussed as the girl swiped the card through the till. But my heart was racing. I checked behind me anxiously. My hands were trembling, so I pushed them inside my jacket pockets. But the girl had already seen.

Oh God!

She immediately stopped what she was doing.

'Erm, I just need to call my manager.'

Oh God, here goes …

My leg trembled along with my hands as I tried to concentrate on keeping calm. But something in the girl's voice told me she didn't believe me.

She knows.

My tongue rested, fat inside my mouth, as I tried to think of something – anything – to say.

Get out of here.

The girl pressed a buzzer as my mind went blank. Frozen, I stood there, my eyes darting everywhere, looking for an escape.

Get out of here!

My heart throbbed inside my throat as fear took over.

What the fuck do I do?

As we waited for the manager, I sensed the girl staring at me, taking me in. I smiled, but it was a thin, watery smile. A smile that said, 'I'm guilty.'

Do I run? Do I stay? Fuck, fuck, fuck!

Normally, Ali and Sal would only be feet away, waiting in the car. But they were parked with Bilal around the other side of the shopping centre.

It's too far. Too far to run.

'He won't be a minute,' the shop assistant added.

Was she trying to stall me?

I looked for Barry, but there was still no sign of him.

That's good, isn't it? Maybe this is routine?

The rest of the world carried on as normal as we waited and waited. Finally, after what had felt like an eternity, the manager appeared. He wore a white shirt and it set him apart from the rest of the staff dressed in identical jersey tops.

'Sorry about your wait,' he said coldly.

I knew what he was thinking. *Why is this schoolgirl using a credit card?*

Even with all the make-up on my face, I realised I couldn't fool him. I looked and felt every one of my fourteen years. Although I was certain he'd already sussed me out, to his credit the manager decided to humour me. I checked the ceiling for CCTV cameras.

Was he filming me?

When I glanced back at him, the manager was checking the card. He checked the till before turning to me.

'I'm afraid your card company is asking me to call through for authorisation.'

Authorisation? Christ!

'Oh, okay, what does that mean?' I mumbled, sounding like the teenager I was.

He stared at me for a moment too long, and that's when I was certain; he knew it wasn't mine.

'Oh, I just need to go through a few questions with them and then you'll be good to go.'

I don't believe you. You're lying.

Trapped, I glanced at the door. As I did, a security guard hovered into view.

'I'm sorry,' I said, trying to think on my feet.

I had to make an excuse for a quick getaway. Checking my watch, I pulled a surprised face and acted as though I'd just remembered I had to be somewhere.

'Sorry, but I don't have time for that. I'll just leave it. Thank you.'

I reached out for the credit card, Ali's warning ringing in my ears.

'Do not let them take the card off you.'

I knew he'd be furious if I returned empty-handed, minus the card. I stood there with my hand out, waiting for the card. Trying to adopt my best poker face, I looked directly into the manager's eyes.

'Thank you anyway,' I said.

I wiggled my fingers impatiently as I waited for him to hand it back. Amazingly, he did, and that's when I ran. I ran towards the door as fast as my legs could carry me. The security guard watched as I dashed out and into the safety of the shopping centre.

Lose yourself in the crowd.

So I did. Walking briskly, my eyes darted left and right as I headed for the main exit. I checked over my shoulder, but there was no one there – no one was following me.

Thank God!

Sick with panic, I took deep, slow breaths to try and calm myself down. Soon I was outside. I began to run back to the car. Ali seemed pissed off as soon as he realised I'd returned empty-handed.

'What the fuck!'

'Please, let me get in the car. Quick, Sal, hurry up. Hurry up!'

Sal jumped out quickly as I got in the back and shoved me next to Bilal. The car had already started to move before Sal even had a chance to close the door properly.

'What the fuck …?'

It was Ali. He sounded freaked out, but not as much as I was.

'I'm sorry, but I thought they were going to stop me …'

Ali looked at Sal in horror.

'Why? What happened?'

I was just about to explain, when he fired another question.

'Fuck, they didn't follow you, did they? Cos, if they did, I'm gonna …'

'No. They wanted authorisation, but I said I didn't have time to wait.'

Ali listened and began to nod.

'Sweet, what else?'

'I got the card back, like you told me to.'

I held it up as he stared at it through the windscreen mirror. The card seemed to calm him.

'That's all right then,' he sniffed, rubbing his hand against his nose in annoyance. 'We'll just get another one.'

Another one? What, another credit card? He wants me to try again!

Mentally spent, I pushed myself back into the seat and we drove along the road in silence. We hadn't even driven five hundred yards when the wail of sirens pierced the air.

'Shit!' Sal cursed.

He checked the road behind in the car's wing mirror.

'Fuck, it's the Feds!'

Bilal's head twisted to look behind and Ali's knuckles flashed white as he gripped the steering wheel. Suddenly, the inside of the car was illuminated; bathed in blue flashing light as a police car pulled in front of us, forcing us to stop. The blue light lit up Sal and Ali's panicked expressions in the front as they stared at one another.

It sounds crazy, but even then I didn't register that we might be in trouble. We'd been pulled over by the police before. They'd wanted to check insurance details and other documents. I convinced myself it was just another one of those times. Besides, I still had the card. They had nothing on me.

'Gaia, the card!' Ali gasped, suddenly remembering it. 'Push it deep down between the seats. Do it! Do it now!'

I did as he said as quickly and discreetly as I could as Bilal slid over to one side. Ali ratcheted up the handbrake as a police officer approached his door. He signalled for him to wind down the car window, so Ali did as he was told. The officer leaned in towards the car and began to speak.

'Ali, could you please turn off the ignition, pass me the key and step out of the vehicle?'

How does he know his name?

Ali climbed out, followed by Sal and Bilal. Then the officer asked me to get out. As I did, I heard a commotion at the side of me. Another officer began to give chase as

Bilal made a break for it. Bilal was fast and he soon disappeared off into the distance.

Gobsmacked, I turned to Ali and Sal. They both seemed shifty as their eyes darted between me and the other police officer. Just then, Ali gave me a glance as if to say, 'Don't say a word.' The metal handcuffs clinked loudly as they were put on his wrists and then Sal's.

Christ, they'd arrested them both!

Suddenly, everything seemed frighteningly real. This wasn't a game – this was real life.

'Look, I don't know anything,' Ali said, as he began to protest his innocence. 'I'm just the driver. I didn't do anything. It's nothing to do with me.'

Then he nodded over towards me.

'She's the one you want, not me.'

Bastard!

Just like that, Ali had turned on me and then Sal did the same. With their friend gone, they both decided to sell me down the river. With Ali and Sal in handcuffs, the officer turned to me and began to speak.

'Gaia Cooper, I am arresting you on suspicion of attempting to obtain property by deception. You do not have to say anything, but it may harm your defence if you do not mention when questioned something which you later rely on in court. Anything you do say may be given in evidence …'

But I'd already stopped listening. Shock had rendered me mute.

CHAPTER NINE

APPROPRIATE ADULT

As the officer put me in handcuffs, I bit my lip and tried to suppress an overwhelming urge to cry.

With his colleague still giving chase after Bilal, he called for back-up and another two squad cars to transport Ali and Sal to the station. Before Ali got in, he shot me the same warning look not to drop him in it. I nodded slightly to let him know that I understood. I tried to look at Sal but he had his back turned to me as he climbed into the squad car.

I'd been arrested once before for the phone thing, but it had been nothing to do with me. This did. I'd never had any dealings with the police before, apart from that one time.

Mum. Her face suddenly zoomed into my mind.

She's going to kill me!

The hard, metal edge of the handcuffs bit the thin skin on my wrist. I twisted them to try and make them more comfortable, but I didn't dare complain. I was in enough trouble. The officer placed a flat hand on the top of my head to protect it as he guided me down and into the back of the squad car. I tried to look for Ali, but I couldn't see him anymore. I wondered if I'd see him later at the station.

Yes, I decided. *They'll take me to the station, realise I'm only fourteen and let me go.*

However, I soon discovered that life doesn't work like that because it isn't a fairytale.

The police station was just minutes away from where we'd been stopped. It almost felt as if they'd been lying in wait. As we drove over there, I looked into the front of the squad car. It wasn't like any other vehicle I'd ever travelled in. There was a walkie-talkie-type device mounted on the dashboard with a lead running from it. The officer picked it up and reported back to the station that he was bringing me in.

'We have a fourteen-year-old female ...' he garbled, as the line hissed and crackled.

I zoned out.

I'm in the back of a police car!

My stomach flipped with fear.

This is really happening.

The police radio continued to crackle and buzz as we pulled up behind the back of the town's police station. I spotted a small, inconspicuous metal door at the back of the building as we parked up in front of it. I don't know why, but I'd expected to be led through the automatic doors of the main reception area. I'd expected that, not this.

This must be where they sneak in the criminals, I decided.

It sounds odd, but I didn't consider myself a criminal. Not yet, anyway.

Another officer held the metal door open as his colleague led me down a long corridor. At the end there was a large desk surrounded by a Perspex screen. Behind that stood a tall, grey-haired man with a weary face that indicated he'd seen it all before. He finished typing something into a computer at the side before turning to look at me. As he peered over the top of his black-rimmed glasses, bile rose at the back of my throat, scorching it. I swallowed hard as the senior police officer began to speak.

'Gaia, I'm the custody sergeant. Do you understand where you are?'

I nodded.

'Good. The officer has read you your caution, and he has explained why you are here and why you have been detained. Do you understand what he has told you?'

I gulped and nodded to show that I had.

'Very well,' he said.

He turned back towards the computer to input my details. Although he seemed intimidating by his height alone, the custody sergeant had a kind face. He looked like someone's grandad. The kind of grandad who'd spoil his grandkids on their birthdays and at Christmas. The kind of grandad I'd have loved for myself. He was so calm and gentle that I felt a sudden urge to cry. For the first time I'd felt something. When it dawned on me what it was, it stole my breath away. Shame. I felt nothing but shame. I was fourteen years old. I'd been handcuffed, arrested and was now standing inside a police station. I was a kid playing at being an adult. But I didn't want to be an adult any longer, I just wanted to go home.

'Gaia, did you hear what I just said?'

It was the custody sergeant.

'Sorry, no, please could you repeat it.'

I tried to focus but my heart skittered with panic.

The sergeant sighed and nodded as though he understood.

'Gaia, you need to listen to this next part because it's very important. I'm going to read you the caution again and then your rights. You are entitled to free independent legal representation – a solicitor – but I will need to contact your parents to let them know you're here.'

I swallowed hard. But he hadn't finished.

'One of them will have to attend. They will need to sit with you and be your appropriate adult because you're only fourteen years old.'

I couldn't hold it back any longer; vomit rose again at the back of my throat, and I was certain I'd throw up right then and there on the spot.

'No, no, it's okay,' I gasped, trying to fight back the nausea. 'I don't need anyone to come. You don't need to tell them. You don't need to let them know anything.'

I'd hoped my protests would be enough to ward off the phone call home. I imagined Mum picking up the telephone in the hallway and her face contorting with anger as she was told I'd been arrested for using a stolen credit card.

'Please don't call my parents,' I began to beg.

I hoped he'd take it onboard. I hoped he'd simply accept my word for it, only he didn't. Instead, he shook his head.

'No, because of your age I am duty-bound to let your parents know where you are and that you're safe in custody. To protect your rights and to make sure that you are given a fair interview, an appropriate adult must attend and sit with you. Do you understand?'

Defeated, my heart sank to the floor.

The sergeant was reassuring. It may sound strange, but no matter how scared I felt with the threat of a phone call home hanging over me, I didn't want to disappoint him. I also didn't want to argue with him. He'd been so polite and kind that I didn't want to appear rude. There was nothing I could do, so I decided to accept my fate and the consequences that went with it. However, first I'd have to face Mum or Richard, my stepdad. There was no getting round the fact that one of them would have to come to the station. I prayed it would be my stepdad.

Once he'd read me my rights, the custody sergeant booked me in. I emptied my pockets as he began to list my property. I didn't have much on me, only a lip gloss, a few Sovereign cigarettes, my mobile and a couple of loose pound coins. Placing it all inside a clear zip-tie bag, he jotted my name on the front and bundled the bag inside a locker. That's when I noticed the tower of lockers behind his desk. It was massive – three lockers tall and five lockers across – and all the doors were royal blue. Bizarrely, they reminded me of the ones at the swimming pool, only this wasn't the swimming pool and I didn't get to keep the key. My eyes scanned the custody area. I was just wondering which room they'd take me in to wait for my parents when another officer guided me off towards the cells. I was petrified. I'd expected a telling-off, I'd even expected Mum to turn up, screaming and shouting, but I'd never expected this.

'What? You want me to go in there?' I asked, slightly bewildered.

The officer nodded sharply and held the cell door open. I turned to look back at the nice custody sergeant, but he was busy dealing with the next criminal.

Criminal. Is that what I am?

'Shoes.'

The copper pointed down at my trainers.

I must have looked a bit vacant because he explained things to me in short, sharp sentences.

'Off. Take them off. Leave them at the door.'

I did as I was told and placed my trainers at the side of the doorway. My legs trembled as I stepped inside the cell. The floor was sticky and my thin socks stuck to it before peeling away with each step. The walls were made of thick brick and they'd been painted in heavy gloss paint. I turned to look back at the metal door, equally imposing and escape-proof.

What the fuck am I going to do?

I tried to think of something – anything – to try and change their minds so they'd let me out of there. My thoughts were interrupted by a loud slam as the large, blue cell door thudded shut, cutting me off from the rest of the world. There was a distinct chill in the air, so I wrapped both arms around myself to try and keep warm. The place smelled of stale urine and cheap pine disinfectant mixed together. Someone had tried, but failed, to mask the awful smell. My nostrils widened. There was something else – food. My stomach rumbled, reminding me I hadn't eaten for hours. But it didn't smell like nice food or the kind of stuff to make your mouth water. It smelled of cheap school dinners, only not as good. Needles of anxiety stabbed inside my stomach. If they planned to feed me, then they planned to keep me locked up for hours.

Thoughts of swimming-pool lockers and school dinners swirled around my head as I turned to survey the rest of the cell – my home for the rest of the daytime, possibly the evening too. I felt strangely misplaced, as though this wasn't really happening to me. Using my finger and thumb, I pinched and twisted some skin on my arm. The sharp pain made me wince.

No, this is real. This is really happening.

I scanned the rest of the cell. There was a makeshift bed in the corner placed on top of a wooden base raised half a foot off the ground. A bright blue mat had been laid on top of it, reminding me of the ones we used in PE at school.

I gulped.

School. Wait until they hear about this. The head will refuse to take me back and I'll end up in a pupil referral unit like Scarlett.

I shook the thought away.

No, it wouldn't happen.

As bad as she was, Mum would never let that happen.

I spotted a small metal toilet opposite the bed. It looked uncomfortable and there was no privacy to speak of.

Christ, will they watch me go to the toilet?

Clutching my face, I dragged both hands down it in despair.

This is horrible. What the fuck am I doing here?

I'd been arrested before because of the phone, but that had only been for a few hours. That time, I'd been with Scarlett. This time, I was alone.

I patted my hands along the cold wall in disbelief.

There's no way out.

It sounds ridiculous but the thought of it left me speechless. I was only a kid and, right now, I felt like one.

Why the fuck had I listened to Ali and Sal?

I cursed. I should have listened to Scarlett. She'd tried to warn me, tried to tell me not to do it – and that's when it hit me.

Fuck! What if I go to prison? What if they lock me in a place like this forever?

I doubled over in shock, as though someone had just punched me in the stomach. Even though I tried to slow my thought processes down, my mind raced.

No, they wouldn't put me in prison. They only know about the one card.

To try and calm myself, I lay down on the blue mat. It was freezing cold, tomb-like. Everything seemed alien and terrifying, and I really didn't have a clue what would happen next. The place smelt of fear. The shouts, cries and catcalls of other prisoners penetrated the thick cell walls and door. Footsteps and the constant slamming of metal doors echoed on the other side, making me nervous.

As I stared at the door, I noticed a square shape had been cut into its upper part – an observation hatch. I couldn't see out, but they could see in. Suddenly, the shutter screeched open. There was a rectangle of light and two eyes stared in at me, watching.

I wondered if someone had come to let me out. But, as soon as I'd thought it, the hatch slammed shut again. Footsteps sounded outside in the corridor before fading into the distance. I grew bored and, with nothing else to do, I started to read all the different names that people had carved into the wall. Paint had flaked off where prisoners had used their fingers to pick at it and spell out the letters of their name. It reminded me of the girls' toilets back at school, but this was worse than anything

I'd seen there. It was even worse than the shelters at the bus station.

I traced a finger along each one. There was a Johnno, a Mikey, a Bev and a Rav.

How the hell have they managed to carve their names into solid brick?

I read and traced each one to try and while away the time. When I tired of that, I lay down on the mattress and closed my eyes. I tried to fall asleep but the cell was absolutely freezing and there was no blanket to cover myself with. I didn't want to ask for one because I wasn't sure if the missing blanket was all part of my punishment. Time seemed to stand still as I tried to count each second.

One … two … three …

Christ, I really need a cigarette!

I stopped and started the count again. I was gagging for a cigarette – my body craved what it couldn't have.

I wondered if Scarlett knows where I am? I thought randomly.

Then I remembered Sandy, and my heart plummeted.

She'd be so disappointed.

I couldn't bear the thought of it as I respected her so much. Sandy was decent, kind and hard-working.

Everything I'm not.

I turned onto my side; blood rose into my face as I burned with shame. *Sandy.* I'd always had such a special bond with her because, unlike everyone else, she'd never judged me. I didn't want her to think badly of me. In fact, the thought of it scared me because I couldn't lose Sandy. Not now, when I really needed her.

Mum would be furious. She'd call me a disgrace and tell me how disgusted she was with me. She'd always wanted me out of her hair and now, maybe now, her wish had come true. I'd just handed it to her on a plate.

The police rang home, as they said they would. I was told Mum wouldn't come to the station. I'd not expected much, but I suppose I'd expected more than that. With no appropriate adult, I was forced to wait for the on-duty social worker to appoint one. A stranger took Mum's place.

As I was already in enough trouble, I decided I couldn't drag Ali or Sal down with me. The police tried their best to get me to admit that both men had been involved, but I refused to snitch on them. Besides, I knew my life wouldn't be worth living if I did.

'So, Gaia, how do you know Ali? Is he a good friend of yours?'

I folded my arms defiantly and turned my face to the side, away from the officer.

'No comment.'

'And Sal? Is he a good friend of yours?'

My face flushed pink.

'No comment.'

'And the card – the card is stolen. You do know that, don't you?' the officer said, as he pressed me further.

'Yes.'

My answer seemed to reignite him and he sat up straight in his chair.

'So, you admit the card is stolen?'

'Yes.'

'And who gave you the stolen card, Gaia?'

I stared at him coolly.

'No one, it was my idea. I stole it and I used it in the shop. It was nothing to do with Ali or Sam. They had nothing to do with any of it.'

The officer glanced at his female colleague, who picked things up. Her questioning seemed softer and, somehow, gentler.

Good cop, bad cop.

'Gaia, you do know that we know these men. They are both known to the police. They've been getting into trouble for years, so you can tell us if they stole the card and gave it to you. You can tell us if they made you do it.'

Sal's face flashed across my mind, and I imagined how angry he'd be if I grassed him up.

'They didn't. Neither of them knew anything about the card. I stole it and I used it without them knowing. Just me.'

The woman pursed her lips in frustration.

She knows I'm lying.

She gave her colleague a knowing glance. He placed both elbows flat on the desk and clutched his hands together, as though he was about to pray.

'Look,' he sighed wearily. 'We've had both of those lads in here lots of times for stolen cards and, whenever we've nicked them, they cry like babies. They're not the big, tough men that they make themselves out to be, so you can tell us, Gaia. Did they nick the card?'

I sniffed and looked him directly in the eye.

'No, I did.'

By now both officers seemed exasperated by my misplaced loyalty, but I'd done exactly what Ali and Sal wanted me to. After half an hour of questioning, I was taken back to my cell as I waited for the custody sergeant to bail me. Two hours later he did.

I realised I was done for when I finally returned home. The police dropped me back outside in the early hours.

I'd been gone for hours. Sure enough, Mum was waiting as the squad car pulled away. I could see her outline through the side glass panel as I approached the front door. Curtains twitched as the neighbours snooped from behind them and I stepped inside the house. Mum was boiling with rage. In fact, I'd never seen her so angry. Before I'd even closed the front door, she started on me.

'I'm not tolerating this anymore. You are choosing to do this. It's your choice and I refuse to put up with it any longer. In fact, I won't.'

I rolled my eyes; I'd heard it all before.

'You're nothing but a common thief. Is that what you want out of life?'

I shook my head wearily.

'Well, what do you want out of life? Because, I'll tell you one thing, you're ruining my life. You're ruining my life, your life … and you're ruining our marriage,' she said dramatically.

She looked to my stepdad for back-up. For once, he seemed equally angry – and that crushed me. I didn't care about Mum, but I cared about Richard. In fact, I loved him because he was the closest thing to a father I had.

'I'm sorry, Dad.'

But instead of forgiveness, Richard erupted.

'I'll bounce you off every wall in this house, do you hear me? The police came here and searched the place. They even searched your baby sister's cot. Do you know how that felt?'

I stared at the ground. They were just words, I knew that. I knew he'd never raise a hand to me. It was the thought I'd let him down – that's what killed me. My eyes brimmed with tears.

'Oh no, don't you turn on the waterworks!' Mum began to scream. 'You don't go to school and you spend your time hanging around with that little tramp ...'

Her words made me shake with fury.

'Scarlett isn't a tramp! You don't know anything about her.'

But she refused to back down.

'I know she's a little trollop and I don't want you to be a little trollop like her. And as for that stupid mother of hers ...'

Stop it, just stop it!

I'd had enough. Mum could say whatever she wanted about me, but she couldn't say anything about Scarlett or Sandy.

'Yeah, well, she's a better mother than you! At least I feel welcome over there. I'd much rather live with them than here with you.'

Mum paused, and looked me up and down.

'Is that right? Well, you need to be careful what you wish for.'

And she was right, I did.

████████████████ **Social Services**

Date: June 2000
Time: 8.20 p.m.
Referred: Sgt ██████████ of ██████████ custody

Reason for referral: Gaia has been arrested with three others from a motor vehicle. She has been arrested on suspicion of obtaining property by deception using stolen credit cards. Police have contacted Gaia's mother and stepfather. As she had already discussed the offence with them, police thought they were not in a position to act as her appropriate adults. It also transpired from the conversation that the parents are at 'the end of their tether' and need urgent help with Gaia's behaviour. Background action taken note that case referred to CCT by mother on 24 May 2000, but still awaiting action.

11 p.m.: Was informed that ▬▬▬▬ had contacted custody several times wanting to speak to social worker. Interviews were delayed while police undertook house searches. Spoke to ▬▬▬▬ and ▬▬▬▬ by telephone. Both told me that Gaia is beyond their control and they want her to be accommodated.

They have been in touch with SSD several times, but their understanding is that nothing can be done if Gaia refuses to speak to the social worker, ▬▬▬▬, who had made an appointment with Gaia today at school. Instead of going to school, Gaia has apparently been on a shopping spree. ▬▬▬▬ seems to understand the limitation of the care system, ▬▬▬▬▬▬▬▬▬▬▬▬▬▬▬. However, she says that she can see no prospect of things improving if Gaia remains at home. She says that Gaia steals from home, has lots of clothes etc. which do not belong to her, frequently physically assaults mother etc. Gaia has not attended school regularly for some time. Having transferred to ▬▬▬▬ school because of problems at ▬▬▬▬. There is a lengthy history already known to social worker and Child Mental Health team. I explained that there were no places available for Gaia on an emergency basis and that if the family was determined that they could no longer try and work with Gaia at home, they would have to make a formal request for her to come into care. Parents seem to think that they have made such a request, but they are being ignored.

█████████ said they are worried that she may be using drugs. She uses cannabis and they think she may be trying other substances. With great reluctance they accepted that if bailed, Gaia would return home tonight. They will go through the motions of trying to make sure she attends school tomorrow, although they seem to think it unlikely that she will.

0.45 a.m.: █████████ (appropriate adult) called. Gaia has been bailed to return on █████████ at █████████. She was arrested with a group of Asian lads who are 17+. Police are now taking Gaia home.

This situation seems to be very fragile and the family is in need of continuing support at present.

Signed: █████████████.

CHAPTER TEN

KIDNAPPED

A week after I was arrested, word spread. Scarlett's mum was so appalled that she banned me from their house. I was mortified but I also understood. Scarlett already attended a pupil referral unit, so I realised that to hang around with a 'common thief' like me wouldn't help her. I also knew Sandy had a soft spot for me and I decided to appeal to her better nature. Knocking at the door, I took a deep breath as I waited for her to answer. Her face immediately fell as soon as she spotted me standing on her doorstep.

'Oh, Gaia,' she gasped, looking a little startled.

'Look, Sandy,' I began, as I held out my hand to stop her from slamming the door in my face.

'I know why you don't want me hanging around with Scarlett, and I understand. But if I don't have you and Scarlett, well …'

I looked down at the ground, as I tried to search for the right words.

'The truth is, if I don't have you and Scarlett, then I have nobody. Mum hates me – she always has, and Richard, well, he's furious with me. They both call me a thief and they don't want me in the house, but you ... well, you and Scarlett have always been so kind to me. You're like the family I never had, and I promise, I cross my heart that I'll never let you down again. What happened – the arrest – that thing is all in the past now. It frightened me, Sandy, and I swear I'm going to change. I swear I'll stay out of trouble. I never wanted it to take over my life, but it did. Everything just spiralled out of control – and I couldn't stop it – but now I can, and I will.'

Sandy's eyes searched mine as though trying to convince herself that I meant what I'd said. But I did. Every single word.

'And will you promise me you'll not get Scarlett involved with any of those men you've been knocking about with?'

I agreed, even though it had been Scarlett who'd introduced me to them, not the other way round.

'Yes, I promise. I swear I won't let you down, Sandy. Please ... please can I see Scarlett again?'

She didn't speak for a few moments. I fretted she'd close the door in my face and that would be that. However, she decided to give me one last chance and opened the door to welcome me in. I hugged her gratefully. She grabbed my arms and held me away.

'Now, don't you let me down.'

'I won't.'

'Okay, well, Scarlett is upstairs in her room. She's been moping around without you, so go up and see her.'

I didn't need telling twice. I bolted up the stairs, two steps at a time.

'Only meeee,' I called out.

I tapped a hand against her bedroom door and pushed it open. Scarlett was lying on her bed, listening to Usher and smoking a fag.

'Gaia!'

I wrapped my arms around her as I began to explain how her mum had given me a second chance.

'She's always liked you,' Scarlett smiled.

She passed me her half-smoked cigarette. I took a puff of it and handed it back.

'I know, but I'm done with all that now, Scar. I've learned my lesson.'

'Really?'

Her eyes were wide, as though she didn't believe me.

'Yep.'

This time I vowed not to mess things up. Sandy had thrown me a lifeline and I was determined I wouldn't let her down. So, an hour or so later, when my phone flashed Sal's name, I panicked.

'Shit!'

I turned the screen towards Scarlett to show her.

'Aren't you going to answer it?'

'Nope.'

I'd promised Sandy. Scarlett realised how much Sal's call had spooked me.

'Let's ignore him – tell him to fuck off! We'll go to Hayley's house instead.'

'Hayley?'

'Yeah, she invited me over. There's vodka in the house and her mum is out all night.'

A smile broke across my face. I was just so happy to be back with my best friend.

'Let's go!'

Hayley's house was on the other side of town so it took us a good forty-five minutes to walk there. On the way, I filled Scarlett in on my recent arrest.

'Weren't you scared?'

'I was shitting myself, Scar. Bilal did a runner. The police eventually caught up with him, but they didn't charge any of them.'

'How come?'

'Ali told them he was just the driver. I wouldn't mind, but he was the one who picked out the trainers. They were for him.'

Scarlett shook her head in disgust. She was starting to see Ali for what he really was.

'Oh, babes, I told you you'll get in some serious shit for that, and you have.'

I shrugged and pretended I wasn't bothered but, in truth, I was mortified.

By the time we arrived at the house, Hayley was already drunk. At seventeen years old, she was three years older than me. She was supposed to be babysitting her younger sister, but when we knocked on her front door it was clear she was too far gone to even look after herself.

'Baaaaaabes!' she screeched, as soon as the door opened.

Hayley dipped towards us and clumsily wrapped her arms around us both.

I raised an eyebrow and glanced over at Scarlett. It was way over the top, even for Hayley.

'Come in, come in, and get yourselves a drink.'

A fag hung precariously from the edge of her mouth, dusting the carpet with ash, as she waved us inside. Loud garage tunes blasted out of some tinny speakers in the living room. The music was deafening, but her baby sister was nowhere to be seen.

'We've got so much catching up to do,' Hayley shouted above the din.

Oh God, she's so drunk; I don't want to be as drunk as her.

The house had cream carpets, so we took off our shoes and left them by the front door. Then we followed Hayley upstairs to her bedroom.

'How long is your mum gonna be out for, Hales?' Scarlett asked her loudly, as we all climbed the stairs.

Hayley staggered a little when she turned to look back at us. Thinking she'd fall, Scarlett put out both hands to try and balance her.

'Cheers, darling,' Hayley giggled, steadying herself on the top step. 'Mum? Oh, she's out all night, so we're sweet, babes.'

Hayley had also been involved with lots of different, older men, but unlike me she came from a good home. Hayley's house was spotless and her bedroom was massive, with a vast fitted wardrobe that ran the whole length of the wall.

'What do you keep in there?' I asked.

I pointed over to the wardrobe, so Hayley jumped to her feet, went over and slid open the doors dramatically.

'Clothes, babes. Why, what else would I keep in there?'

I was stunned. Never in my life had I seen so many clothes belonging to one person. Scarlett loved her clothes, but even she didn't own that many. There were dozens of tops, skirts, jackets, all fighting for space. Underneath was a mountain of shoes and trainers. I felt a pang of jealousy as I went over to take a closer look, thinking of the cramped built-in cupboard in my bedroom. It was so small there was barely any room for clothes. I shuddered with revulsion as I recalled how I'd once hidden used sanitary pads inside it.

'You're so lucky, Hales. Look how many clothes you've got.'

I slid each item along the rail as I leafed through them.

'My mum never buys me anything, unless it's my birthday,' I complained.

'Forget that,' Hayley said with a wave of her hand. 'Let's all get pissed on vodka!'

Scarlett squealed with delight, but I didn't really feel like drinking. I'd only ever been drunk twice in my life – both times bad things had happened, and I hated the feeling of not being in control and how vulnerable it left me. Despite all this, I agreed to the offer, and Scarlett seemed happy I'd finally relented. Delighted that we'd join her, Hayley brought up two more glasses from downstairs and poured us each a vodka and Coke. Giggling, Scarlett grabbed her glass and slugged it straight back, while I took small and measured sips.

A short while later my phone rang. It was inside my handbag, so I rummaged around for it. As soon as I saw the caller, I raised an eyebrow. It was Sal again. I ignored it and let it go through to voicemail. Almost as soon as it had, it rang again. And again. In the end, Sal called me five times, but I ignored each and every one.

Sandy, I promised Sandy.

I couldn't fuck things up.

Scarlett looked over as my phone continued to ring.

'It's Sal,' I whispered, mouthing his name.

She rolled her eyes but didn't seem that surprised.

'He lives over the other side of the estate; he's probably seen us walking over here.'

I'd completely forgotten we were just around the corner from where he lived.

'Do you think he's seen us?'

Scarlett shrugged.

'Who knows?'

The calls had spooked me out, and I took a deeper sip of my drink. The next time my phone rang, Scarlett took it from me.

'Don't!'

I panicked. I knew Scarlett was tipsy – and she wasn't frightened of Sal, like I was.

'What do you want?' she screamed down the phone.

My stomach flipped with nerves; Sal would be furious. A moment later my friend began to laugh as she listened to what he had to say.

'Oh, really? Is that right? Well, Gaia isn't coming out tonight, so fuuuuuccccckkkk you!'

My stomach fell away.

Sal's going to kill me!

Only Scarlett hadn't finished. She was still talking.

'What? No, I told you, she doesn't want to speak to you. No.'

It was clear that he refused to give up and insisted Scarlett hand the phone to me.

I backed away and waved my hands furiously, but Scarlett was drunk so she handed it to me anyway. As I took it from her, she dipped forward to whisper something in my ear.

'Remember what you said.'

I nodded.

It was obvious from the tone of his voice that Sal was livid.

'Where are you, you four-eyed little slag?'

I was incensed and sick of him calling me names. Bolstered by too much vodka, I decided I'd had enough.

'Fuck off, Sal,' I replied coolly.

Scarlett was so surprised that she spat out her vodka in shock.

'What did you say, Four Eyes?'

'You heard, I said, "Fuck off." We're at Hayley's, we're having fun and no, we're NOT going to meet you, all right?'

Scarlett snorted, then began to cough and splutter.

There was a slight pause, then Sal answered.

'Is that right?'

He sounded calm – too calm.

'We'll see,' he added.

With that he hung up, as my heart thumped.

'Oh my God, Gaia!'

Scarlett looked flabbergasted.

'What did he say?'

I was just about to tell her when the front door slammed loudly.

'Shit!' Hayley gasped.

She got up and started to try and hide the vodka, but it was too late – her mother came storming into the room. As soon as she saw the state of us, she went spare.

'Turn that racket off now!'

She pointed downstairs to the front room, where the walls were still throbbing with garage music.

Hayley ran downstairs to turn it off and within seconds the house was deathly quiet. Her mother scanned

Hayley's bedroom – and us. I gave Scarlett a sideways glance, but she seemed preoccupied with staring at the ground.

'Right,' Hayley's mum said.

She turned to address her daughter, who'd just come running back up to her room, breathless. 'You clear this lot up, and as for you two ... OUT!'

With the party over, Scarlett and I left our drinks half-drunk, and made our way downstairs to our shoes and the front door.

'Er, thanks, Hales. See you later,' Scarlett called.

She didn't reply. Instead, we heard Hayley's mother screaming, her words drifting through her bedroom window and out into the night air.

'... treat this place like a hotel ... and you better not think you can have those two over here again ...'

Scarlett grabbed the top of my arm.

'Come on, let's get out of here.'

Laughing, we ran off down the street and into the darkened night. For all my earlier bravado, the cold air sobered me. In my head I rewound my earlier conversation with Sal.

'Shit! Scar, I told him where we were, and he knows where Hayley lives.'

Scarlett stopped and thought for a moment as we came up with a plan. We decided it would be far safer to walk down the back alleys home to try and avoid him. It was almost 10 p.m., so we began to walk with purpose. As we did, my eyes darted all around, searching in the shadows, looking for Sal. I knew what he was like, and I knew he'd make me pay.

The sound of my phone ringing broke the night's

silence, making me jump. Reluctantly, I pulled it out of my bag, knowing full well who was calling.

I turned the screen to Scarlett.

'Why does he keep ringing you?'

I shrugged. I didn't have a clue. I just wanted to be free of the pair of them, but now that they had me, it was clear they wouldn't let me go.

Scarlett stopped abruptly in the middle of the alleyway, with her face dimly lit in the orange glow from a nearby street lamp.

'Look,' she said. 'If we ignore him, then he can't make us meet him.'

Scarlett was right. If I didn't answer, then Sal couldn't make me do anything.

But it didn't stop him from calling, the screen on my Nokia mobile repeatedly lighting up green with his name and number. Determined, I continued to ignore him as we made our way over towards a playing field in the middle of the estate. The field was surrounded by a ten-foot wire fence, and we were just looking for a hole in the side of it to cut across the field when two blinding car headlights picked us out.

'Shit!' I panicked.

I lifted a hand to try and shield my eyes. Although I couldn't be sure, I was certain it was Sal.

'Fuck!' Scarlett cursed. 'You think it's him?'

I nodded.

'What the fuck are we going to do?'

Suddenly, the headlights dipped from full to normal beam. Then the car began to move as it drove along and around the perimeter towards us. As it drew closer, I sighed with relief because I didn't recognise the car.

'It's not him. That's not Sal's car.'

'Are you sure?'

'Yeah!'

However, just as it was about to pass, the driver screeched to a sudden halt.

'Come here, you pair of cheeky little slags.'

I froze. It *was* Sal. His face simmered with anger as my eyes met his. He was sitting behind the wheel of a car I'd never seen before – a car he'd probably stolen. My breathing quickened. I knew we had two choices: we could either go over and try to pacify him, or we could run. We decided to run. Tearing around the outside of the field, we ran until we found a broken piece of fence and scrambled through it.

'Oww!' Scarlett cried.

I turned back to help her. She'd caught her foot on something and had tumbled over.

'Quick, Scar! He's coming.'

We heard a car door slam as Sal began to give chase. Pulling Scarlett to her feet, we continued to run, our shoes slipping in the mud as we tried to escape.

'Come here, you little slags.'

I knew he was gaining ground. His feet thundered as they closed in on us.

I desperately wanted to look over my shoulder, but I knew it'd only slow me down.

Run. Keep running.

Thud, thud, thud. Sal's trainers hammered hard against the ground behind us.

'He's coming!' Scarlett screamed.

I willed my legs to move quicker, but I was already running as fast as I could. My muscles ached as cold air burned inside both lungs. There was a tug from behind and I found myself being pulled backwards by the strap of my handbag. Sal had grabbed it, dragging me towards him. With the bag in his hands, Sal unzipped it and emptied the contents onto the playing field. I'd stowed both mine and Scarlett's phone inside the bag, but Sal grabbed them and tucked them inside his jacket pocket. Then he grabbed Scarlett and frogmarched us both across the field and back to his car. He emptied the rest of my bag along the way; a booklet of stamps, my favourite lip gloss, a hairbrush, tiny compact mirror and some loose tampons scattered as we went, lost in the night. He stopped and shook the last of the contents free. Metal tinkled as a handful of loose coins cascaded to the ground, scattering in the long grass.

'Don't, Sal. Please don't!'

He wasn't listening. Sal wasn't interested in what I had to say, he just wanted to punish me. Wrapping his fingers around my wrist he twisted hard.

'Owww! You fucking prick!' I screamed in his face.

Sal stopped and stared, and I immediately cowered. I waited for him to hit me and I think he would have done so, if it hadn't been for Scarlett.

'We didn't want to meet you! We can meet whoever we fucking want! It's a free country,' she screamed.

But he didn't stop. Instead, he hauled us back to the car. He momentarily let go as he opened the door. I thought about making a run for it, but I knew I couldn't leave Scarlett.

God only knows what he'd do to her if I did.

You're evil, I decided.

His dark brown eyes glinted with anger as he shoved Scarlett and then me into the back seat. We fell like a pair of rag dolls. Fear and adrenaline pumped through my veins as he started up the engine and began to drive fast into the dark night.

'Where are we going?' Scarlett asked.

I knew from the way her eyes darted from me to him that she was frightened.

Sal glared at us in the rear-view mirror.

'You'll see soon enough, you pair of cheeky bitches.'

The car continued to travel at high speed along the back roads, the street lights whizzing by in a long orange blur. I glanced through the side window, trying to work out where we were. It was impossible – all the houses looked the same. Soon the street lights petered out and faded behind us, and that's when I realised.

We're not in town anymore. We're in the country.

The feathered outlines of hedges and trees passed by and then blank, darkened fields. There were no landmarks and no buildings, just dark land.

My heart throbbed as I tried to muster enough courage to speak to Sal.

'What are you doing? Where are we going?'

His eyes stared back at me in the mirror before shifting to the road ahead.

Silence.

I tried to placate him.

'We just didn't want to come out tonight, we wanted to chill with Hayley, that's all. It's nothing personal.'

Silence.

I glanced over at Scarlett; she looked as terrified as I felt right now. I was certain Sal was capable of anything because he'd always had a cruelty about him. I didn't want him to have any more power. Power over us – two frightened schoolgirls pinned to the back seat of his car as we drove at frightening speeds. *Speed.* I glanced at the speedometer. The needle dipped and rose as it nudged 70mph. Still, he showed no sign of slowing down.

Scarlett tapped my forearm urgently.

'Do you think he's going to dump us somewhere?' she whispered.

I mouthed for her to 'shush' as Sal's head twitched suspiciously.

'What's that, Four Eyes?'

'I didn't say anything. We just wondered what we're doing and where we're going?'

But my trembling voice betrayed my nerves. Miles upon miles of pitch-black nothingness whirred by outside as we drove deeper into the countryside.

Is he going to hurt us?

I held Scarlett's hand and gave it a reassuring squeeze. At least we were together.

Suddenly, I could see lights in the distance. They glowed a warm yellow against the dark night sky. Sal indicated, the car turned and began to drive up a long, bumpy driveway. There was the square outline of a building up ahead. It had a pitched roof. I spotted a sign hanging outside as it swayed in the breeze.

A pub. He's driven us to a country pub!

Relief flooded my veins.

Gravel crunched beneath the car tyres as Sal brought the vehicle to a halt.

'This is where you two mouthy little slags are getting dropped off.'

My friend looked at me and I knew what she was thinking. Being dropped at a pub in the middle of nowhere wasn't great, but it could have been worse. However, our ordeal wasn't over.

'Guess what? You're not having your phones back either, you dumb little bitches. Let's see how mouthy you are now.'

Sal smirked maliciously and gestured for us to get out.

He's bluffing. He won't leave us here with no money and no phones.

Only he wasn't. He climbed out and pulled the back door open.

'Get out!'

'No,' Scarlett said, trying to stand her ground.

Sal drummed his fingers impatiently against the car roof.

He was winding us up, wasn't he?

But Sal wasn't laughing. The joke was on us because he'd tossed all my loose change across the playing field. It hadn't been much – 70p at most – but at least it would have paid for a single phone call.

Fear kicked in as we both realised he was being serious. I gestured towards the headrests in front and wrapped my arms around one of them. Scarlett did the same.

'I am not playing with you, get the fuck out my car.'

We clung on for dear life and refused to budge. Sal grew angry and pulled our clothes and hair to try to get us to move. A struggle followed as he unceremoniously dragged us both out and threw us onto the gravel. Scarlett was screaming but I was livid. First, he'd kidnapped us and now he was going to abandon us miles from home.

'You fucking prick! What are we supposed to do?'

But he didn't reply. He walked around to the driver's side, climbed in, and roared off as we sat there choking on dust churned up by the car wheels. We had no choice but to go inside. We approached the pub door together and pushed it open. A raucous din hit us, followed by the warmth of the bar. Standing inside the pub, we were unsure what to do; a fourteen-year-old and her sixteen-year-old pal, with no money or way of getting home.

'All right, girls, lost yer mum, have ya?' a butch-looking woman shouted across the bar.

The other punters looked up and another woman snorted with laughter. Middle-aged men propped on bar stools turned to stare at us, making me feel uncomfortable.

'Come on, Scar,' I said, as I walked over to a cigarette vending machine.

It was fixed to a wall at the side of the bar so we stood there as a couple of the men began to fire drunken remarks our way. It soon became clear we'd be the butt of their jokes for the evening.

How the hell can we ask them for help? What would we say?

I knew if we told them we'd been kidnapped and dumped they wouldn't believe us. I thought of Sandy and how she'd never forgive me for dragging Scarlett into such a mess.

Staring at the vending machine, I tried to gather my thoughts. I'd only ever bought cigarettes from a shop, so I'd never seen a machine like this before. The neatly stacked rows of cigarettes fascinated me. I was still staring at them when I had a brainwave. Checking over each shoulder, I pushed two fingers into the change dispenser to feel around for change. By some miracle, I found a lone 20p piece. I took it and held it up to show Scarlett. Her eyes widened and her face lit with hope that the coin could somehow transport us back home.

'You want a fag, darling? I got baccy,' the butch woman called over.

Right then, I'd have killed for a fag but I had bigger fish to fry.

'Do you have a phone box?' I asked the sullen-looking barman.

He grunted once and motioned to a hallway outside the bar through a set of double doors. With the 20p piece in my hand, I went through and dialled Sal's mobile. I knew I couldn't ring Mum and I certainly couldn't call Sandy, and there weren't any other numbers that I knew off by heart. I dialled his number and waited. I knew the payphone wouldn't swallow my money unless he answered, but his phone rang out. He'd obviously spotted the area dialling code and decided to ignore it. I tried again only this time he answered and then hung up, which sent the call through to voicemail.

This is the Vodafone voicemail service for 0-7-7-6-5-9-6-…

Livid, I slammed down the receiver. It had swallowed the 20p piece – our last lifeline. Downcast, I wandered back into the bar. The butch-looking woman took pity and kindly rolled a fag for me and Scarlett to share. The woman was horrendously drunk and had to cling to the underneath of the bar to try and stop herself from toppling off her bar stool.

I thanked her for the cigarette and wandered back outside, followed by my friend.

'I asked that woman which way we should go to get back into town,' Scarlett announced. 'She said to follow the main road and keep walking straight until we passed a garage.'

'And then what?'

Our hot breath rose up in clouds as we spoke.

'She said there'll be signs from there, pointing towards town. She said to follow the A-roads.'

Christ, we must be miles away.

The cold night air bit through our thin clothes as we walked along the darkened road. There weren't any street lights, just the blackest of nights. The only light was the glow of the warm pub we'd left behind. I pulled my jacket around me and linked my arm through Scarlett's to try and keep our spirits up. The country road was edged with a bumpy grass verge on an incline that dropped towards a thick hedge. The branches caught Scarlett's clothes as I walked on the outside.

'Gaia, you keep pushing me into the hedge,' she complained.

'Yeah, and you keep pushing me into the road!'

The verge was so narrow that we decided to walk single file as we stumbled along, but my shoes were thick and heavy.

'Fuck!' I howled moments later.

I doubled over in pain and fell to the ground.

'What the fuck, Gaia, are you okay?'

'I've tripped on something.'

I stretched out a hand and began to feel around.

'It's a metal grate; I almost broke my fucking ankle!'

Thankfully, no bones were broken, but I'd twisted my ankle badly. To make matters worse, the fall had ripped a hole in my jeans at the knee. A sharp pain stabbed through my leg and I dabbed my fingers against it. When I pulled them away, I spotted blood.

'Babe, you okay?' Scarlett asked gently.

I nodded, even though I felt far from it. As soon as I stood up, the ripped denim flapped against my skin.

'That fucking bastard! How could he just leave us here?' Scarlett screamed in anger.

But no one could hear her.

'If only Hayley's mum hadn't come home when she did then we'd still be there – inside a lovely, warm house.'

I cursed her, even though I barely knew her.

In the end we walked for miles, moaning and occasionally crying at the injustice of it all. Each footstep felt like agony. Blood had congealed against my knee and my feet were numb with cold. Finally, we spotted a BP garage up in the distance. The illuminated green and yellow sign felt like a beacon of hope in the barren landscape. We walked towards it, our footsteps growing faster because we knew we were a step closer to home.

Just then, a passing car beeped his horn loudly. My heart pounded.

Sal?

Scarlett looked scared.

'You think it's him?'

I didn't have a clue. The beeping continued as we looked on in confusion. It didn't look like Sal's car, but it was dark and hard to see. Just then, the car turned back and drove towards us, its headlights picking us out against the hedgerow. It drew up alongside and a man I'd never seen before wound down his window and began to shout.

'What the hell are two little girls doing walking out here on these roads at this time of night? Who are your parents?'

His anger shocked me as we didn't even know him.

Who the fuck does he think he is?

However, his fury stemmed from the fact he'd almost hit us.

As Scarlett began to explain where we were from the man nodded knowingly.

'Yeah, I'm from the same town but that doesn't answer my question. Why are you out here at this time of night? You could've been killed!'

We explained that a man had dropped and abandoned us there as the motorist shook his head in disgust.

'What was the name of the man who dropped you here?'

I was nervous telling him, but reasoned that it was a big town so there was no way he'd know Sal.

'His name is Salim, but they call him Sal. You won't know him.'

The man thumped his hand against the steering wheel. I looked at Scarlett.

'Know him?' the man said in a rage. 'I know him all right. I trained that little twat! I was his football coach and trained him since he was five years old.'

I gasped, but he hadn't finished.

'Right, my name's Dave,' he said by way of introduction, before he gestured over to the passenger seat.

'Get in, both of you. We're going straight to his uncle's house. See what he's got to say about this.'

Although we didn't know him, we realised we didn't have much choice. It was either get in the car or walk another eight miles home.

'Come on, Gaia,' Scarlett said, making the decision for us. 'Let's get in.'

I wasn't sure if the man was a serial killer, but the thought of walking any further in my stupid shoes was too much to bear. I knew it probably wasn't one of my better moves, but Sal hadn't left us with much choice. There was no Plan B. We were tired, scared and half-frozen to the bone. We got in the car.

'Belts,' Dave said, urging us to fasten them.

It made me feel a little better; a serial killer wouldn't care if we wore a seatbelt or not. We'd only been driving for a few minutes when Dave mentioned Sal's uncle by his first name.

I breathed a sigh of relief. He *did* know him.

Twenty minutes later he was banging on his door, but there was no answer.

'Don't worry,' he insisted. 'I'm not leaving it; I'm going to call at his shop now.'

Dave was so incensed at Sal's reckless actions that, within a short space of time, he'd gone from being a stranger to our hero. Deep down, I knew Sal wouldn't want his uncle to hear what he'd done. But then again, how were we supposed to know that Dave – a random stranger who'd rescued us from the roadside – would know Sal's family? I could hardly believe that, out of the handful of cars that had passed, Dave would be the only one to stop and help. I'd just started to wonder how protective he must be over his own kids when he parked up in a side road. He climbed out and walked fifty yards over to Sal's uncle's shop. I watched as Dave pushed open the shop door and disappeared off inside. Ten minutes later he reappeared, only this time he seemed much calmer.

'Right, that's all sorted. Now, where am I dropping you two off?'

We didn't ask what had been said. We didn't dare. But I was terrified it would land Sal in a whole heap of trouble and he'd take it out on me. The pair of us were still a little subdued as my mate directed Dave through the estate and back to her house. Five minutes later we pulled up outside her front door. He waited until we were both safe inside and then he drove off.

'Gaia,' Scarlett whispered. 'I think he knows Mum.'

My mouth fell open. As if the night couldn't get any weirder.

'Are you sure?'

'I'm certain.'

I knew there was nothing else for it; we'd have to come clean with Sandy. She stood there in the hallway and listened intently as we explained how a boy we knew had abandoned us 'as a joke' in the middle of nowhere.

'Just wait till I get my hands on him. I'll wring his bloody neck!'

Sandy was furious and demanded to know his name, but then she caught sight of my bloodied knee.

'Gaia, what the hell have you done? Oh, come on, come in here,' she said, leading me into the kitchen. 'I need to bathe it. That looks nasty.'

By now it was the early hours of the morning. We were cold, tired, hungry and all out of excuses. I'd fucked up again, and I knew it. Sandy's kindness made me feel even worse. I'd broken my promise to her, and I knew she'd never trust me again. It made me feel less than worthless. It made me want to weep.

CHAPTER ELEVEN

THE RAVE

Weirdly, the next time we saw him, Sal didn't say a word about Dave calling at his uncle's shop to complain about him. I wasn't sure if anything had been said but, if it had, then Sal didn't tell us, and I certainly wasn't going to bring it up and ask him. If he'd been given a bollocking by his family, then he didn't let on. Maybe his male pride wouldn't let him – I have no idea. But, afterwards, the kidnap was never mentioned again.

One night, the four of us had been hanging out together but no one wanted to go home.

'Let's go to a rave,' Ali suggested.

'Yeah!' Scarlett squealed.

She waved her hands about in the back of the car as though she was already there. I glanced at Sal in the windscreen mirror, almost as though seeking his permission. I waited for him to say something, but he shrugged as if he didn't care either way. He was driving for a change, so, I suppose, the final decision rested with him.

'Gaia, you up for it, the rave?' Ali asked.

'Yeah, why not?'

In truth, I didn't want to go back home to Mum. I was desperate to join in and had a teenage fear of missing out. Ali turned to Sal.

'Come on, bruv,' he began to plead, in a tone of voice I'd never heard before.

Sal thought for a moment, then nodded in agreement, turning the ignition and firing up the car. We drove for miles, looking for a specific field in the middle of nowhere, but we didn't need a map or road signs; the stream of people and the thump of music showed us the way. The car rocked and dipped from side to side as we travelled down what appeared to be a dirt track. My mate and I were thrown around the back of the car like straw dolls with every pothole we hit, and we cursed as we both banged and bashed our heads against the car's interior. I could hear the rave before I saw it; the throbbing music grew louder and I knew we were only a matter of minutes away. My stomach fluttered with excitement. I grabbed Scarlett's hand and gave it a squeeze.

I can't believe we're doing this. It's so exciting!

The place was packed with haphazardly parked cars, but we eventually managed to find a spot. Sal yanked up the handbrake and snuffed out the headlights. It was pitch-black outside, and with the lights off it felt even more forbidden.

This was my first illegal rave – Scarlett's too – and we were both giddy with excitement. It reminded me of when I used to go camping with Mum: the dark night, the bumpy and uneven ground, torches and headlights as cars drove around, searching for a pitch in the dead of night. Only this time there were no fly sheets, tent pegs or guy ropes to trip us up. We hadn't packed sleeping bags or pot noodles, and there were no enamel mugs for hot chocolate. It was just us, the night ahead and a giant marquee lit up like a castle in the distance. I didn't know what to expect. I'd only ever heard about illegal raves on the news, of people dying and police arrests. But that only made tonight more exciting.

The beat of the music crept along the ground and vibrated beneath our feet as we reached the marquee.

Thud, thud, thud.

I usually preferred R&B to electronic dance music, but as soon as we entered the tent I realised it was going to be a night like no other. The place was hot, sweaty and heaving with bodies. The lights, sounds and atmosphere were electric. I stood there captivated as all around me people danced and moved in time to the beat. Dancers had stripped off to the bare minimum as bodies pulsated everywhere. Everyone was smiling, high on the music and having a great time. The atmosphere felt so uplifting that Scarlett began to dance and join in, but I couldn't. No matter how much I wanted to, I was just unable to let go. I hated the feeling of losing control because it absolutely terrified me.

Despite my reservations, the rave was a joyous and unthreatening place to be, as strangers hugged one another. Although we were an hour's drive from home, I spotted a few familiar faces in the crowd. I recognised a lad called Alim from town. He was a big-time drug dealer who usually dressed in the most expensive clothes and drove the flashiest car, much to the envy of Ali and Sal, so I stared in disbelief as he began to do the 'running man'. Alim was laughing his head off. It was clear he didn't give a toss what anyone thought of it or him.

I couldn't believe it because he was usually such a hard man. People feared him but he was so immersed in the music that he didn't give a shit. No one did. Everyone was hellbent on having an amazing time. There were a few more small-town gangsters in the crowd but here they weren't anything special. They were just like everyone else. Ravers danced and jumped around without a care in the world because here, music was God. Just as it reached its frenzied peak, the pace suddenly dropped, slowing to a pulsating Bob Marley reggae bassline. Once everyone had been given enough time to catch their breath, the beat sped up once more, a huge cheer rang out and whistles were blown as the crowd went crazy. It was one huge, exuberant party.

Scarlett came over and grabbed my hand. Her eyes were wide in wonder as we both stared out at the sea of bodies. She felt the same as me – we were both hooked. I was still watching when I felt a tap on my shoulder. I turned to find Sal standing there. He gestured for us both to follow him out of the tent. Neither Scarlett nor I wanted to leave, but because he'd brought us here, we knew better than to disobey him. We trudged back to the car with our ears still ringing with the music's insistent pulse.

Sal turned to speak to us.

'We're just gonna smoke a zoot and wait for my cousin,' he explained, as he lit a spliff and passed it over.

He blew smoke out of both nostrils.

'What do you think?'

'It's incredible,' Scarlett replied.

She was grinning like a Cheshire cat. I was just about to agree when a random man passed and began to shout something at the top of his lungs.

'Pilllsss … pilllsss!'

Bemused, I looked at my mate and then at Sal.

'What's he shouting? Is he a bit crazy?'

Sal tipped his head back and snorted with laughter. For a change, he wasn't being cruel. He was genuinely pissing himself.

'Nah, it's normal for these places. He's just doin' his thang, selling pills, ya know.'

'Pills?'

Scarlett sounded so young and horrified that Sal rolled his eyes in annoyance, as though he was dealing with a right pair of kids.

'Yeah … E's.'

I must have looked baffled because he decided to elaborate.

'It's E's – ecstasy, girls. They're all over this place.'

Scarlett's eyes widened.

'Yeah,' Sal continued. 'I might drop one in a bit. Why, you girls want one?'

I exchanged a glance with my pal.

'Um, maybe,' I said, nudging her with my elbow.

Scarlett made an L-shape with each hand to form a square, but I was being cautious. My only knowledge of ecstasy was stuff I'd gleaned from the news. I remembered hearing about a girl called Leah Betts on the TV, who'd died only a few years earlier. The young girl's face had been everywhere on TV and in the papers, and I remember thinking how normal she appeared. She looked like me and my friends – in fact, like half the girls at my school, and that scared me. I'd had the odd spliff, sure, but I hadn't tried 'hard' drugs. I'd never even considered taking pills before, but then I'd never been to

166

a rave. This was a whole new territory. So, a little later, when Sal offered us each a tablet, I hesitated.

'What is it?' I whispered in Scarlett's ear.

Sal overheard.

'It's a Mitsubishi, Four Eyes. Take one, it might help you relax.'

I glanced at the pills in his hand and it immediately became clear why it was called a Mitsubishi. The tablet had three diamonds carved into it and looked exactly like the car logo. Scarlett took one from Sal. She popped it on the tip of her tongue and washed it down with a slug of water.

'Come on, Gaia, it'll be fun!'

Although I felt out of my depth, I didn't want to be the boring one, holding everyone else back. Sal's eyes were on me as I rested a pill on my tongue and swallowed it down.

'Sweet!' he grinned.

I felt relieved I'd done something right for once.

'Come on, let's parrrrrttty!' Scarlett screamed loudly into the night.

She grabbed my hand and we ran back to the tent. As we entered, Scarlett turned to say something, but her voice was drowned out by the music. Huge speakers, stacked twenty feet high, blasted through us and above our heads as the whole tent pounded in unison.

Even though I'd just swallowed ecstasy, I refused to dance because I was terrified that I'd make a fool of myself. Undeterred, Scarlett disappeared into the centre of the throng as I stuck to the edges. Everyone was having the time of their lives, arms flailing in the air as people waved and pounded their feet in time with the beat. Each tune seemed to blend seamlessly into the next as strobe lights flashed in time, picking out the rising steam from the dancing bodies. Scarlett danced back towards me, then Ali and Sal came in to join us. Moments later they'd wandered off somewhere, but I didn't care about them or what they were up to. All I cared about was this – the music and the blissful state of happiness I found myself in.

It had been a hot summer's day and the air was still, with no breeze to speak of. Although it was evening and I was only wearing a T-shirt and jeans, I was baking hot. Sweat soaked me as I stood and watched strangers dance. I'd never met any of them before but these ravers felt like my people – my tribe. The sense of belonging and acceptance ignited something deep down inside. I never wanted to go home.

At one point, Scarlett came over to stand next to me.

'I don't want this to ever end,' I hollered over the music.

She turned and smiled serenely. She was already high.

We were two young schoolgirls, who'd bunked off class that day and had just taken pills at an illegal rave.

I've found my place. This is where I belong.

The effects of the ecstasy rolled on, long into the night. At one point I turned to look for Scarlett. She'd been dancing for what seemed like ages, but time felt elastic and I couldn't honestly say if we'd been there hours or just a matter of minutes. My head and body swam with the effects of MDMA, heightening my senses. I felt elated that I'd found this place, this field. I'd finally found my happily ever after. Just then, I opened my mouth and gasped like a fish stranded on the sand.

I went over and grabbed Scarlett's arm.

'Water … I need water,' I said, mouthing the words.

Scarlett nodded and ran her fingers across her soaking wet hair, dragging it off her sweaty face.

'Me too!'

We left the tent and found a litre bottle nearby that someone had either abandoned or forgotten. We gulped it down greedily, sharing it between us. Once it had all gone, we found someone selling bottles of water so we bought another and drank that one too.

'I'm still thirsty,' I complained.

'Me too,' Scarlett agreed.

We bought another and continued to gulp mouthful after mouthful. Just then, Ali and Sal reappeared. They were with two guys I'd never seen before. One of them watched me as I glugged half a bottle down in the space of a minute.

'Hey!' he called.

Reaching out, he snatched the bottle from my hands.

'Give it back!' I shouted angrily, thinking he'd stolen it. But he hadn't.

'No, you can drink too much water. It's not good for you. You need to slow down!'

I refused. I was hot and thirsty – I needed to drink. This man was clearly chatting shit. I stretched forward and tried to take the bottle back, but he pulled it away sharply.

'No!'

'What's your problem?' I screamed, exasperated.

I turned to Ali for back-up. To my surprise, he backed the stranger.

'He's right. If you drink too much water, it'll kill you.'

I laughed because I'd never heard anything so ridiculous in all my life. But my laughter annoyed Ali.

'It's true. You drink too much of that shit too quickly and your brain will swell up. It's like that girl, innit?'

'What girl?'

'The one who drank too much water after dropping ecstasy. It killed her … Leah something.'

My heart stalled inside my chest as I recalled her face on TV. I panicked, and began to try and calculate how much we'd already had to drink. I turned to my friend.

'Scar, how many bottles have we drunk?'

But she couldn't remember, and nor could I. Over the next few hours, I was petrified and paranoid that we'd slip into a coma from water intoxication. Thirsty, but now too scared to drink, my mate and I wandered over to the speakers. We began to scramble up them and perched ourselves right at the top. Scarlett shuffled up next to me as we both looked out across a landscape of writhing bodies, all shifting in time with the music.

Thud, thud, thud.

We were watching the crowd dance when the strangest thing began to happen. At first it was so slight that I thought I'd imagined it.

Thud, thud, thud.

My heart began to pound.

Thud, thud, thud.

The music continued.

Thud, thud, thud.

My heart thumped until soon it exactly matched the beat. I took a deep breath to try and separate the two.

Thud, thud, thud.

Only I couldn't. As the music began to speed up, so did my heart. It felt as though the pulsating bassline streaming from the speakers had taken control of me.

Thud, thud, thud.

The vibration tingled against the backs of my legs, tickling my skin and working its way through dense muscle, into my major organs and up towards my heart.

Thud, thud, thud.

Now terrified, I clutched a hand against my chest to try and make it stop.

Thud, thud, thud.

Everything throbbed in time as I reached out and grabbed my pal by her shoulder.

'Scar, I think I'm having a heart attack!'

But she couldn't hear me. All she could hear was the music, so she smiled back serenely.

Thud, thud, thud.

I stared at the ground twenty feet below us. The earth seemed to rise towards me at a frightening speed before it zoomed away again. I blinked hard and tried to concentrate.

Speakers … I must get off the speakers.

Thud, thud, thud.

I honestly believed I was about to die as I scrambled back down to the grass below. I needed to stand still on solid earth, to escape the music, the beat and the sickening vibration. But as soon as I planted my feet on soil, I realised the feeling was still there.

Thud, thud, thud.

It spread from the soles of my feet up both legs. I shook them to try and rid myself of the sensation. Scarlett must have realised I was in trouble because she'd jumped down to try and help me.

'Need to sit down … think … I think I'm going to die!'

My friend hooked her arm underneath mine, then led me out and away from the tent. At one point she ran off to look for Ali and Sal so she could get the keys for the car. Helping me onto the back seat, Scarlett stopped and checked me over.

'You okay?'

'I think so.'

But I wasn't. The whole episode had frightened the shit out of me. That's when I realised I'd not eaten. I'd not been for a pee either, even though I'd drunk all that water. Eventually, I must have dozed off for a split second, sitting upright in the car. Tired. I was dog-tired.

Sometime later, Ali and Sal returned. Sal tapped a hand against the glass, waking me with a start. Then he opened the car door.

'Here,' he said, handing me a sizable packet of pills, 'you carry these for us.'

For a split second I wondered where he'd got them. But I knew what he was like and thought better than to ask. It was obvious they'd been stolen, probably from someone too stoned to realise.

Although time seemed irrelevant, I later discovered I'd been at the rave for three days solid and had been awake almost seventy-two hours. I had no clue I'd been gone so long. It was only when I returned home that it became apparent.

'What the hell do you think you're playing at?' Mum screamed as soon as I stepped in through the front door.

It transpired that both she and Sandy had reported us missing to the police. Officers had been dispatched. They'd taken detailed descriptions and recent photos of both Scarlett and me, and everyone had been out looking for us. I'd no longer come through the door than a couple of policemen were there, knocking. They wanted to speak to me. As Mum invited both in, one dipped down and stared at my face. I automatically backed away.

'She's taken something,' he told Mum. 'Look at her eyes; they're glazed over and huge, like dinner plates.'

They asked me lots of questions but I refused to tell them a single thing. I felt tired and emotionally spent; I needed to sleep.

The police said I should probably get checked out at the hospital, but I couldn't be arsed because I just wanted to lie down.

After they'd left, Mum stood and surveyed me. I was half-slumped in an armchair in the front room.

'Look at the state of you! Is this it? Is this what you want your life to be – one long disappointment? I'm ashamed of you, Gaia Cooper. I'm ashamed you're my daughter.'

I didn't answer. I knew there'd be no point – I'd never win the argument.

But Mum hadn't finished.

'Well, I've had enough of you bringing trouble into this house. I've had enough of you, and this time I'm going to do something about it.'

And she did. In fact, she'd already done it, secretly and behind my back. Unbeknownst to me, Mum had been speaking to people behind the scenes. Something was about to happen, and it would change the course of my life forever.

CHAPTER TWELVE

RIOT VAN

By now, I felt too far gone. I'd become too entangled in my new fast-paced life, working and hanging out with much older men who only wanted two things – to use and abuse me.

One day, Bilal wanted to meet up so I could help him with some 'work'. He picked me up from the middle of town and, as we rumbled along the A-roads, the inside of the car clouded up with blueish-grey cannabis smoke. It had a strong chemical smell, and I could feel my eyes and chest burning as I breathed it in. We drove on for a while before turning off from a slip road into a picturesque little village. En route, we'd picked up a kid called Johnno, who I'd met on jobs before. I didn't know much about him other than he lived in a children's home. Bilal used him just like Ali and Sal had used me – for crime. Kids like us, I was beginning to understand, never got stopped. Shopkeepers didn't suspect us because we looked fresh-faced and were well presented. In short, we didn't look like stereotypical criminals. Johnno was young – around sixteen years old – and eager to please. In many ways he reminded me a little of myself.

Criminally speaking, Johnno was always ready and able, but more importantly, he was willing to do whatever anyone asked of him. Today was one of those days. Like me, Johnno was the underdog. I listened as Bilal bossed him around and treated him like shit. He'd be sent to steal things – laptops, cards or whatever he was told to get. Even though he'd stolen things worth hundreds of pounds, Johnno would only be 'paid' £10 for his trouble. It was exploitation in its purest form – Johnno took all the risks while Bilal took the lion's share of the rewards.

I felt for Johnno because he was a sweet boy and a nice person; he'd just had a shit start in life, and the men – Bilal and his associates – exploited it and him. Like me, Johnno had desperately wanted to belong to something – anything – because it was better than being alone. I'd been on jobs with him a couple of times before, with me playing the part of the female back-up. Johnno could do the job, but he was often sloppy and sometimes he'd slip up. Whenever that happened, Bilal would beat him.

After driving around the chocolate-box village for ten minutes, Bilal pulled up outside a Budgens store. He turned to Johnno and gave him his instructions.

'I want you to go in there and get some more cards, understand? Try the staff room, and for fuck's sake don't get caught.'

Johnno nodded dutifully and climbed out of the car without a second glance. By now I realised how the gang operated. They didn't only target hospital waiting rooms and doctors' surgeries for unattended handbags, they also stole from staff rooms and prohibited areas inside shops and small supermarkets. It wasn't an elaborate deception sting, just a shifty-looking kid committing petty theft by scratching around for spoils.

As we waited in Bilal's car, he began to blather on about how fantastic and good-looking he was. I was bored so I zoned out as he continued to boast.

'I wear the best clothes, have the prettiest girlfriend and the biggest dick. But you know that, don't you?' he added, with a wink.

My stomach turned over because Bilal made my flesh creep. I'd been 'gifted' to him by Sal, who'd ordered me to do stuff with him. As I listened to him brag, I decided he was just an insecure bully.

I stared down at my nails and began to pick at them. It was a nervous habit and one I'd adopted following the credit card frauds. I would bite them, gnawing against my nails with my teeth until my fingers bled. Pain was good because pain helped me to feel something. It was my release. I'd begun to self-harm too, slashing my arms. By damaging myself, it helped release some of the self-loathing that had built up inside. Hatred bubbled and boiled deep within me. I'd become a volcano of misery and anger, waiting to erupt.

'Gaia, go see where that thick bastard is, will ya?'

My thoughts were broken by Bilal's voice.

'He's been fucking ages. Could you go and check on him, please?'

At least he said, 'Please'.

'No problem.'

I got out of the car and walked towards the shop to try and track Johnno down. Stepping through the doors, I surveyed inside. There was a mirrored window at the back of the store beside a door with a sign on it that read 'Staff Only'.

He'll be in there.

I had absolutely no intention of going in there myself. To try and blend in, I pretended to shop for items. Wandering along one of the aisles, I picked up a tin of beans and checked the other tins stacked on the shelves. That's when I spotted Johnno. He'd walked past me with his eyes focused straight ahead on the door. Seconds later, he was outside it. I quickened my pace to try and catch him up. As I grew close, Johnno caught my gaze and motioned for me to walk ahead. Once we were both sufficiently far enough away from the store, Johnno caught up with me. He was grinning broadly as if he'd just discovered he'd won the lottery.

'I fucking smashed it in there!'

He checked over one shoulder towards the Budgens, which was now far behind us.

'Yeah, I clapped three cards and some cash.'

He was clearly delighted with himself, but I realised this could mean trouble. Inwardly, I groaned.

'Did you put everything back as it was?' I asked. 'You didn't take a purse, did you?'

I'd said it out of concern for my own safety more than his. From bitter experience, I knew that once a shop assistant had realised their purse had been stolen, they'd quickly cancel all their bank cards. However, if everything else had been left intact then they were less likely to notice one card had gone missing until later. This would buy us a few precious hours to get the 'shopping done', get out of there, and be home and dry.

I'd learned quickly, which was strange because I'd never ever been exposed to theft or crime when I was growing up, a little bit of hash back in the strange flat with Mum being the extent of my involvement with anything remotely criminal. Now deception and credit card fraud were my life and my job. I'd become entangled with a set of extremely unsavoury men who I wrongly considered to be my friends. I was young and foolish, as well being so blinkered and bullied that I didn't see the bigger picture until it completely engulfed me.

By the time we reached the car, Johnno was buzzing. He couldn't wait to boast and show Bilal his prized haul.

'You fucking prick!' Bilal roared as soon as he saw it.

He was beyond angry and cursed Johnno as he climbed back into the car. Bilal passed the stolen cards to me and pocketed all the cash.

'I'm taking that,' he said, pushing it inside his jean pocket.

Johnno seemed confused because he didn't understand what he'd done wrong.

'I got the cards, just as you said.'

Bilal's eyes flashed with anger.

'Yeah, but as soon as they clock the cash is missing, they'll report the card too.'

The young boy's shoulders sank as if he was completely deflated. He'd messed up again and he knew that Bilal wouldn't pull any punches when it came to his 'punishment'. The car engine started up and we roared off in the direction of town. I knew what I had to do. I'd be taken to a different area to use the cards in various shops. We'd just begun to discuss which shops we'd target when the familiar two-tone wail of a police siren pierced the air.

Johnno twisted in the front seat to check which direction the sound was coming from.

'Behind,' he mumbled.

Bilal checked it himself, using the windscreen mirror.

'It's the fucking Feds,' he shouted.

He banged his hand in anger against the steering wheel and glared at Johnno as though he was going to kill him.

'Here,' he said.

Bilal passed the small wad of banknotes – the ones he'd just stuffed inside his jean pocket – to me in the back.

'And this,' he added, as he popped two lumps of hash into the palm of my hand.

They were unwrapped and loose. I started to panic as I tried to think where I could stash them, especially when blue lights flashed inside the car as the police began to gain ground on us. I continued to fret about where I could hide the hash and cash.

Think, think!

For a moment I considered pushing it down in between the padded car seat, but quickly ruled it out.

They're bound to search the car.

I looked down. I couldn't put it in my pocket.

But where?

Then I remembered my bra. Tugging down the neck of my T-shirt, I pushed the hash and cash into the cup on my left side.

They'll never think to look for it there.

I wasn't sure why the police were following us. It wasn't unusual to be pulled over and asked for routine documents – a tax disc or an MOT certificate. If so, the officers would simply hand Bilal a pink slip, ripped from a police pad, and he'd be asked to appear at the police station within twenty-one days with proof of his MOT and insurance. Only this didn't seem like a routine producer. Anxious, I glanced behind – this time there was a riot van as well as a squad car.

No, this is something else.

The squad car pulled in front of us, slowing us down as the riot van parked close behind, wedging us in. I felt confident; I hadn't done any cards that day, so I was sure that whatever it was, it had nothing to do with me. I was wrong.

A police officer approached the front passenger side and bent forward so close that his forehead was almost touching the trim of the door frame. His eyes flitted between Bilal and Johnno before he looked over at me. He pulled his radio forward and mouthed something unintelligible into it, then he asked us to get out.

'I haven't done anything wrong,' I protested.

The officer wasn't listening. He pulled out a pair of handcuffs and fastened them around both my wrists.

'Gaia Cooper, I am arresting you on suspicion of theft. You do not have to say anything but it may harm your defence if you do not mention when questioned something which you may later rely on in court. Anything you say may be …'

I zoned out as other police officers read out the same caution to Johnno and Bilal.

One led Johnno over towards the squad car while another cuffed Bilal. Together, Bilal and I were put in the back of the riot van. We sat on opposite sides of the vehicle, facing each other. We were still parked up when Bilal lowered his voice and began to whisper.

'Fuck's sake, can you believe it? That fucking Johnno, he's such a fucking halfwit. I should've never trusted him. He's fucked everything up!'

I listened as Bilal spoke in a hushed voice, acutely aware I was carrying both the stolen money and the cannabis inside my bra. I told myself I'd be fine as long as I kept my mouth shut.

I stared down at both hands and then I realised something. Lifting my head, I stared at Bilal until he made eye contact, then I gestured down at my hands. With Bilal looking on in astonishment, I folded my thumb under the palm of my hand and slipped the cuff off. If I was double-jointed, then I'd never realised it until that moment. It was either that or the fact the arresting officer hadn't tightened my cuffs enough. It had smarted and dragged against my skin, but my fourteen-year-old hands were still so small that the cuffs slipped off easily.

Bilal grinned mischievously and indicated towards the left pocket of his jeans.

'Guy, get my phone out for me, I'm going to call my mum.'

The van was cramped but I dipped forward and retrieved his mobile phone. Bilal recited a number as I punched it in and waited for it to ring. As soon as it did, I held the phone against his ear. He began to speak in Moroccan Arabic, so I didn't understand a single word. Just then the doors at the front of the van slammed and we began to pull away. Bilal quickly ended the call and I pushed the phone inside his pocket. Then I shoved my right hand back inside the cuffs and sat down.

'Gaia, you're a gangster, you know that?' Bilal said, smirking in admiration.

My chest flooded with pride. I thought of Sal, and I hoped Bilal would tell him just how smart I'd been.

The road bumped along beneath us as the riot van trundled back to the county where Johnno had committed the crime. Once we'd parked up, the doors of the riot van opened as natural light came flooding in, blinding me. I stepped out into the daylight, still slightly dazed, as we were led into an unfamiliar police station. Once we'd been booked in by the custody sergeant, we were taken to separate cells. As I lowered myself down onto the bed, I decided this cell was way better than the ones down the local nick. My eyes wandered and I realised to my utter amazement that I hadn't been asked to remove my shoes. A thought entered my head.

Should I hide the cash and hash in them?

But almost as soon as I'd thought about it, I discounted the idea.

No, it's much better to keep it stashed in my bra.

With nothing else to do and time to kill, I pulled the itchy woollen blanket over me and up to my chin. I stared at the yellowing ceiling tiles above my head. I must have dozed off because the next moment I was being woken by someone calling my name.

'Gaia … Gaia …'

I thought it was Mum and that I was back at home. However, as soon as I opened my eyes and the stark surroundings of my cell zoomed into focus, I remembered exactly where I was. I glanced over at the opened door hatch as a pair of blue eyes stared down at me.

'Gaia, we're coming in. You're going to be taken to be searched.'

With that, two female officers entered my cell and helped me to my feet. The strip lighting blinded me and I tried to shield my eyes as I was led away. Although my heart was pounding, I tried to keep calm and composed. I knew any protest would be a sign of my guilt. Instead, I decided to remain nonchalant.

One officer held my arm as she guided me out of the cell and along the corridor outside. I glanced down at the navy-blue, Brillo-style carpet tiles that covered the floor and wondered who else had walked over them.

Killers, rapists?

I shuddered slightly. We stopped by a dark wooden door at the end of the corridor. I gasped when they opened it and I peered inside. The room looked exactly like an examination room in a doctor's surgery. There was a medical examination bed, a bright yellow sharps bin, a sink and a tall, hospital-style waste bin with a bright yellow liner. It looked and felt clinical.

What the fuck! What are they going to do to me?

I was petrified as I was led into the room. One officer turned and locked the door behind her, sealing the three of us inside.

'Gaia, can you remove your clothes? We will start with the top half and go from there,' the second officer instructed, as she pulled on a pair of blue latex gloves.

What the hell?

My mouth was now parched with fear.

The two officers stood and watched as I slowly removed my top. Blood whooshed inside my ears as a burning shame crawled over my skin. I felt hot, so hot I thought I might faint. As my T-shirt dropped to the ground, I clutched at my greying, daisy-embroidered bra as though my life depended upon it. I was utterly terrified and I suddenly felt every single one of my fourteen years.

But the officer hadn't finished.

'Take your hands down and unfasten your bra, otherwise we'll remove it for you,' she said in a stern voice that left me with no option but to obey her request.

I groaned and rolled my eyes like the petulant teen I was. Fumbling a hand behind my back, I managed to unfasten the hooks. I pulled down both straps and the bra dropped from my body until … there they were – as clear as day – a neatly folded bundle of banknotes and two lumps of hash on the floor by my feet.

The officer wearing the gloves swooped down to pick them up and placed the 'exhibits' to one side. Thinking they would be satisfied, I dipped down, grabbed my top and covered my naked torso. I slipped both bra straps over my shoulders and decided to fasten it back up when I returned to the cell. However, as I turned to leave, the gloveless officer made me go back to the spot where I'd been standing.

'Now the bottom half,' she said, pointing at my black trousers. 'You can just pull your knickers down to your knees. That will be enough.'

That's when I lost it.

'You've got all there fucking is. What the fuck else do you want from me?' I screamed.

I felt beyond humiliated. Hot tears threatened to spill down my face, but I refused to let them. This wasn't right; I was fourteen years old. I'd never felt as exposed as I did in that moment. I'd just entered hell.

One of the officers stepped forward and grabbed my arm firmly.

'If you carry on and don't do as we ask, then we'll have to do it by force.'

'You fucking weirdos!' I screamed in horror.

The tears I'd fought so hard to try and hold back began to spill down my face, adding to my humiliation. My throat ached from my sobs as I undid my trousers and allowed them to fall to my ankles in a puddle.

The gloved officer nodded her head, indicating that my knickers were next.

Closing my eyes, I pulled the tiny thong down until it hung around my knees.

'There you go,' I hissed through gritted teeth. 'Are you both fucking happy now?'

CHAPTER THIRTEEN

CARE

My behaviour was getting worse. When I wasn't getting myself arrested, I was hanging around with different men. I didn't recognise it as abuse because of the way I'd been groomed. It was as though the men and the drugs had twisted and frayed the wiring inside my brain until I couldn't think straight or see the situation for what it was. I'd convinced myself that these men were my friends and, right then, they felt like the only ones I had.

Following the rave, I'd been pretty much banned from Scarlett's house. Sandy was adamant that I'd led her daughter down the road to destruction, and by now I was certainly on a fast-track there myself. I'd often stay out all night and reappear in the morning, bleary-eyed and uncommunicative. School became a thing of the past as I embraced my 'new life' with these men. Mum had all but given up on me, which didn't surprise me because I'd given up on myself. Once she became so irate that she threw a can of hairspray at me, but I didn't feel any pain. I was numb. I was broken.

Following my arrest for obtaining goods by deception, Mum refused to come to the police station again. Instead,

I was appointed another stranger as my appropriate adult. By the time the police released me, she was apoplectic.

'That's it, enough. I'm not tolerating this anymore. You're choosing to do this, to live this way.'

I shook my head in despair.

Tell her, tell her about the men – the ones who force you to go into shops and buy things for them. The ones who give you alcohol and drugs. Go on, tell her. Tell her now.

But I couldn't, because I didn't understand why all these awful things had happened to me or how to escape from my situation. Mum wouldn't understand; she never did. She'd blame me for everything, like she always did.

I'd not been to school for over four months. Instead, I'd leave and go out for the day, spending on stolen credit cards as I sat in the back of strange men's cars comatose through drugs and lack of decent sleep.

'You need to stop gallivanting with these friends of yours …' Mum snapped, breaking my train of thought.

But I didn't have the words or the maturity to try to explain.

The following morning she left for work as usual. However, as she did, she stopped for a moment and curled her fingers around the edge of the door.

'You need to be in today. Someone is coming to see you. It's important.'

I rolled my eyes.

Yeah, sure.

So later that afternoon at around 3 p.m., when a woman called Pauline knocked at the door and asked to speak to Mum, I didn't think anything of it.

'Hi Gaia, could I speak to your mum? Is she in?'

'Yeah,' I said, inviting her inside before I shouted to Mum, who was busy in the kitchen.

It was only as I climbed the stairs to my bedroom that I wondered how she'd known my name; I'd never met her before in my life.

I'd only been upstairs for a short time when I heard a knock at my bedroom door. Thinking it was Mum, I barely glanced up as the door opened. I was stunned, therefore, when Pauline walked into my room and told me she was a social worker. She explained that due to my bad behaviour I'd be leaving with her immediately.

'Your mum thinks it's best all round if you come with me and we take you to live somewhere else.'

'You what?' I gasped, unable to compute what she was saying.

For a moment I thought she'd just said I had to leave my own house.

Pauline repeated herself.

'Your mum thinks it's for the best if you come with me.'

I was so stunned that, for once, I was lost for words. I stared at her in disbelief as Pauline asked if I knew a girl called Rebecca, who lived in the same town and was a similar age to me. I nodded because I knew Becka well. The social worker began to explain how Rebecca had been hanging around with a man who was a well-known criminal and one of the most violent men in town.

'She lets him rape her rather than take a beating.'

I was gobsmacked because it was clear that Pauline knew I'd been hanging around with undesirable men, although I wondered why she'd confide in me about someone else's misery. But at the time Rebecca was the last person on my mind. Right now, I was more concerned about myself.

'So, Mum wants me to leave and go with you?' I asked, trying to get the situation straight in my mind because I was certain I must have misunderstood.

Pauline nodded.

'Yes.'

Utterly horrified, I ran downstairs to confront Mum, expecting that she'd tell me it was all a mistake and there was no way she'd let me leave with this stranger. Instead, she simply stared down at the ground.

'You've brought it upon yourself,' she mumbled.

Her words left me sucker-punched.

'It's Richard,' she said, trying to pin the blame on my stepdad. 'He doesn't want you in the house anymore.'

Just then Pauline came downstairs and joined us in the kitchen.

'But … but where am I supposed to go? Where are you going to take me?' I asked, looking at her for answers.

'We've found a foster placement. It's not far from here.'

'What?'

Time stopped. It was too late, it had all been arranged. As the shock settled it sucked the air clean from my lungs. Breathless, I turned to Mum, but she refused to look at me.

'I'm doing this to make you safe.'

Traitor.

That's when it dawned on me. She'd been speaking to social services about me for a while. Every time I'd left the house, gone missing, bunked off school or come home late – she'd rung them and tried to persuade them to take me into care. Although a sense of dread filled me as my eyes burned with tears, I refused to let Mum see she was breaking me, so I turned and in complete silence left the house alongside Pauline with minimum fuss. We walked down the front path and climbed into her car, parked just outside. I didn't even get the chance to pack or say good-bye. To add insult to injury, Pauline made me sit in the back seat as though I'd just been arrested. It certainly felt that way, because my freedom had been taken from me.

As we drove, Pauline tried to make small talk. When this didn't work, she brought up the subject of my recent arrests. I folded my arms defiantly and kept my eyes fixed firmly on the road ahead.

'These men, Gaia. They're not your friends, you know. They're just using you.'

Pauline twisted to look back at me and try to gauge my reaction. But I refused to give her one.

'These men … they keep getting you into trouble. You're getting into trouble the whole time. They're not your friends, Gaia.'

'But they are my friends,' I screamed.

Hot, angry tears finally began to spill down my cheeks as the reality of what was happening to me began to sink in. I was being taken into care. We'd only driven a short distance when Pauline parked up, climbed out and waited for me to join her on the pavement.

'We're here,' she said, as she gestured towards a house that was barely any distance from my own home. Just then, a goofy-looking woman called Angela opened the front door to welcome me with a smile. It was clear she was expecting us.

'Hello, you must be Gaia. Come in, come in.'

Angela stepped to one side and invited us inside. But I felt utterly numb; I'd been whisked from my old life just minutes earlier and placed bang in the middle of a completely different one.

There were two other girls waiting to greet me. One was called Jessica, and I disliked her on sight. It was clear that, at eighteen years old, Jessica considered herself top dog in the household. She was Angela's adopted daughter, and therefore – as she never tired of telling us – the 'wanted' daughter. The other girl was called Chelsea. Like me, Chelsea had also been in foster placement, but that's where all similarities between us ended. Chelsea was fifteen, and a whole school year older. It turned out she was also a total brown-noser. Not only did she go to the same school as me – the one I'd hardly ever bothered going to – but we also had to share a bedroom. She wasted no time in giving me a guided tour. The bedroom was small and it had a bunk bed shoved up against one wall.

'You're in the bunk. The single bed's mine. I've been living here for a year, so I get the best.'

To be honest I didn't care either way, as long as I didn't have to engage with her. Later that evening, as we both lay in our beds and I texted Sal to let him know I'd moved, Chelsea started to complain.

'Gaia, can you stop texting. It's late and I'm trying to go to sleep.'

I rolled my eyes, sighed and turned to the wall.

Fuck's sake!

I knew then she was going to be a royal pain in the arse.

With Chelsea, Angela and the social worker all on my case, I was forced to return to my old school. To make matters worse, Chelsea and I were expected to walk there together. On my first day back I stopped halfway and lit up a cigarette.

'Want some?' I offered, as I held the cig out to Chelsea. I knew I'd have to try to buy her silence.

'Sure.'

I was flabbergasted.

Maybe she's not so bad, after all?

Up until that point I'd been living a different life, mixing in an adult world. In comparison, school had seemed even more pointless. Still, I discovered that most young Asian boys at my school knew and respected both Ali and Sal, so I became 'cool' by association.

The days soon turned into weeks as I tried to adjust. The worst thing about living in my foster home was the fact I'd have to pass Mum's house on the way to school every single morning. I'd deliberately slow my pace whenever I passed by, but I never saw her. Her van would occasionally be parked in the driveway and I'd wonder if she was home. I often thought of my stepdad and half-sister. I missed my half-sister Laura more than I realised. She'd just turned five and, for the first time, had started to engage with me, showing me her favourite dolls. But that had all gone. Now I was stuck with Chelsea and her annoying ways.

I wonder what they're having for breakfast? I thought one morning, as I paused outside Mum's house on the opposite side of the street.

Without crossing the road, I tried to peer inside the front window but all I could see were shadows. It seemed strange – an outsider in my own street – as I watched my old life carry on without me. It was as if I'd died and was now a ghost. That's when I had an epiphany; if they didn't give a shit about me then I really had nothing to lose.

Shockingly, Mum hadn't even firmed up any contact arrangements, so as far as she was concerned I was firmly out of sight and out of mind.

I might as well be with Ali and Sal. At least they give a shit about me.

Without realising, Mum, the social worker and all those who were supposed to care for me had just pushed me back into the hands of my abusers.

CHAPTER FOURTEEN

THE GOLD CHAIN

Three months after I was taken from my family home, I heard that Mum and my stepfather had split up. Pauline told me Mum wanted to leave the area. I asked why, and that's when Pauline dropped another bombshell.

'She says your stepdad hit her.'

My mouth fell wide open.

'That's bullshit, he'd never raise a hand to her.'

Whatever the truth of the situation, it enabled Mum to take my half-sister and leave the area for good. Now I really was on my own.

Mum requested a place in a women's refuge but there were none available, so she'd gone up to stay with my aunt and uncle in Newcastle. I asked if I could go and join them, but I was told in no uncertain terms that I wasn't wanted. It seemed my lovely relatives no longer trusted me in their own house following my arrests. It left me feeling like shit. My own family didn't trust me, not anymore.

As I'd already been labelled a thief, I decided to up my 'work' with Ali, Sal and Bilal. Soon, Bilal's brother Temel wanted to get in on the act. Temel, who'd just been released from prison for fighting, realised just how lucrative the stolen credit card game could be. Before long I found myself caught up on a carousel of crime. The men would use me to procure goods in the day. They'd groomed me and psychologically dismantled me and my self-confidence to the point where I truly believed it was all I deserved. Mum's disappearance only served to confirm this fact. I'd just reached rock bottom, but I couldn't find my way out.

The weeks passed by quickly, and soon I started to hang out with a white girl called Zara. She'd also been in foster care and, like me, had also previously lived with Angela. After leaving care, Zara had met an Asian man called Bizhan. They'd had a baby together and lived in a council house on the other side of town. Zara was a naturally large girl, and because she was a mother she seemed well liked and respected by the men in the Asian community. With so many mutual friends between us, Zara would invite me and a stream of other young girls to her house along with the men to smoke weed. We'd been sharing a spliff and enjoying a chat when a group of men I'd never seen before called round to see her partner. Among them was a guy called Chamali, or Cham for short. He was charming and seemed like a nice guy, although he was already extremely drunk when he arrived. As we chatted, he remarked on some gold rings I was wearing. They were cheap – 9 carat gold – and I'd recently bought them from Argos, along with a thin gold chain. At one point Cham dipped forward, revealing a heavy gold chain around his neck. I'd never seen anything like it because the gold was as thick as my little finger and it had been studded with tiny diamonds and rubies. I looked down at my own jewellery and felt embarrassed.

'Your gold chain is lovely,' I said, pointing at it.

Cham grabbed it between his fingers and pulled it away from his neck.

'You like it?'

'Like it? It's absolutely gorgeous. Where's it from?'

He unclipped it and dropped it as a coil into the palm of my hand. The gold felt even heavier than it looked.

'It's been in my family for years. It belonged to my dad. It's worth a fortune because it's 22 carat Indian gold and it's covered in tiny diamonds.'

The precious metal shone beneath the light as I twisted it.

'I'll tell you what. Why don't we do a swap? You wear mine and I'll wear yours?' I suggested, only half-joking.

To my amazement, Cham grinned and, fuelled by booze, began to warm to the idea.

'What? Swap that for yours?'

He cracked up laughing and looked over at his friends, who'd started to egg him on.

My eyes glinted mischievously.

'Go on, I dare you.'

I waited to see if Cham would rise to the challenge. He thought for a moment, looked down at the chain and then made a suggestion of his own.

'Okay, but it's only a loan; I want it back, understand? You can borrow it, but that's it. You have to return it.'

Squealing with delight, I quickly undid the clasp on my own and handed it over before he changed his mind. For the first time in my life I was up on a deal.

'Promise?' Cham added.

'Promise. Cross my heart and hope to die!'

'Well, you will if you don't give it back to me tomorrow. Tomorrow, understand?'

I nodded and fastened the precious gold around my neck. Then I wandered over to a mirror to admire it.

'And you bring me mine back,' I smirked as I winked at Cham.

He laughed along, enjoying the joke.

An hour or so later Cham and his mates left the house. He was horribly drunk. In fact, he was so far gone that I think he'd completely forgotten about the chain and our agreement. Later that evening Sal and Bilal picked me up from outside Zara's house. Sal had texted to let me know he was waiting, so I immediately jumped to my feet.

'Bye, Zara!' I called back, as I ran out the door.

I knew they'd be waiting for me to do another job and I didn't want to keep them hanging around. Stepping out into the cold, damp evening I felt ready to go to work. I'd only just climbed into the back of the car when Sal grabbed the top of my arm.

'What's this?'

I winced as he pulled at the thick gold chain around my neck and twisted it so tight that it bit the skin on the back of my neck.

'Oww, stop it, you're hurting me!'

I struggled, trying to shake him free but Sal tightened his grip. His eyes narrowed as he pulled me over and inspected the chain closely.

'I don't give a fuck. Where did you get this?'

He pulled it harder until his fist was pressed up against my windpipe.

'It's Indian gold,' I gasped, struggling to breathe. 'It belongs to a guy called Cham. You know him. He's a friend of Zara's. We did a swap, but I've got to give it back …'

Sal erupted. Yanking my head forward, he undid the chain and took it.

'What? You been shagging some P*kis now, is that it?'

I secretly hoped it was jealousy on Sal's part, but I knew it probably had more to do with the fact he thought he owned me.

'I … I … no. He's just a friend. He let me borrow it and …'

Sal refused to listen. He placed the chain in the palm of his hand as though he was feeling the weight of it, then he dropped it inside his jacket pocket. My heart pumped furiously inside my chest as I watched him.

'No, Sal, it's not mine. I have to give it back, otherwise …'

His leather jacket squeaked as he twisted in the passenger seat and glared at me.

'Otherwise what? It's mine now. It belongs to me, so you can tell your boyfriend that he's not getting it back. Understand?'

Bile rose at the back of my throat and I tried to swallow it down. A single thought flashed across my mind.

Cham is going to go mad!

For the next week I avoided Zara and her partner Bizhan because I knew I couldn't run the risk of bumping into Cham. I also realised I couldn't betray Sal, who'd almost certainly kill me. Caught between a rock and a hard place, I decided to try and lie low, hoping Cham would forget all about me and the gold chain.

A few days later I was lying up in my bedroom listening to some music when I heard Angela's voice shout up to me.

Rolling my eyes, I got to my feet, wondering what it was that was so bloody urgent.

'What?' I hollered down the stairs.

The front door was half open and Angela was standing there, talking to someone.

'Come down,' she urged.

Angela looked up to me, standing on the top step.

'There's someone down here who wants to speak to you.'

At first I thought it must be Pauline or another social worker. But I paused when I realised that Angela would have invited them inside. This must be someone else. My stomach clenched with unease as I dipped down and tried to peer through the glass panel at the side of the door. There was a distorted outline of a person, so it was difficult to tell who it was.

'Who is it?' I whispered.

Angela pushed the door, closing it slightly without fully shutting it.

'I don't know. It's some man. Says he wants to speak to you … says it's something about a gold chain?'

My breathing grew shallow and my palms began to sweat, the wooden banister rail now slippery beneath my hand.

Cham.

'No, no, Angela … I can't go. Please tell him to go away. Please tell him I'm not here.'

She rolled her eyes and seemed beyond exasperated.

'But he knows you're here. He heard me call you and then heard you answer.'

199

I felt close to tears.

'Please, Angela. Please make him go away.'

But she refused.

'No, Gaia, I'll not have you bringing trouble to my door. If you have this man's gold chain then you need to give it back. I'm sick of you taking things that don't belong to you. It stops right here, right now.'

My body quivered with dread.

I don't have his chain; he's going to kill me!

'Please don't make me go with him.'

My voice sounded whiny and pleading but Angela remained unmoved.

'It's time you realised actions have consequences. Now, I've asked the young man outside and he has sworn to me on his mother's life that no harm will come to you. But you do have to sort this out. It's what adults do. They sit down and sort things out, and that's what you're going to do right now.'

With that, she opened the door wide and pointed over towards me as Cham peered inside. Frozen to the spot, I knew there was nothing else I could do – I'd have to leave with him.

'Hi, Gaia, how you doing?' he said.

He'd sounded charming and gave me a friendly wave, but it was all for Angela's benefit. I knew as soon as I stepped out of that front door I'd be as good as dead.

'Go on then,' Angela said, shooing me outside.

The door slammed behind me with a resounding thud, a guillotine hacking my place of safety away. We'd only taken a few steps when Cham started to interrogate me.

'Where you been hiding, Gaia? I want my gold chain back. Where is it?'

I couldn't look at him; terrified, trapped and alone I didn't know what to say. I didn't have it and I had no way of getting it back.

'I don't have it. I'm sorry, but your gold chain has gone.'

I closed my eyes in anticipation, waiting for Cham to hit me or erupt with anger, but he didn't. Instead he remained unnervingly quiet. Grabbing me by my arm, he led me to his car parked outside in the street.

'Get in.'

I paused, and lifted my face.

'But where are we going?'

'You'll see.'

My hands shook. I was too scared to open the car door, so Cham did it for me. He pushed me into the passenger seat, climbed in and we sped off. Cham didn't say a word. I longed for conversation because his silence terrified me.

Why isn't he saying anything, and where is he taking me?

Houses and street lights passed by as telephone wires cut against the sea-blue sky. We drove fast – too fast – through the estate until Cham indicated and we pulled into a familiar-looking road.

Zara's! He's taking me to Zara's house. Thank God!

My galloping heart began to steady as he parked up outside.

'Get out!' he ordered, pulling me towards the front door.

Cham didn't knock; he just let himself in, as though he owned the place.

They must be expecting him.

I prayed Zara would be there to protect me.

She'll stick up for me. She won't let them hurt me.

Thankfully Zara was there, but there was no welcoming smile. In fact her eyes looked dead as she stared at me, and that's when I realised she'd told Cham exactly where to find me.

She gave him my address.

She seemed almost as furious as Cham. To be fair, I suppose she hadn't asked for any of this. Her small front room was crowded with around half a dozen men – faces I'd never seen before. Cham turned to me as the others stood there, watching. His eyes were wild with fury as he demanded to know where his chain was.

'I don't know, I swear. I lost it!'

It was a lie. But I feared Cham far less than I feared Sal. I knew that as soon as I gave him Sal's name, then all hell would break loose and I'd be at the centre of it all.

'You sure you don't know?' Cham hissed, spitting out each word.

He turned to Zara, who loomed ominously behind him.

'She says she'll beat you up if you don't tell me.'

Zara stared at me and nodded sharply. I gulped because she was massive – she'd pulverise me. At first I wondered why she hadn't taken my side, then I remembered – she and Cham went way back. She continued to glare as I stood there on full alert, wondering what she'd do next. Just then the group of men parted, and a huge Asian guy stepped forward and stood directly in front of me. The man had long, black, greasy hair that he kept trying to drag off his face as it flopped back down. He panted with anger, as though he was crazy and spoiling for a fight.

'Where's the gold chain?' he demanded.

I realised that he must have been visiting the area because he had a distinct Brummie accent. His voice was so deep and loud that it seemed to rattle the walls.

'I don't know. I lost it.'

SLAP!

The side of my face stung as a searing pain ricocheted through my body. I held a hand against my cheek to try and protect it.

'I'll ask again. Where is it?'

'I told you; I don't know.'

SLAP!

My eyes brimmed with tears as I winced in pain. The force of the second slap had caused my glasses to fly off my face and across the room.

'You do know you're gonna have to pay for it, don't ya?'

He slapped me a third time. My jaw ached with pain as I begged him to stop and give me back my glasses.

'I can't see. Please, please!'

I stretched out my hand pathetically, but he refused. Soon the slaps turned to punches, and he started battering my face to a bloodied pulp until it felt as raw as an open wound. Metallic-tasting blood flooded my mouth and I began to choke on it. Although I spluttered up crimson blood, I refused to give him Sal's name.

A skinny man stepped forward from the rest of the crowd.

'Do you know what burning flesh smells like?' he said menacingly.

He stepped away from me and sneered. As he did, I noticed his teeth were yellow and crooked, like a rodent's. I shivered and continued to gag on my own blood.

'Pig!' the man said. 'It smells like pig and that's exactly what you're gonna smell like by the time we've finished with you.'

I began to sob with terror until soon I couldn't stop myself. The men laughed and Zara joined in.

She's as bad as them.

I was fourteen years old – a schoolgirl – being held captive by a gang of men who wanted me dead.

They continued to push and punch me until every part of my body pounded with pain. Finally I collapsed to the floor. Just when I thought I couldn't take any more, Cham towered over me.

'Come on, get up.'

He grabbed me roughly and pulled me to my feet.

'You're coming with us.'

Desperate cries racked my body, stealing away my breath.

'Please, please don't hurt me. I promise I haven't got it. The gold chain. I lost it and I'm sorry, I'm so sorry, Cham …'

He ignored me. Instead, fired up with fury, Cham and his cousin Mo dragged me to the car outside. That's when I realised it hadn't been Cham's car after all – it belonged to Mo.

Maybe they're going to take me home. I've had my beating. Maybe they're finished with me.

Only they weren't. Cham barked at me to get in the car as he slid into the passenger seat, trapping me in the back. Mo climbed in and started up the engine. As we pulled away from the kerb, Cham continued to interrogate me. Still, I refused to give him Sal's name. At one point he became so enraged that he grabbed my neck and squeezed his fingers tight, crushing my windpipe.

'Please!' I rasped.

My face turned purple as I fought for each breath.

'Can't ... breathe ...'

Cham's fingers loosened slightly before he let go. Relieved, I wrapped both hands around my neck and greedily gulped in air. Cham wasn't finished. As I panted, he pursed his lips and spat at me once ... twice ... three times.

'Fuck's sake, cuz,' Mo began to protest.

Annoyed, he stared in disbelief at the windscreen mirror. But it wasn't for my benefit.

'It's a new car, for fuck's sake. Save it for when we get this thieving slag out of here.'

I tried to catch my breath as we drove to a different part of town and an estate I'd never been to before. We turned into a narrow avenue and pulled up outside an unfamiliar house. The door opened and a weaselly-looking man stepped out and came over towards us. He was carrying a spade and a broom. He nodded at Mo, who duly opened the boot of his car. I heard a dull thud as the man threw both things inside the boot and slammed it shut.

Why has he got a shovel and a broom?

My mind raced with different scenarios – none of them rational.

Cham jumped out and the man climbed in the back seat next to me. Even though I couldn't see him clearly without my glasses, I could sense him staring. My head felt hot and wet with blood as my eyes had already begun to swell up. Soon, they'd swollen to thin slits, my eyesight reduced to narrow, blurry windows on the world.

'Look at you, you Moroccan-shagging whore, you ugly white slag! Where is it?'

It was the man who'd brought the spade and broom. He began to shout as I flinched and waited, poised for the next punch. Only it didn't come.

'You tell her, Tony,' Cham called.

He was egging him on from the front of the car. I knew the man wasn't really called Tony, it was his nickname and one I'd heard before. Everyone had heard of Tony because his reputation for violence preceded him.

'Do you know what those are for?' Tony asked.

He gestured back towards the boot with a nod of his head. I shook my head blankly.

'You are a dirty kuffar bitch. Do you know what dirty kuffar flesh smells like when it's burning?'

Fear bolted through my body, zapping my nerve endings.

'It smells of bacon.'

I continued to weep.

I'm going to die ... these men, they're going to kill me!

'And the shovel. Remember the shovel? That's for you to dig your own grave, you filthy fucking whore.'

The more I howled with fear, the more they laughed. Distressed, but high on adrenaline, my senses were on full alert as I anticipated what was yet to come. My body felt numb until soon I couldn't feel the pain, only fear.

Tony's body heat trickled against my skin. He was sitting too close to me, his flesh pressing against mine. We drove past some tall black gates; I could just about make out the shadows of trees as they swayed in the breeze. My ears pricked up as I heard Mo say something about a key to the park hut.

'It's in the glove box, cuz. Look there.'

'Got it!' I heard Cham announce triumphantly a few minutes later.

Why have they brought me to the park?

I remembered the shovel.

Are they going to make me dig my own grave?

I began to shake all over.

'Stop fidgeting, you kuffar bitch!' Tony screamed.

Fear stole my breath from the back of my throat. I was petrified because I knew why they'd brought me here. There was a lad – a park gardener – and everyone knew him well. He'd often give his mates the spare key to the park hut so they had somewhere to go to smoke their weed in peace. Ali and Sal knew about the hut and used it often.

Ali and Sal! I wonder if they'll be there?

A faint glimmer of hope rose inside me, but it was soon dashed as we slowed and then parked. The place was deserted. Cham and Mo climbed out and flipped the seat forward to let Tony out. A cool breeze blew against my skin, which by now was drying and tightening with dried blood, as they dragged me from the car by my hair. Each strand stabbed at my scalp like needles. I lifted my hand up to try and stop the pain and tension as I was dragged along the gravel towards the hut. Tony disappeared around the back of the car and I heard the boot click open. I saw the shovel in his hand. Partially blinded, there was a rattle – metal against metal – as Mo unlocked the door. They dragged me into the hut, with Tony bringing up the rear. He turned and locked the door behind him, sealing us in.

Cham was holding something in his hands. I blinked and tried to focus as he pulled it from behind his back and back into the light. Tape – he was carrying two rolls of tape. One was a roll of thick silver gaffer tape, the other a roll of parcel tape.

What's he going to do with that?

'Put her over there and tape her,' he ordered.

I expected Tony to stick some over my mouth, only he didn't. Instead, he signalled to Mo. A moment later they'd knocked me over. I was flat on the floor as both men kneeled against my back and pressed my face into the cold concrete floor.

'Please don't …'

They proceeded to pull both my arms outwards and strapped the broom handle against my back in a make-shift crucifix. Then they tied me to it as they bound both wrists with tape, rendering me completely helpless.

'Tell me where my chain is?'

It was Cham. I shook my head wearily and continued to cry.

'I told you; I DON'T know!' I screamed.

PUNCH!

The right hook connected directly my jaw, throwing my head backwards.

'Where's my gold chain?'

'I don't know.'

Blow after blow followed, but still I refused to say. There was a pause – a brief silence – as I waited to see what they'd do to me next. My breath quickened and I twitched from side to side expecting another punch. My nostrils flared with terror as I waited and waited. The smell of damp grass and soil filled the air as I tried to remember the other things stored in the hut.

A sit-on lawn mower, more spades … gardening shears … an axe!

I gulped as pain dragged the breath from my lungs. Just as I wondered what they'd torture me with next, Cham signalled to the others and the door was unlocked. Half-beaten and as limp as death, I was hauled back to the car, a hand shoving hard against the small of my back as I was twisted and pushed prone onto the back seat of Mo's car. We set off again, only this time I was on my front, my back taped to the crucifix. My bloodied face pressed against the seat, so I shifted it sideways to try and breathe. As I did, I bled against the upholstery. I wiped it purposely against the back seat.

At least they'll be able to find a trace, if they kill me.

Blood seeped from my wounds as my arms burned. I longed to pull them away and rest them against my body. With both my arms taped out, I had no way of protecting myself against these monsters.

'What are you going to do to me?'

A silence was followed by a short murmur, then muffled laughter. My eyes were so swollen that the men were now only blurred shapes. Blood trickled down my face and inside my mouth as I shook it away and tried hard not to choke.

They're going to kill me …

I panted as my breathing grew shallow. Vomit rose at the back of my throat but I fought hard to swallow it down. I pleaded for my life, but the men just laughed at me.

'Ready?' Cham asked.

The car pulled to an abrupt halt.

'Ready,' Mo replied.

'Please don't hurt me. I'll pay you back; I'll do whatever it takes to pay you back. I'm sorry, Cham.'

'Anything?' a lone voice mocked.

It was followed by a ripple of laughter and more murmurs.

'Flat …' I heard someone say. 'We'll take her to the flat.'

With both arms still taped to the broom-cum-crucifix, the men carried me up a metal staircase. I wasn't sure where they'd brought me, but a distinct smell of grease and stale kebab meat hung in the air. My stomach heaved. The men continued to taunt me until I soon found it hard to distinguish one voice from another.

'Do you know what burning flesh smells like?'

My gut twisted with revulsion as my mind raced with horrible possibilities.

Someone knocked against a metal door and I heard a fourth voice, as another man answered and let us in. They twisted me sideways to bundle me through the doorway. I was led into another brightly lit room. By now all my strength had faded and I was struggling to stand. The men hooked their arms under my armpits and propped me up either side. From there, I was taken to a back bedroom, where they balanced me against a wardrobe. I was so exhausted that, once they'd let go, I fell backwards, wedging myself against it. With my spine pressed up against the slats of the doors, Cham's blurred face suddenly zoomed into view as he approached.

'Tell me where the chain is.'

His voice thundered above me as he stood poised, ready to strike.

'I told you, I don't …'

SLAM!

I felt the force of the adjoining wardrobe door as it smashed against my face, the protruding slats biting against skin and muscle before smashing into my cheek-bone. A white-hot pain splintered through me.

'Tell me.'

I couldn't.

SLAM!

The men tortured me for the best part of an hour. I felt hot and feverish until soon my knees gave way and I sank to the bedroom floor. My eyes and face throbbed as dark bruises began to bloom across my skin.

'What are we going to do with her now?' a voice asked.

I recognised the smell of Cham's aftershave as he pulled me to my feet.

That's it. It's finally over.

I wept with relief because I truly believed my ordeal was finally at an end. Tony left the room as Mo and Cham looked at each other knowingly. Tony returned moments later holding a stainless-steel pipe, the type you'd normally attach to the end of a hoover. With the pipe in one hand, he grabbed my hair and pulled my head back.

'Open your mouth,' Cham shouted.

Tony held up the pole at the side of my face.

My eyes flitted between it and them. I shook my head furiously.

Please don't kill me!

My body went into full panic mode as I watched Cham shake three tablets out into his hand – two blue, one white.

'Please, please don't!'

He nodded to Tony, who grabbed my face and forced the metal pipe inside my mouth. Thin skin at the corners of my mouth had stretched so tight that I was certain my face would split open. I began to gag as the metal scraped hard against my tongue. My jaw had been prised so wide open that I felt it would dislocate or shatter. Tony gave the pole an extra shove to make sure it was fully inside.

A strange echo noise sounded – my breath amplified – as it ricocheted inside the pole. Still panting, my eyes darted anxiously from Tony to Cham, and down to Cham's hand. He lifted it and, one by one, dropped a tablet into the top end of the pole. They slid down before landing at the back of my throat, making me gag. I didn't want to swallow the pills but I had to, because it was either that – or choke to death. Once I'd swallowed all three, Tony removed the pole. I immediately doubled over and gasped for breath. Both my arms were still attached to the crucifix as Cham suddenly twisted me and threw my body against a filthy unmade bed. The pole pressed into my back as I landed against the cheap, soft mattress.

'Right, you need to pay back your debt – and you will,' he decreed.

Just then, he glanced over his shoulder and began to address someone who was standing just outside the room. I tried to lift my head to see but it was almost impossible.

Cham turned back to me.

'You'll have sex with lots of different men until you've paid me back. Understand?'

I shook my head.

'No, no, please, Cham. I'll do anything, just not this …'

He turned towards the unknown person and gave the order.

'Let them in. They're welcome to her.'

With my eyes almost swollen shut and my vision distorted, I blinked in terror. Cold air brushed against my thighs as someone pulled both my trousers and knickers down in one go.

'No!' I yelled.

A queue of disgusting, old men shuffled into the room and lined themselves up against the wall to wait their turn. Their eyes gathered into one collective stare as I closed mine and braced myself for the inevitable. Cold and exposed, I'd never felt so vulnerable in my life. I waited for the tell-tale smell of body odour and bad breath, the weight of the men's bodies on top of mine and fat tongues pushing their way hungrily inside my mouth. Hot, humiliated tears rolled down my face and dripped onto the bed below as I waited and waited. But there was nothing, just silence. I opened my eyes as far as I could, unsure of what I might see next. But the queue of old men had vanished. They'd left the room, leaving only Tony, Mo and Cham. His face came into view as he dipped down to check I was still breathing.

'Untie her,' Cham said quietly.

Tony and Mo went to each side and began to unbind both my wrists. The tape glue ripped against my skin, refusing to unstick. Then I saw Cham. He was standing at the foot of the bed. I watched as he took out his phone and began to dial a number. I couldn't hear the other person, but I heard Cham's reply.

'We've got her here. Yeah, that's right. She's here. Now, where is it?'

A garbled conversation followed until some kind of agreement was reached.

'Okay, but he better have it.'

Cham hung up and looked down at me. I flinched, waiting for him to belt me again, but he didn't.

'Enough punishment. You're free to go but I'll be back again tomorrow, so go and look for my chain.'

My face was bloodied, my eyes almost swollen shut and my glasses long gone. Blood rushed back into both arms as I struggled to prop myself up.

'Thank you,' I gasped.

They were my torturers, but I'd never felt so grateful. My stomach heaved as I pulled up my trousers and knickers in one go. I tried to stand, but I felt woozy because my balance was still off. Heavy with pain, my head throbbed as I staggered to my feet. I wobbled from side to side as Tony sniggered cruelly. But I was determined. They were letting me go and I had to get out of there as fast as I could.

Stretching out both arms to try and anchor myself, I took one step and then another as I stumbled, bloodied and beaten, out of the bedroom.

CHAPTER FIFTEEN

UNWANTED

Exhausted, I staggered past a kebab shop half-blind and unsure where I was. The shop was at the front of the flat – the place I'd been taken, held and tortured. With my arms out, I stumbled along the unfamiliar street as though I were blind. I sensed people turning to look at me, but I didn't care. I just needed to escape.

A voice called behind me. I froze.

'Wait!'

It was Cham.

A dark shadow passed over my heart as the sound of footsteps grew louder. He was trying to catch me up.

'Please don't hurt me,' I whimpered.

Cham backed away from me, a little affronted.

'Hurt you? I was giving you some money for a taxi home.'

He took my hand and placed three pound coins in my palm.

'I've called you a cab. It'll be here in a minute, if you hang around.'

With that, he disappeared off into the night as I stood there in disbelief. I could barely see, but I could just about make out the coins in my blood-smeared hands.

If the taxi driver was shocked when he picked me up, then he didn't let on. In fact, he didn't say a word.

I wonder if he's a friend of Cham's.

I also wondered who he'd phoned back there in the bedroom – my torture chamber. I didn't care; whatever they'd agreed, it had secured my release. I felt grateful to the person on the other end of the line. Eventually, the taxi pulled up outside Angela's house. There was a squad car parked outside and I knew the police were inside, waiting for me. I decided I couldn't and wouldn't tell them who'd meted out my punishment. If Cham could do this over a gold chain, then God only knows what he'd do if I led the police directly to his door.

Nothing, say nothing.

I walked to the front door and pushed it open. The noise of it opening brought Angela running into the hallway.

'Oh Gaia, what has happened? Look at you! Are you okay?'

I could barely look at her, as she'd been the one who'd handed me to my attacker. With two police officers waiting to speak to me, I realised she was in full arse-covering mode. I turned away from her. I didn't want her anywhere near me. She was supposed to be my protector – it was her role as my surrogate mum – but she'd failed, just as my own mother had done before. It was clear Angela was shitting herself because she knew exactly who'd done this – the man she'd almost pushed me out of the door to go with.

'There was a man,' Angela gasped, as the police took note of my injuries. 'But I didn't know he was going to do this to Gaia.'

Didn't know or didn't want to know?, I thought bitterly.

The police drove me to hospital, where my stepdad Richard arrived shortly afterwards. As soon as I saw him through the hospital doors, I burst into tears. Although I was grateful to see him, I really needed one person – my mum – but she was hundreds of miles away.

'Gaia, what the hell! Look at your face!' Richard cried in horror.

Despite my tough exterior, I allowed myself to be comforted as he pulled me into his arms and hugged me. Eventually I peeled myself away and pulled out my mobile.

'I need to speak to Mum.'

Richard nodded and went off in search of a hot drink.

I scrolled through the list of stored names until I found her number. I paused and, for a moment, almost changed my mind. However, I realised the severity of what had happened and I knew that as my mother, she needed to know. The phone rang a couple of times before she picked up. But before she'd even had a chance to say hello, I blurted everything out – the kidnap, the torture, the fact that Angela had handed me over to the man who'd beaten me black and blue. There was a short silence on the other end as Mum listened. Swollen, angry tears streamed down my face as I pictured her horrified expression and her urgent need to be with me.

'Richard's here but, I need you. Please, Mum, I really need you.'

There was another pause, then a deep sigh before she answered.

'Well, you've got yourself into all this so, you can get yourself out of it.'

Her heartless reply left me absolutely floored.

'What? Is that it?' I croaked. 'Please, Mum, I need you.'

But she was adamant.

'No, Gaia.'

With that she hung up, and I stood looking down at my phone as though it had just bitten me. My mother, the woman who'd given me life and brought me into this world, had given up on me for good. She didn't seem to have a single maternal bone in her body.

Richard reappeared, holding a couple of hot drinks.

'Did you speak to her?'

I nodded.

'She's not coming.'

He didn't say a word, but he didn't have to. It was written all over his face.

I was taken for an X-ray to check that I hadn't suffered a fractured cheekbone. Then a nurse treated and dressed my face – I had two black eyes, and was covered in multiple cuts and bruises. Then I was released home, wherever that was. That evening I chose to stay with my stepfather. The following day the police arrived to drive me to the station, and take a statement and photographs of my injuries. I refused to answer any of their questions. With no cooperation from me and only a scant statement from Angela, the police dropped their inquiries.

A couple of days later I was told Ali's dad had handed Cham his gold chain back. The beating they'd given me had all been for nothing.

The lad who'd supplied the keys to the park hut had also heard what they'd done. He was so outraged and disgusted that he came to see me.

'Bastards!' he cursed, as soon as he saw my injuries. 'That's it, I'm taking that set back. I'm so sorry, Gaia.'

But it wasn't his fault. This was down to them.

A few days later I was walking along the street when a car slowed and drove alongside me. The window dropped down and I immediately froze when I spotted the man with the Brummie accent staring straight back at me.

'What the fuck happened to your face?' he said, before he started to laugh.

I couldn't believe it. He knew what he'd done to me and, in my opinion, he was as guilty as Cham. Just then, Tony dipped his head forward to get a good look at me.

'I told you, bruv, she's *qisam* [meaning 'kind' in Urdu]. She's a soldier. She's strong.'

Both men laughed as the car accelerated away, leaving me standing there, throbbing with pain.

████████████████ **County Council Social Services**

Detailed Contact Sheet

Name: Gaia Cooper
M/F: Female
Address: ████████████████████
Date: 2 August 2000

Telephone call from Angela to inform EDT that Gaia had been involved in an 'incident' today in which she had been 'abducted' by an Asian man who had taken her back to his flat, threatened her, tied her to a chair &

'beaten her up'. He had accused her of stealing a gold chain from his flat. Gaia denied all knowledge of this, but he took all her jewellery in 'compensation' & told her to go and look for the chain, as he would be back to see her again the next day. He then put her in a taxi & sent her back to her foster-parents ███████. Angela thought this was a bit 'strange' (? Weird) & tried to find out more from Gaia, who refused to talk to anyone anymore about her 'experience'. She was quite distressed and tearful. Said she now wanted to be put in touch with her mother (who is in ████████ & who is not answering her phone). She made no immediate mention of her stepfather, who is still in ████████.

Police were already involved (spoke with WPC ████████) who had been called to house, but had great difficulty in getting Gaia to say anything or make a complaint.

... Angela felt they were all very vulnerable (especially Gaia) & felt she ought to be moved to a safer place – tonight, if possible. DSW needed to check this with a manager & get back to Angela with a plan.

████████████ **Social Services**

Detailed Contact Sheet

Name: Gaia Cooper
Date: 4 August 2000

Gaia accommodated at Angela ████████. Made an appointment to visit.

Date: 7 August 2000

Home visit to Angela ███████████.

Angela was fairly upset since the recent events of Gaia being assaulted and held hostage and drugged.

Gaia said: 'It's a shame it has taken this to get a social worker.'

Gaia talked about her feelings for her mum and how she feels Mum is very inadequate. She says she doesn't want to move out of the ██████████ area. It would appear Gaia is fairly entrenched in offending with famous known criminals in ███████████. I feel Gaia is so vulnerable and has been for many years. She is feeling at present so unworthy of being loved. She says she loves these men and they fulfil the needs she so desperately wants.

CHAPTER SIXTEEN

RAPE

A month or so after we'd first visited Heidi's house, Ali drove us all back there. I'd not been living at Angela's for long, but I'd already stopped listening to her and refused to tell her where I was going. After all, she wasn't my mum. Mum didn't want me either, so I reasoned that no one did. No one apart from the men. If anything, this made me gravitate towards them even more.

Scarlett and I smoked a spliff as Ali drove us over to Heidi's. Her mum was away again so the house was available, ready to be used as a meeting point and general doss house until her return. This time I wasn't worried because we'd been before, so I thought I knew what to expect. Only this time, everything was about to change.

Scarlett and I had been sitting inside the front room on the sofa getting slowly stoned when Ali approached. He stood in front of Scarlett and held out both hands to pull her up to her feet.

'Come on, babe,' he said sweetly.

She seemed thrilled he was paying her so much attention and willingly extended her arms. The two of them disappeared outside, but I wasn't worried because my friend was with Ali.

He'll look after her.

I assumed that Scarlett would return when she was ready, but she didn't. I tried to stand to go and look for her, but found I couldn't. My body had been marinated in dope, and my legs felt weak and useless.

I'm so stoned, I thought, as I swayed and fell back onto the sofa with my eyes closed.

Just then a hand gripped my arm. I opened my eyes and traced along the arm to the elbow and up to the face. It was Sal. My stomach flipped with excitement. He raised his eyebrows and gestured with a nod of his head for me to follow. Again, I tried to stand but found I couldn't.

I wonder what was in that last spliff?

Sal's hands gripped my wrists as he pulled me up and held me there. Then he proceeded to half carry, half drag me over towards the stairs. Raising my head, I took in the row of steps. It looked as steep as a cliff face. He continued to prop me up as I shook my head.

'I'm sorry … I can't … too tired.'

My words had been splintered by the dope as I struggled to stay upright and focus. Determined, Sal continued to lift me, one step at a time, until soon we'd reached the landing. A single lightbulb hung above our heads, lighting up a series of half-closed doors.

'Come on.'

It was Sal again. The sound of his voice brought me back into the moment.

'Sorry … here … where are we going?'

He didn't reply. Instead, he pushed a hand against one of the doors and pulled me inside a small bedroom. I could just see the dark outlines of a bed, wardrobe and a small set of drawers. I stumbled on for a few more steps before Sal let me go. I lifted both arms out as I began to tumble backwards before landing softly on top of a bed. The light from the landing seeped into the room and Sal stood before me half-lit and in a half silhouette. He turned, crossed the room and closed the door, snuffing out all the light. It was so dark that I could no longer see his face. I could smell his breath, however, and feel the sensation of his greedy hands as he tugged at the waist-band of my trousers. The clasp came undone and the metal teeth of the front zip parted as it gave way and peeled open. Sal grabbed me; his hot breath brushed against my neck as his weight pinned me down against the mattress. The cheap, fake leather jacket I'd borrowed from Scarlett stuck against my skin as he held me down and brutally raped me. I was just fourteen years old.

Once he'd finished, the weight on top of me shifted as he stood up. There was the slight rustle of fabric and he pulled up his trackie bottoms as though nothing had happened, then left the room. I lay there feeling battered and numb. I was unsure what to do. It had been sex, but not as I knew or understood it. For a start I hadn't consented, and Sal was a grown man. But I didn't see it as rape, not then, anyway. I thought I loved Sal, only now I wasn't so sure. My self-esteem was so low that I almost accepted it as my fate – as though it was all I deserved. The truth was that, although I fancied Sal, I also feared him – and he knew it.

The effects of the dope began to subside as I pulled up my knickers and trousers, then made my way downstairs to the front room. It was exactly as we'd left it. Everything seemed normal, only it wasn't, because everything had just changed upstairs. I looked across the room and spotted Sal sitting alongside the rest of the men, smoking as though nothing had happened. As though he hadn't just raped me upstairs in that grotty bedroom.

Taking my place back on the sofa, I kept my eyes focused warily on him. Just then a huge smile broke across his face. One of the men laughed and replied, saying something funny in Arabic. He patted Sal on the back and then looked over my way.

Did he just tell him what happened?

My skin felt itchy, as though a thousand ants were crawling across me. I wanted to sharpen my nails and claw it all off, strip myself back to muscle and bone so that I could feel clean again. I didn't want to be trapped inside this filthy house, sitting on a cheap sofa surrounded by these awful men. I wanted to go home. Sal continued to laugh as paranoia washed over me.

Was he laughing at me?

I grew so uneasy that when someone poured me a strong vodka and Coke, I knocked it straight back. I didn't usually drink alcohol, but I needed to forget – forget what had just happened. As the booze and dope mixed inside me, my insides began to churn.

'I'm going to be sick,' I said to no one in particular.

I clasped a hand against my mouth, got up and dashed outside to throw up. Soon I couldn't stop retching. At one point, someone stood beside me, watching as I continued to heave violently.

'Sal?' I mumbled.

But it wasn't Sal. It was a man I'd never seen before.

'Are you okay?'

I shook my head. I felt far from it. The man wrapped his arm around me and gave my back a concerned rub.

'Better?' he asked.

I nodded gratefully.

'Good.'

I'd just wiped my face with my sleeve when he lifted me up.

'W … w … where are we going?'

Drugs and alcohol had scrambled my brain as he carried me off into the dark night.

'No … no … I need to go back to the house. I need to find my friend,' I insisted, as I began to struggle.

But he wouldn't let go; if anything, he tightened his grip.

'Please … please, don't hurt me!' I said, sobbing.

The stranger, who I later learned was called Taj, took me over to a parked car. The alarm bleeped and lights flashed as he unlocked it and bundled me onto the back seat. Then he pinned me down and anally raped me.

I'd been raped twice within the hour, although I didn't realise what the men had done to me was illegal. They'd both had sex with a child – me – and that was rape. I hadn't given my consent because I couldn't – I was a schoolgirl.

I don't know how long I lay there, but goosebumps prickled along my skin as the cold night set in. I was battered and bleeding, but somehow I managed to get my clothes back on in the orange glow of the streetlamp. As I pulled my trousers up my legs I noticed they were covered in Taj's semen. But I couldn't think about that just now. My main concern was to find Scarlett and get the hell out of that house. I still felt unsteady on my feet as I climbed out of the car and headed back inside, to my abusers. I had to find Scarlett. The front room was full of men and swirls of smoke as they continued to chat.

Where is she?

The attack had sobered me up and I just wanted to get away as fast as I could. With my back against the wall, right next to the door, I waited for my friend. I was on high alert, poised in case another man tried to have a go. Suddenly, the ongoing chat was broken by loud wails and screams.

Scarlett?

Just then, the door swung open and Scarlett burst into the room. Her hair and clothes were dishevelled, and it was clear from her tear-stained face that something awful had just happened. Channels of mascara-black tears streamed down her face. They dripped and soaked as greyish black splodges against her satin top. She staggered over to the stairs and slumped down onto the bottom step.

I was about to go to her when Ali walked in and addressed the room.

'Yeah, Bruvs,' he announced, punching the air.

The men stopped what they were doing and looked up.

'I've just taken her virginity!' he said, as a huge cheer erupted in the room.

One by one, each man stood up to slap Ali's back in a congratulatory manner. The noise was deafening. I glanced over at Scarlett in horror as she sobbed quietly to herself.

Ali was standing there like a hero when Bilal got up and waved both hands to try and hush the room.

'You're too late, bruv. I had her earlier.'

Another loud cheer and another celebration followed as my eyes darted between the men and Scarlett.

Animals…

Ali smirked at Bilal and pretended to spit on the floor, as the others fell about laughing. I immediately ran over to Scarlett; her face was in her hands and her body convulsed as huge sobs tore through her. She was crying so hard that I thought she'd never stop. I wrapped my arms around her and pulled her towards me, cradling her head in my hands. That's when it hit me. My friend hadn't been outside having a drunken fumble with her so-called boyfriend. She'd been raped by Ali and Bilal. They'd taken advantage of her wasted state, just as Sal and Taj had done with me.

The two men continued to laugh and joke as the others congratulated them. I felt sick to my stomach and held Scarlett's head against my chest. I remembered Jack, and how I'd lost my virginity to him. Suddenly I felt grateful – grateful that I'd had a choice in the matter, not like now. This had been premeditated. Somehow, we'd unwittingly stepped into a sleazy new underworld – a world to which we didn't belong. We didn't stand a chance.

The following day Ali, Sal and Bilal were still laughing and talking about how Taj had 'taken' me in his car. I felt ashamed. Humiliation burned inside me as they laughed and called me a slag. Word must have spread, because a few days later I was approached by a girl I'd never seen before. It was Taj's girlfriend, and she was furious that I'd 'had sex' with her boyfriend. She didn't even give me a chance to explain; she just punched and beat me in the street.

'That'll teach you for cheating with my boyfriend,' she spat, as she walked away, leaving me bloodied and battered on the ground.

I wanted to shout out that it had been him, not me. But there wasn't any point. I was only a kid, and therefore I was nothing.

Sal and Bilal continued to intimidate me after that day and forced me to have sex with them. Neither of them ever wore a condom, so I ended up catching several sexually transmitted infections, although I was still only fourteen years old.

Despite this, I kept going back for more.

██████████████████ **Social Services**

Detailed Contact Sheet

Name: Gaia Cooper
Date: ████████ 2000

The placement is very rocky. Gaia is not abiding by the rules. She was hurting and angry. Angela believes that she's still seeing ████████ and when she came in last Sunday she had semen stains on her trousers. Gaia says she is unhappy, very unhappy at Angela's and wants to live with her stepfather. Also, Angela asked for her mobile number and Gaia is refusing.

CHAPTER SEVENTEEN

THE REFUGE

I decided I desperately needed to see Mum or, more accurately, she needed to see me. I asked a social worker if I could move in with my mother. Before I knew it transport had been arranged, and on 23 September 2000 I left town for good to start a new life.

Of course, Mum was a little wary when I arrived. In addition, I was still hurting and extremely angry at her because I felt she'd abandoned me. The social worker arranged for all my stuff to be moved over to hers, which meant that Mum's living conditions became even more cramped. There were other women living at the refuge who really needed to be there, including two women who'd had acid thrown in their face by disgruntled ex-partners. But I knew Mum was only there to try and get away from Richard. She'd seen it as a fresh start and had decided to go for it, using whatever means necessary to make her wish come true.

Of course, things didn't run smoothly, and after a short while – only six days – we had an almighty row.

I'd heard that a lad I knew from back home had taken his own life and I desperately wanted to go back for his funeral, but Mum wouldn't let me. With the blue touch paper already lit, an explosion followed. It ended with me slapping Mum around the face in a temper. As she was a victim of 'domestic violence', I was immediately banned from living at the refuge. I was now deemed a threat to everyone. I'd just unwittingly sealed my own fate.

With nowhere to go, I called at Scarlett's house. Sandy had helped me in my hour of need before, so I hoped she'd come to my aid now – and she did. For the first time in months I felt safe and in a place where I was wanted. A few hours later, we'd just got changed for bed when we heard a loud knock at the door. Scarlett ran over to the front window and peered through the blinds.

'Shit! It's the police!'

I was so terrified they'd take me back to Mum's that I hid behind a large wicker chair in the front room. However, once Scarlett had opened the front door, the police stormed into the house, found me and shone a torch in my face. They dragged me out from behind the chair, and I was wearing just a T-shirt and my knickers.

'Go upstairs and get dressed,' I was told.

The officers took me to the police station, where I was detained in a side room until the following morning. As soon as she'd heard what had happened, Sandy, who'd been working nights, had cycled over to try and get me released. I could hear her sobs as she begged the police to let me go home to her house. But because Sandy wasn't my legal guardian, they couldn't authorise it. My legal guardian had washed her hands of me so, unsure what else to do, the two officers drove me back to Angela's. Her face fell as soon as she opened the door.

'Oh, I'm sorry,' she said, a little shocked that I'd turned up like the proverbial bad penny. 'But I can't take her back for long. I'm going on holiday.'

To be fair to Angela, my placement with her was only supposed to have been for six weeks, but it suddenly turned into a much longer stay.

My fifteenth birthday was only a few months away and I'd never felt more unwanted in my life. Angela took me back, but it was only a matter of time before I started to reoffend.

In my head I convinced myself that I was in a relationship with Sal. Although he constantly called me names and put me down in front of the others, I'd go back for more. Sal treated me like shit and in no way like his girlfriend, but I'd fallen for him – and I'd fallen hard. I'd been groomed by both men although I didn't see it then. Ali would keep me on board, offering a snapshot of kindness to get me to comply, and I would. I'd have sex with all these other men to try and keep Sal happy.

One day, Sal pressured me into having sex in the back of his car. Afterwards, he removed my glasses and I watched as he studied my face. I held my breath and waited in anticipation of him saying how much prettier I was without my glasses, the way people did in the movies. I was expecting Sal to shower me with compliments, only he didn't. Instead, a wide smirk broke across his face.

'I'd keep those glasses on all the time if I were you,' he said, as he pulled up his trackie bottoms.

'Why?' I asked, as I fumbled to put them back on.

Sal's face zoomed into view and he began to snort with laughter.

'Because you're even uglier without them.'

The insult cut me to the quick, and after that day I vowed never to take off my glasses again. I even slept in them. The men understood how much I relied on my glasses, so whenever they wanted to intimidate me, they'd rip them from my face. Whenever this happened, I'd hide my face in my hands so no one could look at me. Just when I thought I couldn't feel any more vulnerable.

I'd steal for the men by day, and they'd demand sex by night. It was relentless. Sal was twenty-one years old, but whenever he'd had sex with me, he'd make derogatory comments about me in front of the others. It was mortifying. Bilal and Ali would laugh and call him a bastard. Sometimes Ali would tell him he was out of order, but it didn't stop me from feeling worthless. I was still a kid; I didn't know about sex or what I was supposed to do or how I was expected to be. But it didn't stop him from molesting me night after night. Sal would drive me to the middle of nowhere, hold me down and rape me. It would only last thirty seconds because he wasn't much of a man, but then neither was Bilal.

Ali slagged Scarlett off too. He'd make derogatory comments about her pubic hair and the others would howl with laughter. I never told her because I knew how much it would hurt her. The men didn't like pubic hair and seemed to prefer girls on the brink of puberty. I wondered why a grown man would want to hang out and have sex with a young girl. None of them seemed to have girlfriends their own age, and I wondered why. It took me a while, but I eventually realised they didn't choose women their own age because they couldn't control them. But they could control a child. I don't even think it was about the sex. I believe it was more to do with the power it gave them. It was also why I was the one standing in the firing line when everything finally came undone.

██████████████ Social Services

To Whom It May Concern

Re: Gaia Cooper, D.O.B: ██████████

I am writing as I understand Miss Cooper is due to attend court to answer criminal charges on ████████████████ 2000.

This department has been working with Gaia and her family regarding some complex family difficulties. Gaia has been at severe risk of violence and exploitation from adult males in the community. Gaia's mother has left the area in order to try and keep her children safe. Gaia has been adversely affected by some quite sophisticated grooming and, as a result, was extremely reluctant to leave the area. It took the combined efforts of the police and social workers to get Gaia reunited with her mother.

This is a very tenuous situation, and I am deeply concerned about the possibility of Gaia absconding if she returns to the area too soon. I therefore respectfully request that the court give consideration to adjourning Gaia's case for three weeks to give her time to become more established in the new area prior to her returning here for court.

I hope you will look favourably on this request and thank you for your consideration in this matter.

Yours sincerely,
██████████████ Team Manager

Information for EDT

Name: Gaia Cooper
D.O.B: ████████
Composition of household: Mother and six-year-old sister
Tel. number: ████████
Legal status: No orders
Ethnic origin: W/B
Referred by: ████████

Brief description of present involvements: ████████ has moved to ████████ today to stay in a women's refuge due to D.V. Gaia refused to leave with her mother although she is at high risk as a result of her involvement in the local drug scene. Gaia was staying at the home of ████████ but has now gone missing. The police have been informed she is missing.

Anticipated problems leading to EDT's involvement: Gaia is now officially missing and may be found out of hours. She is refusing to leave ████████ and may request to be taken back to ████████. But ████████ does not want Gaia to stay at this address. ████████ has arranged transport to take her to ████████.

Preferred course of action: Gaia should not be accommodated but transferred to ███████████. ███████████ can be contacted on her mobile for exact location of women's refuge.

Signed: ███████████████████
Youth & Criminal Justice

Placement Monitoring Panel Application

Name: Gaia Cooper
D.O.B: ███████████
Address: Refuge in ███████████
Ethnic origin: W/B
Address: (care provider) Angela ███████████
School: ███████████
Designated teacher: ███████████
Social worker: ███████████
Team manager: ███████████
Reason for application: accommodation/move (with brief statement)

Gaia has been at severe risk of violence and exploitation from adult males in the community and has been involved in offending, drug taking and unlawful sexual intercourse. However, Gaia has been unwilling to make a statement to the police and press charges, and these problems escalated to the point of her stepfather saying that she could not remain at home.

███████████ was also having difficulty in a relationship with her husband and left the family home to escape domestic violence. It was suggested to ▆▆▆▆▆ by both the SSD and police that she will be best advised to leave the area to enable Gaia to be in a safe environment.

▆▆▆▆▆, left the area and went to the refuge in ▆▆▆▆▆ at this time. Gaia was refusing to go with her mother and went missing from home. However, when Gaia was located, she was taken by social services to her mother in ▆▆▆▆▆. Gaia initially seemed to settle but during an argument with her mother, Gaia assaulted her. Gaia then absconded from the refuge and returned to ▆▆▆▆▆ on 30 September and was placed with Angela, her foster carer by EDT.

Due to the incident that occurred at the refuge, they asked ▆▆▆▆▆ and Gaia to leave as they do not tolerate any violence. ▆▆▆▆▆, however, remains at the refuge but Gaia is unable to return.

Education: Gaia was on roll at school until she went to ▆▆▆▆▆ on 23 September, and we understand that she is still on the school register.

Gaia has been a non-school attendant for some time. The school reports that Gaia is a bright, articulate student who is underachieving due to the difficulty she's experiencing at the present time.

Gaia is keen to cooperate, and I intend to make an appointment with the school to discuss an integration programme to enable Gaia to go back to school.

Health: Gaia does not eat properly and is prone to weight loss. Gaia has admitted that she was using cocaine but says that she is not using it at the present time. Gaia has mentioned flashbacks, which she believes are drug related. Since being back with Angela, Gaia is eating well and has put on weight.

Angela, meanwhile, had her holiday to go on, so as I had nowhere else to go, a decision was made and I was taken to my stepfather's home. As soon as the social worker knocked on his door and explained the situation, he invited me in. By now I felt broken and bedraggled, standing there on his doorstep in the rain.

'You know you're always welcome here,' he said.

I smiled gratefully but he hadn't finished.

'You're always welcome here, as I say, but if you reoffend then I'm afraid you're out. Do you understand?'

I nodded. I was just happy that someone had finally agreed to take me. But I was hardly home and dry. I had multiple charges for deception and several impending court cases hanging over my head and I wasn't even yet fifteen.

Confidential School Report

Name: Gaia Cooper
Form: ▮▮▮▮▮▮

Achievements: Very able student. Gaia is an intelligent student who is currently underachieving due to her low attendance and her situation outside school. Homework is rarely completed.

Attendance/punctuality: Gaia has only recently returned to school. She moved to ████████ for a while. Since her return she has been on a re-integration package. Her attendance this term until her return was nil.

Behaviour: Very good, a pleasant student. Sometimes lacks concentration and on occasion gets easily distracted.

Parental contact: Gaia's mother and half-sister are now living in a women's refuge in ████████. Gaia's relationship with her mother has broken down. ████████ has needs of her own, which often conflict with Gaia's. She is in foster care in ████████.

She does not know the identity of her (natural) father and this causes Gaia a lot of heartache. In many ways, she feels that she does not know her true identity.

Signed: ████████████

Angela was determined to try and make it up to me, and before she left, she bought me a box set of Garage Nation 2000 tapes. I listened to them on my Walkman over the Christmas break. With Mum gone and Angela away, I continued to live at my stepdad's house for a while.

Just after Christmas 2000 it was Eid, the Muslim festival. Ali, Bilal and his brother paid for a hotel room so we could all hang out to celebrate. It was then that I met Syed. Unlike the others, Syed was utterly charming and he seemed genuinely interested in what I had to say. He talked about his life and how he'd recently been bullied in jail. I couldn't believe he'd been jailed for fighting because he didn't seem to have a bad bone in his body. Syed wasn't a typical hardened criminal; if anything, he scolded me for hanging around with the group.

'You deserve so much better, Gaia.'

Nor did Syed seem to want to use me for credit card fraud or even sex. Instead, as the others drank and smoked, we drifted into an adjoining room where we sat for the rest of the evening, chatting about our lives. At one point, Syed almost broke down as he told me that his brother had taken his own life.

'It was tough, you know, not having him around anymore. I miss him, Gaia. You only get one family, so you need to treasure them. Do you know what I mean?'

I knew exactly what he meant. As fractured as my relationship was with Mum, I still missed her and my heart ached for my baby half-sister.

Syed and I met up several times afterwards, and I'd feel like I was floating on a cloud whenever his name flashed up on my mobile phone screen. Soon, I found myself falling for him. The fact that he'd revealed his vulnerabilities to me marked him out as different. It also made him seem irresistible because I could identify with every single thing he told me. A few weeks later, I was still living at my stepdad's when Syed texted.

Wanna meet 2day?

My hands were shaking as I typed out my reply.

Sure. Come here. I'm all alone.

I knew we'd have the house to ourselves because Richard was at work all day. Sure enough, shortly afterwards, the doorbell rang and there was Syed standing on the doorstep. I checked both ways to make sure the neighbours hadn't seen him and dragged him inside. He'd brought a bottle of Moët champagne with him so we opened the bottle, drank a bit and then fell into bed together. Afterwards, Syed pulled out a spliff and lit it, but it didn't smell like any other spliff I'd smelled before.

'It's got coke in it,' he said, offering me some. 'Wanna try?'

I'd tried cocaine before with some of the other men and I decided I liked it. The coke made us both giddy and euphoric. I felt as if I could conquer the world as it gave me the confidence I'd always lacked. In many ways, it'd felt like the missing part of the jigsaw, and I immediately became hooked. We must have fallen into a deep sleep because the following morning I awoke to find Syed still lying next to me in bed.

'Syed!' I whispered sharply. 'Wake up, you've got to go. My dad will be back.'

It took him a few moments, but Syed woke, sat upright, rubbed his eyes and let out an almighty yawn.

'Shussssh!'

But it was too late. Richard had been crossing the landing on his way to the bathroom when he heard a man's voice in my bedroom. Suddenly the door opened.

'Who the hell is this?'

It was Dad. He was standing in the doorway as Syed and I squinted against the light.

Syed realised he was in trouble and quickly leapt to his feet. Thankfully, he was almost fully dressed as he'd planned to leave hours earlier. Dad didn't care, he just wanted the stranger gone; gone from my bedroom, gone from the house and gone from my life.

'Get out!' he roared.

Syed scarpered as Dad stood there staring at me in astonishment.

'It's not what it looks like … I can explain.'

But he wasn't buying it.

'Who the hell is he? He's not part of that group you've been hanging around with, getting into trouble with? Because if he is, I swear I'll …'

I sat upright in bed.

'No, I promise. His name is Riccardo and he's Italian. He's just a friend. He's Mia's brother.'

My stepdad knew I had an Italian friend called Mia. She was a little bit older than me, so he completely bought into my lie. I realised that with his dark hair and olive skin, Syed could easily pass for Italian.

Although he wasn't happy, at least Richard seemed satisfied that Syed wasn't part of the bad company I'd been keeping. He must have scared Syed off because I didn't see or hear from him again for ages. The fact I found myself alone once more left me feeling down. I considered what he'd said about family and realised I didn't want to go back to live at Angela's when she returned home. I needed to be with my mum.

I mentioned this to Pauline, the social worker, who agreed. She explained that Mum had since left the refuge and had moved to another town, three hours' drive away, where she'd secured a three-bedroom council house and was willing to take me back again. She said I'd have to move over there because my half-sister was already settled in school. I agreed to give it another go because I was desperate to try and turn my life around. Somehow, I'd become everything I didn't want to be.

Pauline drove me to Mum's in her bright orange car. As soon as we pulled onto the motorway and the car gathered speed, there was an almighty whooshing sound as the car boot flew open. A bunch of loose clothes that I'd stuffed on top of my bag whipped up and off into the air behind us as Pauline turned to me in horror. She quickly indicated and pulled the car over onto the hard shoulder.

'Don't move!' she said, before getting out to close the boot.

When she sat back down in the driver's seat I asked what was missing.

'Just a shirt … nothing much.'

'Not my Moschino shirt!'

I wanted to cry because it was the nicest thing I owned.

Pauline turned the ignition and started up the engine.

'Sorry, Gaia, but I can hardly go back and get it. It'll be lying in the middle of the motorway somewhere.'

I was thoroughly pissed off. I didn't realise it then, but the disastrous journey must have been an omen. I didn't last very long in Mum's new house, only a matter of months. I pined for my old life; I missed it all, even the men I considered my friends. I missed Syed, Sal, Ali. I even missed creepy Bilal and his jailbird brother. I didn't realise how strong the grooming had been. They'd well and truly got their hooks into me and now, I decided, it was all I knew and all I ever wanted. It was time to leave and return 'home'.

Placement Monitoring Panel Checklist

Gaia Cooper
DOB: ██████████
Social worker ██████████
Accommodation agreed

Issues arising: Gaia's mother is currently in a refuge in
██████████. issues of DV. Gaia has been involved in
serious drug taking, i.e. use of cocaine. Gaia has also
been involved in unlawful sexual intercourse with a
number of older men. Gaia is currently cooperating with
the foster carers placed since ██████████ and working with
the care plan. Gaia has been at the refuge with her
mother, but has had to leave due to her violence towards
her mother.

Panel chair: ██████████

Panel members: ██████████ ██████████ ██████████ ██████████

Panel agreed to short placement for six weeks for core
assessment to take place.

CHAPTER EIGHTEEN

ESCAPE

Sal, Ali, Bilal and his brother Temel were delighted that I'd come back to live at Angela's. Temel had just been freshly released from prison, where he'd been serving a term for fighting, I think, although I didn't care. I'd missed them all, and now I was free it felt good to go and see them again. It wasn't long before I found myself caught up in more sophisticated and organised crime. Things had moved on and I was no longer using stolen cards but cloned ones. It was the dawn of internet banking, and new online banks seemed to be opening every other month. The gang members were delighted, especially if they found themselves in possession of an Egg or Marble bank card, as both had a much higher credit limit.

On one occasion I was given a gold card I'd never seen before. There was a picture – almost a hologram – of an older woman's face imprinted on it. Obviously, I looked nothing like her, so I popped the card inside my mouth and used my teeth to scrape off the picture. I was certain I'd be stopped – that the cashier would notice the scraped-off picture – but no one said a word.

One afternoon, Temel – Bilal's brother – or Tem, as he preferred to be called, decided he needed me. He turned up unexpectedly at my stepfather's house and banged at the door. My stepdad was out at the time but Ruby, my step-sister, was there because I was supposed to be looking after her.

'Don't tell Dad, will you?' I made her promise.

I headed to the door to see what he wanted. His face broke into a warm smile as soon as I opened it.

'Hey, Gaia.'

'Hi, Tem,' I replied tersely.

My eyes scanned the street. I was acutely aware that my stepdad might return home at any moment. However, Tem didn't seem in a rush. In fact, he seemed positively chilled. I watched as he lit up a cigarette, took a drag, then tilted his head back to blow the smoke up into the air. The grey smoke thinned as I waited to see what he wanted.

'So, I need you to do a job with me.'

My gut clenched and my immediate reaction was to say no. I didn't like Tem and I didn't want to do a job with a small-time thug like him. But, after my beating from Cham, I was wary because the men intimidated me, and they knew it. They had full control and they knew that I'd do whatever they asked of me. I desperately wanted to slam the door in Tem's face, but I was in too deep. He wasn't my friend, like I considered Ali and Sal to be. I convinced myself I mattered to them. I wanted to believe it because I didn't feel I had anyone else on my side, apart from my stepdad.

Richard – he'd kill me if he could see this.

'Sorry, but I can't right now,' I whispered to Tem.

He nodded knowingly and leaned against the door frame.

I glanced over my shoulder to check that Ruby wasn't earwigging our conversation.

'Later then? Later tonight. I'll meet you. Usual place.'

I knew he meant the shops near Scarlett's house. I quickly agreed because I just wanted him gone before my stepfather returned.

'Good girl,' Tem leered. 'See ya later.'

And then he was gone.

A few hours later I climbed into Tem's car. As usual, I was given a stolen credit card in another woman's name. I looked at it carefully to try and familiarise myself with the person it once belonged to.

Miss Katie Rogers.

Today, I would be her.

'You need to practise the signature?' Tem asked.

'Nah, I'm good.'

By now I was an expert at forging signatures, and I could become a different person almost instantly. I studied the black biro swirls, memorising the upturn of the 't' and the shape of the double 's'. Like a fingerprint, everyone's signature is unique to them; however, unlike a fingerprint, your signature can be copied almost exactly.

Tem seemed edgy, and with good reason. He knew that if he was caught with a stolen card he'd be sent back to prison – this time for a much longer stretch. Unlike Sal, Ali and Bilal, who were all well practised in the art of obtaining goods by deception, Temel was a little rusty, but he expected the biggest gain.

'Where are we going?' I asked, as his car tore along the road.

He turned his head.

'PC World. I want you to get a laptop.'

I gulped. I knew from experience that trying to buy high-cost items was super-risky. I'd cut my teeth on deceptions under £100, but laptops, camcorders and other portable electronics were expensive, and they usually ran into thousands of pounds.

'Right,' Tem said as we pulled into a retail park on the outskirts of town.

He ratcheted on the handbrake and looked at me.

'Laptop and video camera.'

'Both?'

'Yeah.'

My stomach plummeted because goods that expensive usually required a ring through to the bank. But I was good and, I reasoned, an expert at making up bogus addresses.

I'll be fine; I can pull this off.

The PC World store was bustling as I stepped in through the door. The place was crammed with parents and teenage kids, shopping for phones and computers to set them up for university. From my viewpoint by the main entrance, I spotted a line of new TVs playing to themselves over by the back wall. The computers were on the right. To the left of me was a table of video camcorders out of their boxes but attached to security wires. As they were the closest, I wandered over there first. I chose the smallest camcorder I could find; it was also the most expensive, so I made a note of it and headed over to look at the laptops, spread over many display tables. I didn't really know much about computers, so I adopted the same principle. Smaller meant it would be easier to conceal, especially if I had to make a run for it. I was just about to go and find a sales assistant to bring me both items from the stockroom when I spotted Tem. I watched as he paced up and down nervously outside the store. Then, shielding his eyes, he pressed his face against the glass and stared through the window.

Christ! He's going to get both of us in the shit!

Our eyes locked and I nodded sharply to the left, signalling to him to get back in the car. He must have taken the hint because he stubbed out his cigarette and climbed into the driver's seat.

With the coast now clear, I approached an assistant, pointed out the items and asked if he could fetch both from the stockroom. He returned a few minutes later and placed them behind the till. The shop was about to close, and it was clear that all the staff wanted to do was shut up shop and go home. The metal shutters juddered and partially closed as a polite reminder for the last of the shoppers to finish shopping and leave. I approached the cash till to 'pay'. As I did, the female cashier looked up at me suspiciously as she inputted the prices. Her face was stern, and she gave me a look that suggested she didn't believe I had enough money to buy either.

'Is that everything for you?'

'Yes, thank you.'

I gave her the credit card in the hope she'd ring the sale up quickly so she could go home. But something told me it wasn't going to be that easy. A larger sale meant bank authorisation. Previously, whenever a card had been declined, I'd bluff my way out, offering an excuse that there probably wasn't enough money in my account. But I couldn't use that excuse when 'buying' a high-value item.

Instead, I had to rely on the shop being slack or the person at the bank not checking thoroughly enough. Sometimes it worked and sometimes it didn't, but I'd never done it standing inside a shop with the shutters half-closed.

Sure enough, the £2,500 price tag triggered an alert on the till and the assistant had to ring the bank for authorisation.

'Won't be long, Miss Rogers,' she said frostily.

She looped her red varnished nails around the coiled phone wire as I smiled politely and tried to think up a bogus address. By this time, the few remaining customers had made their final choices and a small queue had started to form behind me.

As I turned back to look at the cashier, she glanced furtively in my direction out of the corner of her eye. Paranoia flooded through me and my heart began to clatter. I tried to look nonchalant over the slight hold-up.

She knows. She knows it's a stolen card.

I was almost certain that this was a ruse and she was trying to stall me to buy extra time to alert the police.

'Postcode, please?' she said finally.

Her voice broke the tension between us.

I made an address up as she relayed the information down the phone. The light outside had begun to fade as I watched and waited for her to process the sale, only she didn't. My instincts screamed.

She knows. Run!

I glanced at the exit and the waist-high chrome barrier I'd have to navigate to try and make my escape. Just then, another assistant went over to the barrier and locked it. Then he started to pull at the shutters as though locking us in.

Run!

'Could you wait a moment, please? I just need my manager to authorise the sale,' she said, stalling me further.

But I didn't want to wait. I wanted to be out and as far away from there as I could get. A male assistant began to redirect other shoppers over towards the store entrance. His colleague, the one who'd locked the barrier, pulled something out of his pocket.

A key?

I watched as he turned something at the side of the exit doors.

Get out!

A burning heat rose from my toes up towards my face, as my eyes darted everywhere.

'Won't be a moment,' the cashier mumbled. 'The manager will be here in a second and …'

They know.

I didn't hear the rest because I ran, sprinting as fast as I could towards the store entrance. I was running so fast that I almost took out a family with a pushchair as they were leaving. There were loud voices – shouts from behind me – as a security guard began to give chase.

The car. Get to the car!

It had just started to rain as I bolted outside. The cool night air brushed against my skin, heightening my senses, as my pulse raced and my heart pounded. I heard the screech of car tyres against tarmac as a car emerged from the darkness – a police squad car. Two officers jumped out.

Run!

Turning, I raced through the freezing rain as it whipped against my face. Both my legs pumped like pistons and air burned inside my lungs as I sprinted over to Tem. I heard footsteps behind as the police began to close in on me. The car engine was running; grey fumes spat from the exhaust and Tem watched in horror as I approached. His eyes were wide and his face a trickle – distorted by rain against the windscreen – as he stared through the glass.

'Tem, oh, thank God!' I cried through the half-opened window.

But as I went to grab the car door handle, he revved the accelerator and began to pull away.

'Get the fuck away from the car!' he screamed.

The vehicle roared as it took off; away from me, the police and the scene of the crime. Seconds later I felt the familiar sensation of cold metal – handcuffs clinking shut around my wrists. As the police arrested and began to caution me, I lifted my head and watched the red lights of Tem's car, two small red dots in the dark before they vanished into the night.

Detailed Contact Sheet

Name: Gaia Cooper

Home visit to Angela ████████.
████████ did not attend because she was sick.
Date: 29 December 2000

Angela very concerned for Gaia. She doesn't want her moved, but Gaia seemed to think I was there to remove her. Angela and I spent some considerable time exploring why Gaia is doing what she is doing. She is back taking cocaine and has been involved with credit card fraud ▉▉▉▉▉ ▉▉▉▉▉, so she believes Gaia is with ▉▉▉▉▉. Gaia is wearing only stolen clothes and some of her jewellery (gold earrings and necklaces) is stolen too. They make her go into the shop and buy goods with the credit card that they have previously stolen. They go all over the place and have recently been to ▉▉▉▉▉ and ▉▉▉▉▉ ▉▉▉▉▉.

Gaia abides by the rules in the house and is managing to come in on time. She can be half an hour late. She tells ▉▉▉▉▉ the other foster child what she is doing and wonders why ▉▉▉▉▉ tells Angela. She has had a few communications with her mum and ▉▉▉▉▉ is down with her father ▉▉▉▉▉ and ▉▉▉▉▉ has said to Gaia she can visit.

Gaia came in and we shared our thoughts with her. Gaia must try to come home during the day and not be staying out for twelve-hour stretches. This is when she is offending.

... Gaia was very angry and states ONCE AGAIN she wants to go straight. We give her options to try, and she just gets angry. Also, we asked her to remove all the stolen things from the house and I made it clear that if we thought she was bringing in stolen goods in future we would report it to the police. Gaia really cross at this! Gaia still refusing any counselling for drug abuse or her past experiences.

CHAPTER NINETEEN

ORGANISED CRIME

As soon as he heard about my arrest, Syed offered to come to the police station to be my appropriate adult. He was twenty-two years old – in other words a grown man – so I knew the police would allow it. But I didn't want him there to witness me being questioned for fraud. I felt ashamed. So I asked my Italian friend Mia to come instead. Of course, because of my age, I was charged and bailed again, which left me free to commit even more crime. My life was in a negative spiral and I knew I was out of control. I urgently needed help, so I confessed everything to my stepdad. Unsurprisingly, he went mad.

'You know what this means, don't you?' he said calmly, as he sat across from me at the dinner table.

I nodded reluctantly. It meant I was out. I didn't blame him – I knew he was only trying to protect my step-sister. She was younger and at a vulnerable age, and he certainly didn't want her to follow in my footsteps. My stepfather contacted Pauline, the social worker, who drove me back to Angela's house. In many ways, being put back there made things worse because everyone knew where she lived. I was ripe for the picking, and I hated myself because I seemed unable to say no.

Word soon spread, and instead of working for petty criminals like Ali, Sal and Bilal, I was now being summoned to do jobs with big-time crooks and major drug dealers. One of them was called Masud.

It was early 2001, just weeks before my 15th birthday, but I was due to appear in court for credit card fraud totalling £8,000.

Around this time, Scarlett had started seeing a friend of Masud's, a lad called Adnan. Both men were part of the local gangster scene, but they soon set their sights on us – a pair of compliant schoolgirls. One day, Scarlett told me she'd arranged to meet up with Adnan at a nice hotel in town.

'Come along, Gaia.'

I rolled my eyes because I didn't want to play gooseberry.

'No, it's not like that. Just come, it'll be fun. We can smoke, drink and chill.'

After much persuasion, I finally agreed. For starters, it sounded way more exciting than going back to Angela's alone. We'd not long been at the hotel room when Masud knocked and then came bursting into the room. It was obvious he'd been drinking heavily. I'd been sharing a spliff with Scarlett, but she and Adnan had already drunk their way through half a bottle of Moët. Masud was overly loud and began to show off, so Adnan started to take the piss out of him. Everyone was laughing when Masud's mood seemed to change in an instant. He pulled me to my feet, and dragged me off and away from my friends into the bathroom. Masud turned and locked the door behind him before trying to force himself on me. The bathroom was tiny, so it was difficult trying to fight him off in such a tight space. It was obvious he expected to have sex with me. I'd turned fifteen a few days earlier, and somehow the fact I was now a year older helped me find my voice.

'No!'

I pushed my hand against Masud and he momentarily lost his balance, staggering backwards and falling heavily against the sink. He seemed shocked. It was clear he wasn't used to anyone saying no to him, particularly a young girl.

'You don't want to?' he raged in disbelief.

A fury boiled inside him, taking him over.

'Well, tough. I do, so you will!'

With that, he lunged forward to try and grab me. But I was sober and quicker, as I shifted to the side.

'No, you don't understand. I can't. I'm on my period.'

It was obvious he didn't believe me, although it was true. Masud staggered away from me as though I were filthy. Islam teaches men that sex is forbidden with women when they bleed, so I knew that Masud couldn't have me even if he wanted to. He swayed slightly and narrowed his eyes suspiciously.

'I don't believe you.'

I was stunned.

'You don't believe me?'

Masud shook his head.

'Nope. Not a word of it.'

Wedged up against the wall with the bath on my left, I had no way of escaping and he knew it. He lunged at me and grabbed both my wrists in one hand. Then he snaked the other one under the waistband of my trousers and into my knickers.

'Please don't,' I begged.

But he didn't care. Seconds later he withdrew his hand, then studied his bloodied fingertips.

'Fucking dirty kuffar bitch!'

Masud threw me back against the wall, turned to the sink and ran both taps to wash his hands. Once he had, he stormed back into the room and over to the mini bar. He pulled the door open with such force that I thought he'd ripped it off.

'Dirty fucking whore!' he began to rage, as Scarlett and Adnan looked on in shock.

Pulling a box of Malteser chocolates out of the fridge, he ripped the box open and threw the contents across the room at me. Small brown balls skittered across the carpet like chocolate marbles and rolled off into the shadows in the far corners of the room. Taking the bottle of champagne, he went to smash it against the wall. Adnan sat upright on the bed to try and protest.

'No, bruv, don't …'

SMASH!

Dark green glass splintered against the wall and scattered onto the carpet below. Champagne bubbles foamed against the wallpaper before fizzling away. The glasses were next and then the teacups, as Masud's rage intensified. He didn't finish trashing the room until there was nothing left to throw. Shaking with rage, he turned to me, still cowering in the bathroom doorway.

'Do you think I pay money for a hotel for a two-dollar ho like you, and I don't get what I want?' he shouted.

He spat on the ground, left the room and marched off down the corridor. Scarlett tried her best to console me, but I was petrified and humiliated. Even Adnan couldn't believe it.

'He's way out of order,' he muttered under his breath as we began to pick broken glass and crockery off the carpet.

To make sure the coast was clear, I waited a little longer and then made my way back home to Angela's. I realised I'd just made a mortal enemy in Masud. I hoped and prayed he'd been so drunk that he wouldn't remember. These men were nothing like Ali and Sal; these men were not nice people. My mate and I had initially been impressed by their apparent wealth – the champagne and nice cars – but, as we were beginning to realise, the stakes were much higher. We didn't stand a chance.

A week or so later I had a meeting with my probation worker, and I was just heading back through town when I spotted a man staring at me from the opposite side of the street. It was Masud. Although I was in the town centre behind the back of some shops, I knew I was in trouble, particularly as I was wearing platform shoes and knew I'd never be able to outrun him. Instead, I stared at the ground, buried both hands inside my pockets and continued to walk.

Masud shouted something over, but I pretended not to hear. Inside I panicked, my heart hammering fast.

Don't look up. Don't react.

Quickening my steps, I hurried along the street. Moments later, a hand grabbed my shoulder and soon I was spinning, spinning towards him as he stood in front of me, throbbing with hatred.

'You dirty kaffur bitch!'

I felt a slap and then a punch; blow after blow until I curled up in the foetal position to try and protect myself. Shoppers stopped and stared as he continued to kick, slap and punch me as I lay folded on the ground. A fifteen-year-old girl being beaten up by a grown man in broad daylight.

'Bitch! You fucking bitch! You owe me fifty fucking quid.'

SLAP.

I howled in pain as the thumps and slaps grew harder.

'Please … please don't. My glasses, please don't break my glasses.'

Breathless, the park hut and the broom flashed across my mind.

'Breathe … I can't breathe!' I cried.

I was having a panic attack. Masud was beating me senseless, but no one did a thing. Shoppers stood and watched open-mouthed as I took the beating. Just when I thought I'd pass out from the pain, I heard footsteps, then a lone voice.

'Enough! Leave her alone, Masud.'

Blinking and trying to focus through swollen eye sockets, I put down a hand and felt all around for my glasses. I'd recognised the woman's voice but her outline was blurry, moving as she dipped down and hooked a hand beneath my armpit to help me back up.

'It's okay, Gaia, it's Milly,' the voice soothed.

I felt her let go as she knelt to pick up my glasses from the floor.

Please don't let them be broken.

The world zoomed back into sharp focus as I put them back on my face. Just then, I spotted Masud and backed away.

'You fucking dirty ho!' he spat.

'Enough,' Milly said, as she formed a barrier between us.

For a second, I wondered if he'd start on her, but Masud knew better. Milly had children to a friend of his – a friend who must have been far bigger and nastier than he was. With Milly here to protect me, my ordeal was over. Masud was still furious when he finally walked away. As he did, he turned and pointed straight at me.

'Don't forget, you dirty fucking bitch. You still owe me £50.'

Then he left. I was still in a state as Milly guided me to a nearby bench and made me sit on it to try and catch my breath.

'You okay?'

I lifted my head; she wasn't much older than me, but she was more powerful and respected than I could ever hope to be.

'Yeah, I'm a bit sore but I'll be fine.'

My heart galloped as I tried to calm myself down. With nothing left to see, the shoppers picked up their bags and left.

Milly came to my rescue that day. In her, I realised I'd found a pal. I was later proved right when we became lifelong friends.

The beating seemed to be the final straw. Then I heard that Sal – the man I'd always adored – had got himself a new girlfriend. The girl was twenty-one, had a good job and owned her own car, all of which made me feel intensely jealous.

'That's why he's seeing her,' Bilal later remarked. 'He's just using her to get a car.'

The truth was, Sal and Ali drove lots of cars but none belonged to them. They were either borrowed from friends or stolen. I was distraught. I liked Syed, but I'd always loved Sal, and one day I hoped we'd make it official and I'd become his permanent girlfriend. Pulling my mobile out of my pocket, I dialled his number. I pretended I was ringing for a chat, but when he told me his girlfriend was there I became hysterical.

'I'm going to kill myself!'

The words came blurting out of my mouth before I could stop myself. Sal laughed as though I were just some daft kid making empty threats.

'Do it, Gaia! Slit your wrists, then me and my girlfriend will come and piss all over your grave.'

Each word felt like a body blow.

He doesn't believe me.

But I'd never been more serious in my life. I had nothing to lose.

Everyone leaves me. No one gives a shit.

It was true, no one did.

Initial Assessment Record

Name: Gaia Cooper

Gender: Female
D.O.B: ██████████
Address: ██████████
Telephone number: ██████████
Date initial assessment commenced: 21.2.02
Date completed: 21.2.02

Reason for initial assessment: Gaia requested support assistant re. accommodation; she is currently being provided with short-term accommodation by a friend at the above address.

Health: Gaia states she's slightly depressed though is not taking any medication. She is not currently registered with a GP.

Education: Gaia is not currently attending school. She last attended school in March 2001 while living with her mother in ██████████. She stopped attending school as she had a lot of absences previously and was finding it difficult to keep up.

Emotional and behavioural development: Self-care skills: has 4/5 concurrent supervision orders. Most recent has very recently expired. She also previously had a combined order with which she did not comply.

Family and social relationships: Gaia's mother lives in ████████ with Gaia's seven-year-old half-sister ██████████. Her mother will not allow Gaia to return to live with her, as Gaia states she did not agree with the things that Gaia had been getting herself involved with. Gaia had lived with her mother for nine months before returning to ████████ two weeks before Christmas.

On 22 February 2002 I calmly popped each Nurofen tablet out of the blister pack until I'd formed a small white pile on my bed. Then I swallowed each and every one of them. Thankfully, I'd told Milly what I'd planned to do, so she called round and took me to hospital. As I'd taken a handful of tablets, the consultant decided to keep me in for observation and monitor me for any adverse symptoms. True to form, none of my family came to see me in the hospital. Not Mum, nor my stepfather. Even Angela didn't bother to pay me a visit.

I was put in a children's ward but, at almost sixteen, I felt oddly out of place surrounded by childish drawings and colourful curtains that had been pulled around my bed.

Besides Milly, my only visitor was Sal's uncle. I think he turned up out of some kind of duty, although he seemed nonplussed when I explained what his nephew had said.

'He's a cheeky little bastard!' he reflected, as though Sal was just being a typical lad.

The uncle had brought me a couple of Kit Kats to aid my recovery, and I remember thinking it was strange to bring them to a hospital.

Don't most people bring grapes?

After a few hours I decided I'd had enough. I got out of bed, dressed myself and, as soon as the coast was clear, I snuck out of the hospital and I didn't look back.

████████████████ County Council Social Services

Emergency Duty Team

Detailed Contact Sheet
Sunday 22 February 2002

22:20. Gaia went to A&E this afternoon after an alleged overdose of Nurofen but has since left without treatment. Stepdad has been contacted but he's on his way to ██████. Mum's phone is engaged. I was unable to provide much current information. Gaia is now a missing person and the police are looking for her.

23:40. Telephone call from paediatrician, ██████, who has been informed by police that Gaia has been found and stepdad is going to collect her. The consultant would like her back in hospital. I discussed options, i.e. police protection or stepdad could persuade her to return. I said I would follow up.

23:50. Telephone call from PC ██████. Police are happy for her to be collected by stepdad. She is alert and does not appear to be adversely affected by the overdose.

I rang stepdad ██████, who said Gaia has just gone to bed. She is alert, said she had taken ██████ Nurofen this afternoon and does not want to go back to hospital. He is happy to have her for a few days and will try to arrange for her to go to Mum in ██████.

Monday 25 February 2002.

13:00. A telephone call from Dr ██████ for update. She said that she was not so concerned at the minor overdose but more concerned that she might repeat it. I pointed out that police and stepdad were happy for Gaia to be in the care of stepdad and that she was more likely to act dangerously if forced into a situation she did not agree with.

Signed,
██████████████, Duty Social Worker

CHAPTER TWENTY

CHOOSING MY RELIGION

Following my botched suicide attempt, I asked the doctor if I could be prescribed some antidepressants but he refused. I found it difficult to articulate what was wrong; I just felt completely and utterly lost. In a cloud of depression, I spent the best part of the following year numb as I flitted between my old town and Mum's new place. Still, I couldn't settle.

As a condition of my probation, I had to stay in Mum's new town and keep away from my old associates. I was living with Mum when I decided to nip into town and have a mooch around the shops. I was just browsing when I realised that I was being followed. At first I thought I'd imagined it, but then I saw that a security guard was monitoring my every move. I turned, quickened my steps and headed over towards the door. He called after me.

'Gaia Cooper.'

I froze to the spot.

How does he know my name?

As he wandered over, I studied his face but I didn't recognise him. In fact, I'd never seen him before in my life.

'How do you know my name?' I asked.

The security guard began to smirk.

'Er, what's so funny?'

'You,' he said. 'Everyone knows you.'

That's when I realised; my young offender's record had followed me like a shadow. I'd just turned sixteen and I was allowed to move into a supported lodgings foster home. It was run by a lovely couple called Gary and Denise Baker. Gary was a pastor, and he and his wife Denise ran a house that sheltered waifs and strays like me. I was given a room but was told I'd have to do all my own washing and cooking. I didn't mind because I was determined to get my life back on track.

A few weeks later I appeared in a youth magistrates' court so that all my outstanding offences could be dealt with. They were so large in number that I'd been told to expect a custodial sentence. Thankfully, the youth magistrate took pity on me and, although I was a cat who'd already used up all its nine lives, he gave me one last chance. I was ordered to pay compensation of £243, and handed a £57 fine. However, before I left court, he had one final warning.

'If you don't buck up your ideas, Gaia, you'll end up in prison.'

I swallowed hard. The thought of serving time frightened the shit out of me.

I wouldn't last a week inside a prison.

The youth magistrate was right; I was sixteen but had racked up seven convictions since that fateful first meeting with Ali and Sal. The offences were mostly for obtaining property by deception or handling stolen goods. However, they were only the ones where I'd been caught and the police had taken many others into consideration. I knew I was heading to prison if I didn't turn my life around. As well as the fine, I was given 100 hours community service. As part of my punishment I had to paint a psychiatric unit. As soon as I arrived, I understood why – the walls were smeared with blood. Once I'd finished that, I did the rest of my community service working inside a café in a church. The place was full of old people and most were incontinent, so the air always stank of piss.

With the youth magistrate's words ringing in my ears, I decided to change my life once and for all. With the pastor's support, I stayed in my lodgings for almost a year. During this period I landed a job at a local fast-food restaurant and, for the first time in my life, had money of my own. More importantly, I'd earned it through my own hard graft, not through theft. Soon, a year had passed and I hadn't reoffended.

With this bit of experience accrued, I was offered a job as a waitress in an Indian restaurant. The manager was a bit of a creep, with wandering hands, so I'd spend most of my time trying not to be left alone with him. There was another lad working there who I knew fancied me. He'd spend all his wages buying me clothes and trainers, without expecting anything in return. It felt like a revelation. However, because of the grooming and abuse I'd suffered, I also spotted an opportunity. One day, I lied and told him Mum's house had been burgled. He had become so infatuated with me that he immediately offered me £1,250 to replace our 'stolen' things.

I spent the lot on a kilo of Moroccan hash. It had been Temel – Bilal's jailbird brother – who helped organise the deal. The plan was I would sell the hash off in small deals, try to turn a profit and save enough money to pay for a place of my own. However, Temal must have told Taj, the man who'd once raped me when I was being sick at a party. Taj contacted me and asked if we could hook up in my old town. At first, I was unsure whether to go ahead with the meeting, but eventually decided I was now older and wiser, and convinced myself that these men no longer had a hold over me. I was wrong. To be on the safe side, I decided to stash the hash inside my step-dad's home while I went out for the day. Although I'd always been a little wary of Taj since the rape, that day he was utterly charming. By the evening, however, he'd changed. He threatened me and told me to bring him the hash. I did as I was told because, in truth, I was still utterly terrified of him. Later that evening, Taj picked me up and drove me to a housing estate on the outskirts of town. He parked in an unlit road and then turned to me.

'Whores like you have chlamydia.'

I was just about to reply when he grabbed my hair, forced my head down and made me perform oral sex on him. Taj realised I was still intimidated by him and he exploited that power. He also used it to steal the hash from me, mentioning he'd tell his girlfriend we'd had sex if I didn't.

'You don't want her to find out, do you? Remember what happened last time?' he sneered.

His dark eyes glinted in the dull dashboard light as I recalled how she'd beaten me black and blue for having 'sex' with him. But it hadn't been sex – he'd raped me, just like the others.

To my horror, I later discovered he'd beaten his girlfriend so badly that she had welt marks across her back. To this day I'm not sure if she'd been groomed, like me. The men continued to exert such power over me that I found it impossible to lie to them. The last time I'd tried that it had led to my torture and much else. But I'd now convinced myself I could go clean and, apart from the hash, I had. However, time and time again, my old life pulled me back and I repeated the same cycles. This time I still wanted to be back with the old crowd, but I vowed to stay out of trouble. I decided to return 'home'.

My new social worker was close to retirement. She was also a complete pushover, just putty in my hands. This time I became a manipulator, and somehow I managed to convince her I'd be better off returning home. I even persuaded her to allow an older man I knew, called Yahya, to act as my guarantor. Weirdly, Yahya was the older brother of Bilal and Temel – two of my abusers. They'd not only groomed me, they'd both raped and criminally exploited me. With hardly any background checks, the social worker rubber-stamped my move and told me that if I found somewhere to live, she'd happily back my plan. So I did.

I was almost seventeen when I enrolled at the college in my old town. I'd planned to take GCSE Maths and English – two exams I'd missed out on. I secured a room in a house, although I had to share it with a single mum. At just nineteen, Alice was two years my senior, but unlike me she was a total scruff. Her baby was just reaching that awkward toddler stage, and whenever I was out she'd let him play in my room with all my things. One evening I returned home to find he'd squeezed a whole tube of foundation all over my bed.

That's it, I'm out of here, I decided.

Less than a week later, I'd gone.

I was just wondering where life would take me next when Sal called to see me. He mentioned a house he knew of where I could stay.

'You'd do that for me?'

I was secretly delighted that he'd offered to go out of his way for me. However, my new flatmate had serious mental health issues and would openly masturbate in front of me. Sal also failed to mention that it was a crack house. I stayed just the one night.

Thankfully, a girl called Ciara – who was married to Sal's brother – heard what had happened. She was so horrified that she came to my rescue. Ciara whisked me back to her flat, even though it was only a temporary measure. With nowhere else to live, I was certain my old social worker would make me move back to Mum's place. I was just fretting what to do when Bilal came up with the perfect solution.

'Why don't you move in with my family?'

At first I thought he'd completely lost the plot, but the more I thought about it, the more it made sense. Bilal suggested I could contribute by buying food for the rest of the household. In return, his family would provide me with a much-needed roof over my head. On paper it made complete sense; in practice, however, it was much more difficult.

To begin with, Bilal's mother looked down on me. The house was already full of young and able Muslim women, who I thought were treated like maids. I was fully expected to pull my weight, but I knew very little about cooking, cleaning or how to 'keep a house'. In fact, I'd often burn food or forget to do my chores. I drove Bilal's mother Yousra to despair.

'You're so lazy, Gaia,' she'd say time and time again as she tutted disapprovingly.

Secretly, I liked and respected Yousra, so I worked hard to earn her approval. Slowly but surely she taught me how to cook delicious Moroccan food and clean the house to her exacting standards. Soon, Yousra became the mother I'd never had. With my place in the household secure, Ciara and I also became good friends. Ciara was white, like me, but she was married to Idrees – Sal's brother.

One night we began to chat as we stood preparing the evening meal together. Ciara described the peace she'd found after she'd converted to Islam. She went on to say how much it had changed her life.

'It's hard to explain, but mainly I just feel part of the family, which is why I converted. Idrees's parents are such strict Muslims. I wanted them to accept me, you see, and they have. I converted a few years ago. It's the best thing I've ever done because I haven't looked back. I was lost before and had no direction. Do you know what I mean?'

The more I listened, the more I found myself nodding along in agreement. I also had questions.

'But don't you mind, you know, having to cover your hair like that?'

I pointed up to her hijab as Ciara rested her hand against it. She looked up from the pot of stew she was stirring and laughed gently.

'No, no, not at all. I just feel I'm now on the correct path in life. Being a Muslim isn't a bad thing. If you read the newspapers and listen to the TV you'd think it was, but all I've found is peace. It's a happy and peaceful religion. I feel …'

She paused for a moment and I found myself leaning forward.

'Go on.'

'Well, I just feel like I've found the true me; the person I always was inside. It's made me a better person, Gaia. Things that used to bother me just don't matter anymore. People matter, and now I have them. When I'm with Idrees, I'm with my family.'

Family. Such a small word but one that carried so much importance, especially to me. I understood completely. Like me, Ciara had been lost, but now she'd found a new inner peace, which she credited to her conversion to Islam. I looked at my new friend; she seemed to have it all – everything I'd ever wanted.

With a renewed determination to keep on the right path, I decided to follow Ciara's example. If she could become a Muslim, then so could I. I realised that it might not only bring me a sense of belonging, the men – all those who'd raped and abused me – would start to view me in a different light. I hoped in time they would come to respect me, as they did Ciara. I couldn't choose my family, but I could choose my religion. I could and would become part of a much bigger family – somewhere I'd finally belong.

CHAPTER TWENTY-ONE

RESPECT

I converted to Islam, and – for the first time in my life – things seemed to fall into place. I felt as though this was what I'd been searching for, the missing part of the jigsaw. I became a changed person and I vowed I wouldn't re-offend, and I didn't. I didn't even waver, because I took my new religion so seriously. Day after day I studied the Quran avidly and became passionate about life because I could finally see a future for myself.

I was convinced my new-found faith would keep me on a better path and help me to turn my back on all that had gone before. I'd tried that life and it had all but destroyed me. I realised that in order to try and move forward I had to let go of my past and change everything. So I did. The men who'd previously abused me also began to view me differently. Incredibly, Sal and I even became engaged, and I joined in with female-only prayer circles to try and learn more and strengthen my faith. I wanted to become a good Muslim wife to Sal, and to love and care for him. Attitudes towards me began to shift, and soon I became so well read in the words of the Quran that I would teach other Muslim women verses and prayers from it, including my beloved Yousra. It was my way of trying to repay all the kindness she'd shown me. But however I framed it, the stark reality was I'd simply replaced one addiction with another. I was certain my old abusers had begun to consider me as their 'sister', yet I couldn't have been further from the truth.

As part of my new faith I followed the teachings of Islam, and as a female Muslim I wore a hijab. I wore it because Islam taught me that the hijab was part of decency and modesty when interacting with the opposite sex. In fact, one of the verses – verse 59 of chapter 33 – says:

> This is more appropriate so that they may be known (as Muslim women) and thus not be harassed (or molested).

I wore it as a symbol of my new faith and because I wanted to become a better person. Not only did I want to change, I wanted to show Allah that I was sorry for everything I'd done in my life up to that point.

One evening I had to sleep on the sofa in the living room because a visiting relative had put her children in my bed. The house was deathly quiet and everyone was sleeping soundly, when I heard footsteps coming down the stairs. I got up to see who it might be and if anything was wrong. It was Bilal.

'What are you doing?' I gasped.

He was standing by the doorway, staring at me standing a few feet away from him. He didn't say a word and lifted a finger against his lips as if to 'shush' me. He then forced me back towards the sofa, wrestling me down onto it.

'Please, Bilal … don't!' I sobbed.

But he did it anyway. Pinning both my arms down, he held me there as his hand began to snake beneath my *abaya*, a long gown. I wanted to shout out, but I knew that if I woke the family they'd certainly blame me and not him. After all, given my past, who was going to believe me? Bilal continued to wrestle me as I attempted to wriggle from beneath him. But he was strong and I was no match. A waft of cold air brushed against my thighs as he lifted the fabric of my gown. Then he pulled my knickers down roughly.

'Please … please …' I begged.

Sobbing uncontrollably, at that moment I truly wanted to die. I'd worked so hard to try and become a good Muslim woman, but as much as I tried to fight him off, I couldn't physically stop him.

'Bilal!' I cried.

Balling both fists, I attempted to punch him in the side of his head. When that didn't work, I sank my teeth into his shoulder – anything to get him off me – but he refused to stop. His eyes were wild – a mixture of fury and lust – as he held me down and brutally raped me. Afterwards, I lay there with my *abaya* ruched up and my body exposed, full of self-loathing. I'd been raped before, but this seemed far worse. This felt like the ultimate betrayal.

I've failed again.

Muffled sobs racked my body as I held a cushion against my face to try and silence them. Bilal climbed off me and pulled up his trousers. His lust now sated, my rapist left the room and went back upstairs. He left me lying on the sofa, battered, bruised and defiled. I wanted to chase after him and claw his skin off with sharpened nails. I wanted to shout and cry for help, but it was pointless. I was a woman in his house, under his roof. Up until that moment I'd been a good Muslim woman who'd adhered to the teachings of Islam. I'd done everything right, but now everything was wrong.

As a Muslim I'd regularly perform a purification ritual called *Wudu*, during which I'd routinely wash my hands, face, arms and feet before prayer. But I couldn't wash now.

After sexual intercourse, Muslims are required to bathe and wash every part of themselves – a full-body purification ritual called *Ghusl*. I needed to wash all over, even my hair, but I couldn't do it, and that left me feeling disgusted and distressed. I even thought about creeping up to the bathroom, but it was the middle of the night and the plumbing was old and noisy. I couldn't take the risk of running a bath because it would wake them all up – my rapist's family.

How would I even begin to explain?

Utterly traumatised, I grew to hate myself because I knew that I'd never be clean again. Bilal had soiled me, and now I was trapped with him and had no one to turn to. I'd failed as a Muslim.

Of course, he couldn't help himself. He later bragged about what he'd done to his brothers, although, of course, he claimed it had been 'consensual'. I realised, because of my past, that no one would ever believe me, but it was the way that Yousra looked at me that crushed me the most; she thought I'd betrayed her. In many ways, it felt worse than the actual rape. Although nothing was said directly, I knew that almost everyone knew – or soon would.

Following the rape, I despised Bilal with every fibre of my being. I wanted to claw the knowing grin from his face every time I saw him. To try and protect myself, I swapped my hijab for a niqab. It covered my whole head and face, apart from a small window for my eyes. I felt the need to cover my 'shame', even though it wasn't mine to own.

Temel, Bilal's older brother, had been sent back to prison, and it wasn't long before he heard. Of course, he was told a different version – one where I'd willingly agreed to have sex with his brother, despite the fact I was betrothed to Sal – their cousin. Although Temel was still behind bars, he gave the order for me to be thrown out of the house.

One afternoon, Yousra was speaking on the phone in Arabic. By now, I'd mastered enough of the language to work out what she was saying. I realised Temel was on the phone, speaking to her.

'What do you want me to do? Kick her out?' I heard her say.

The answer was yes, of course.

Temel had labelled me a 'white slag' – they all did. But I was too scared to try and correct them because they were all I had. I was so traumatised by the rape that I'd taken to wearing gloves, even though it was warm outside. I couldn't stand anyone touching me, not even my hands. I didn't want to have a single part of my skin on display because I couldn't bear it to happen again.

All the respect I'd worked so hard to gain over the past year – everything – vanished almost overnight.

Eventually, someone told Sal, who immediately called off our engagement. I tried to explain but he wouldn't listen. Bilal was his family; I wasn't. Family came first and always would do. I was nothing.

CHAPTER TWENTY-TWO

PREGNANT

Suddenly I found myself back on the street. I was home-less, vulnerable and all alone once more. As a care leaver, social services stepped in again and offered me a flat in my old town. I packed my bags, left Bilal's house and tried to pick up the pieces of my life. The only person to contact me out of all my so-called friends was Syed. He'd always been kind and, unlike the others, had treated me with respect. With nothing to lose, we embarked on a relationship. Although he was eight years older than me – I was still seventeen, and he was twenty-five – Syed seemed different.

One day, I was over visiting Mum when I felt decidedly odd. My periods had been erratic for a while and, instead of a full bleed, I'd been experiencing spotting. I visited my GP, who examined me and asked lots of questions.

'And how long have your periods been like this?' she said, as she waited to type my reply into the computer.

I shrugged my shoulders.

'I don't know. A few months?'

The doctor looked at me as she noted my symptoms.

'And do you think you could be pregnant?'

I laughed and shook my head vehemently.

'Not a chance!'

She seemed unconvinced and arched her eyebrow.

'Are you sure?'

'Absolutely.'

Although I was adamant, my doctor booked me in for a scan at the local hospital. A week later, I took a seat and waited to be called in by the sonographer. She covered my belly in a clear jelly and ran an electronic wand over my relatively flat stomach.

'And why are you here today, Gaia?'

I twisted to look at her as she stared intently at the screen.

'Oh, it's just my periods. They've been all over the place. To be honest, I think I might have some sort of cyst because my periods, well, they've kind of been non-existent for the past few months, and …'

My voice trailed off as the sonographer turned to look at me in astonishment.

'I think I know why your periods have stopped, Gaia.'

With that, she twisted the computer monitor around to face me so I could see it more clearly.

'According to this, you seem to be pregnant.'

'What!'

I was so shocked that I sat upright, knocking the wand out of the way.

'But I can't be! I can't be pregnant.'

The sonographer's face said it all.

'Well, I think you are, and according to what I can see here, I think you may be about four months.'

I was so stunned that at first I couldn't speak. Realising I was in shock, she asked me to lie down so that she could take some measurements for my medical records.

'Someone will be in touch with your GP so they can organise pre-natal care and a meeting with the midwife.'

Midwife.

The word sounded alien. I'd only just turned eighteen and getting pregnant hadn't been in my life plan. As I left the hospital I was still in shock. I walked along the street trying to tally up the dates in my head.

Please don't let it be Bilal.

But I immediately knew it wasn't. There was only one man the father could be – Syed. It sounds odd, but I seemed to drift into some kind of denial, as if this wasn't really happening to me but to someone else. I couldn't understand how I'd finally fallen pregnant after all the years of having unprotected sex with different men. Still in a bit of a daze, I took a train to the coast and, with my skirt hitched up above my knees, I began to walk out into the sea. I still have no idea what I was intending to achieve, but as the cold waves lapped against my skin, I glanced down at my belly.

How can I bring a baby into this world? I can barely look after myself.

I didn't believe I possessed the emotional maturity to look after another human being, especially one reliant on me for everything. The sea sloshed around my legs as I stared out to the horizon. I don't know how long I'd been standing there when something dawned on me; this baby – boy or girl – could be a force for good in my life. I'd finally have something to focus on and to love. The waves lapped around me, brushing the underneath of my stomach, with life now growing inside it. I realised all the shitty things that had blighted my life didn't matter anymore because I'd have a child. I'd be a mother, and I made a promise that I'd be the best mum I could be. Cradling both hands around my stomach, I made a vow to always be there for my child, no matter what life threw at us. Where others had failed me, I'd never fail my baby.

I thought that Mum would go crazy when I told her, but remarkably, she seemed absolutely delighted by my news. In fact, when I told her she was going to be a grandmother, she actually shrieked with excitement. It seemed odd, given that she'd never really been there for me.

Syed was delighted too when I broke the news to him. Unfortunately, a month or so later he was sent to prison for fighting. I was shocked because it seemed completely at odds with the man I loved. I was alone again.

In 2005 I gave birth to a beautiful boy, who I decided to call Harry. My son was perfect in every way. In fact, he was so precious that I refused to take him into prison to see his father. As a result, Syed didn't get to meet Harry until he was almost two years old.

With his father on release, I hoped that we could finally be a family and that I'd found my happy ending. Only, it wasn't that simple. As Harry grew and became a toddler, I began to see a different side to Syed. All the charm he'd once used to woo me vanished. He became aggressive and grew violent towards me. It soon reached the point where I'd keep my sleeves rolled down, even in the height of summer, to conceal the finger-mark bruises on them. I'd just decided I'd take Harry and leave Syed for good when I discovered I was pregnant again. Leaving now would be completely out of the question. I found myself trapped, only this time with a violent bully with a craving for cocaine. Syed's coke addiction seemed to make him even more paranoid than he already was.

In 2008 I gave birth to our second son and we called him George. With two boys to protect and Syed's unpredictable behaviour to manage, I felt constantly frazzled.

One day, Syed and I decided to take the boys swimming. I was cradling George in my arms and Harry was at his father's side when an older, larger lady tried to get by. The changing room area was narrow and, as she pushed past us, she accidently bumped into Harry. Within seconds Syed had exploded and began to scream in the woman's face. She looked petrified.

'You stupid, fat bitch!'

The woman stopped dead in her tracks but remained silent.

'For fuck's sake, watch where you're going. You almost knocked over my fucking kid!'

Her eyes flitted to mine as though she was waiting for me to step in or even say something, but I had no words. Mute with shock, I stood there feeling mortified. I couldn't believe that this monster was the father of my children. Harry seemed to sense the anger coming from his father and he began to cry. Syed's temper had frightened him; it had frightened us all.

'Look what you've done now! You've frightened my fucking kid!' he continued to rage, as his anger spiralled.

By now, other swimmers had stopped to stare at the young family who were causing complete chaos in the changing room. I wanted the earth to swallow me up.

'Come on, darling,' I soothed Harry.

Taking his chubby little hand in mine, I led him over to the pool area to try and diffuse the situation.

'That's a good boy, you come with Mummy.'

But inside I knew it was over; Syed wasn't good for me or the boys. Something had to give.

A little while later, Syed decided we should go out for a family meal. My stomach clenched because I knew it would end in disaster, and I was right. When Harry's baked potato arrived at the table, Syed grabbed the plate and twisted it round to give it a thorough check. Sure enough, he signalled to the waitress and beckoned her back over. I stared down at the table as the poor girl approached. I knew what was coming.

'What the fuck do you call this?' he screamed.

Syed pointed at the food as I squirmed with embarrassment. Other diners turned to look at us, trying to listen in as he began to curse and swear.

Harry was sitting opposite, and I could tell that he was trying his hardest not to cry. Even at that young age he knew it would only make his daddy worse. Harry tried his best to blink away some frightened tears that had pooled in the corners of his eyes as Syed continued to tear into the waitress.

'Look at it!' he said, pointing at the potato.

She leaned to one side to try and see what the problem was, but she still seemed a little puzzled. Syed rolled his eyes as though it should be obvious.

'There's fucking mud on his potato! Who do you think you are, serving my kid a jacket potato with mud on it? What are you trying to do, poison him?'

I could barely look at her as she flushed beetroot. But Syed hadn't finished. His voice grew so loud that it brought the manager scuttling over.

'Thank you, Kirsty, I'll take it from here,' he said, nodding sharply, as he dismissed the waitress.

She seemed relieved – eager to escape Syed's wrath.

'Is there a problem, sir?'

I closed my eyes. Waited. Then Syed exploded again. He leapt to his feet, knocking drinks over and sending our plates clattering. With food spilled across the table, Syed became so threatening that the manager called for police back-up. Our 'nice meal out' had quickly turned into the meal from hell. Syed was still swearing as two police officers crossed the restaurant to try and take command of the situation.

'I suggest you calm down, sir,' one of the officers warned.

By now Harry was crying, setting his brother off, until soon I had two wailing kids to comfort. I rocked George gently in my arms, when Syed lunged forward and snatched him from me. At first I didn't understand, but then it became apparent. The police couldn't arrest him when he was holding a baby. He'd effectively taken our son hostage.

'Sir, please give the baby back to his mother,' the officer said firmly.

His colleague stood there watching and poised, with handcuffs at the ready.

Syed, high on cocaine, believed he was invincible.

'Fuck you!' he hissed.

The police had heard enough. Exasperated, the officer turned to speak to me.

'Could you take the baby?'

I stretched out both arms and wrapped them around George to keep him safe. As I did, Syed kicked me hard and continued to scream obscenities.

'I am arresting you for …'

The words faded to a blur as I clutched George against my chest and started to sob. Harry watched wide-eyed as the officers cuffed and arrested his father. Syed was carted off to the local police station, leaving me behind with two terrified kids and a restaurant full of staring diners.

The meal confirmed what I already knew – it was time to leave. I couldn't put my boys through it any longer. Syed's violent and unpredictable temper had largely been down to his constant cocaine use. But this was no excuse. He was an adult who made his own decisions, while my boys couldn't. They deserved better than this. I refused to let them grow up surrounded by violence. I'd witnessed enough of it in my youth, and I sure as hell didn't want my kids to be exposed to it.

George was still only six months old, but that day I returned home, packed our bags and left, taking both boys with me.

CHAPTER TWENTY-THREE

KNOCK AT THE DOOR

A couple more relationships followed, and while they were fun, I knew they weren't right for me or the boys. As we'd come this far, I decided we didn't need a man telling us what to do.

I'd largely brought my boys up single-handed, and now they were both at school I decided it was time to get a job. However, my past was always there, lurking in the background and following me like a shadow wherever I went. I secured myself an administration role, which required a basic DBS (Disclosure and Barring Service) check of my criminal past. Thankfully, nothing showed up because my convictions had already been 'spent'.

I loved my job. I worked hard and valued the income it gave me to help build a better life for my boys. A few years later, with my confidence growing, I applied for a voluntary position at a school. I assumed I'd be fine, but because I'd be working with kids I needed an enhanced DBS check. Of course, it listed my multiple convictions for fraud and dishonesty so, unsurprisingly, I wasn't offered the position. To make matters worse, both my boys attended the same school. To my horror, I realised that the head and some of the office staff must have seen my record. It left me feeling horrified. Although I was now a law-abiding adult – and had been for years – I still carried the shame of my past like a weight around my neck.

Even though he'd been abusive, deep down I still loved Syed. Abusers do that. They dig so far into your psyche that they can retain a hold on you months, even years down the line. They do this because they shatter your self-esteem to the point where you truly believe you're lucky to have them. Syed did this to me and, foolishly, I decided to give him another chance. I believed him when he promised he'd changed. But he hadn't. In fact, I discovered he'd been cheating on me with another woman, so I ended it yet again.

Two more years passed. I had to keep in touch with Syed so that he could see the boys. My mum had never really been there for me, so I didn't want to make the same mistake with my own children. We got back together again briefly, but Syed beat me so badly that one of my lungs collapsed. On my way to hospital I told myself enough was enough. I'd given him three chances and he'd blown them all. It was over, only this time for good. Syed still had a temper, as well as an ongoing addiction; he'd switched cocaine for gambling and had lost what little money we had left.

I started from scratch again. Although Syed had moved on, met someone else and had another family, I couldn't do the same. I tried, but failed, to have another relationship – deep down, I was too damaged. My past had badly wounded me and I didn't have a clue how to fix myself. I viewed all men with suspicion and always looked for the ulterior motive, even when – as was often the case – there wasn't one.

Slowly I became depressed and, faced with bringing up two boys on my own, I began to withdraw from life. Eventually I suffered a breakdown, stopped speaking and, some days, even struggled to get out of bed. I didn't realise it then, but I was suffering from severe PTSD as a result of the abuse and child criminal exploitation I'd endured.

After almost a year of feeling lost, I decided I was worthless and convinced myself that my boys would be better off without me. In 2010, aged twenty-four, I shook a bottleful of tablets into my hand and swallowed the lot. Thankfully, a friend found me and I was rushed – blue lights flashing – to hospital, where the doctors pumped my stomach out. As I awoke, I wished for death but discovered I was still alive. However, I'd finally done it – I'd reached rock bottom. That's when I decided to seek professional help to deal with the demons of my past. I was immediately assigned a psychiatrist and I began to undergo treatment from a psychologist on a weekly basis.

My son, Harry, had always been a highly strung little boy, and subsequent tests revealed that he had both autism and ADHD. Although I was struggling myself, I was determined to fight for my kids. My depression was managed with medication and I understood that my children needed me. I'd just been so terrified of letting them down – terrified I would fail. The following years were a struggle, but somehow we made it through.

One day in 2015 I answered the door to two female police officers from the National Crime Agency. Although the visit was unexpected, when they said that they believed I'd been the victim of child sexual exploitation (CSE) and child criminal exploitation (CCE), I broke down.

The officer waited as I tried to process my shock.

'Gaia, from what we can see on the missing persons database and the men you associated with at that time, we believe you were a victim of grooming and sexual exploitation. These men exploited you and they got you into a lot of trouble.'

I wiped away my tears as I stared at her in disbelief. The room fell silent as I tried to absorb what it was she was telling me. I understood that I had a past, and that it was something that was still shaping me. However, up until that moment I didn't have a name for it. Now I finally did.

Throughout my formative years I'd been made to feel like the black sheep of the family; the girl your friends' mums and dads didn't want their son or daughter to bring home. I'd been labelled a criminal, and I was the daughter who was never invited to family get-togethers in case I 'stole' something. But I never 'stole' a thing from my family. It didn't matter, because my reputation went before me. I was 'off the rails', unreliable and a bad influence. I was everything that was wrong with the world all rolled up into one person, only I wasn't. I was simply a vulnerable little girl who'd been exploited by some very bad men.

'Gaia, are you okay?' the officer asked, interrupting my train of thought.

'Yeah,' I whispered. 'It's just that nobody, not one single person, has ever told me it wasn't my fault.'

She shook her head in dismay.

'Gaia, none of it was your fault. You were groomed and exploited in the most horrible way.'

I let the news slowly sink in. I allowed myself some moments of reflection when I recalled my fourteen-year-old self – that little girl who played at being an adult. There was a pause, until one of the officers spoke. She had a favour to ask – they wanted my help.

That's when I grew angry. I asked where they'd been when I was a child and I'd needed them most.

'We're here now,' she replied.

A rage boiled inside me.

'Well, I'm sure, as you have so much intelligence on your database, you could have stopped it; you could have done something. I've only been drunk a handful of times in my entire life and one of those times I was fourteen. The police pulled the car I'd been travelling in over for a routine producer. But I was so drunk that I was sick all over the officer's shoes. And do you know what she did?'

The officer shook her head.

'She laughed. She told me off and then let me be driven off into the night with two adult men.'

That's when I realised I'd been shouting. I was angry, but I'd been overtaken by something else – sadness. I was broken-hearted for my poor, vulnerable fourteen-year-old self.

'Gaia, we're here now, and we really want to make these men pay for what they've done to you and other girls like you.'

I desperately wanted to believe and trust the officer. Most of all, I wanted her to take me in her arms and help me. I'd been searching for love my entire life to the point where my body ached for it.

Here they were, promising me the earth with three small syllables: 'We're here now.'

But their words felt hollow. The officer looked me directly in the eye.

'We need to make these men pay for what they've done, Gaia. We need as many girls as possible to speak to us about what they've been through at their hands. We need justice. Wouldn't you like to see that?'

I shook my head.

'No, I wouldn't, and I'll tell you why. There will always be evil people in the world. Even if you locked them up forever, they'll never take responsibility for their actions. And do you know who's even worse? All those people who are supposed to protect kids – my mum, the social workers, police. All these people are supposed to be the good guys, the heroes, the ones I could turn to. But where were they when I needed them?'

Both officers shifted uncomfortably in their seats.

'Where were you – the police? You and the youth courts were too busy, giving me a criminal record, sending me back to court for breaching conditions and handing down community service orders. Everyone – adults who should have known better – repeatedly told me what a bad and silly girl I'd been.'

'Gaia, I can promise you …' one of the officers began, butting in. But I didn't want to hear it; I'd had a bellyful of listening to other people. Now I'd found my voice, and I was only getting warmed up.

'Besides, where would I even start?' I said, looking them both in the eye. 'Should I start with the older men – the ones who asked me to do a one-off card and paid me well – or with the ones who forced me to do it and came knocking for me? And what about those men, the ones who finished their day off by raping a fourteen-year-old schoolgirl?'

By now I was apoplectic.

'No, I don't want to do it. It's far too late. It wouldn't help me one bit to drag it all up again – not me, nor my children. No thanks!'

The blonde officer smiled tightly. She rooted inside her briefcase and pulled out a letter and handed it to me.

'We understand it's a shock, and it's also a lot to be confronted with. We'll leave you to think about it, but we'd like to stay in touch. We'll come back to see you in two weeks, if that's okay?'

So it had been a rhetorical question all along. They'd be in touch, irrespective of my response.

'Sure, you can contact me, but as I have children I know this won't bring anything good into my life right now.'

I stood and led them back towards the front door. In truth, I wanted them gone. It had taken fifteen years for them to come and knock on my door to tell me it wasn't my fault. Fifteen wasted years. Within half an hour of their departure, I received a text from the police. I didn't reply straight away because I was pottering around the house in a daze. I was seething, but surprisingly not with the perpetrators. My gripe went much deeper than the men. I directed my fury at those who were supposed to have been there to protect me, but hadn't been. In my book they were as bad as my abusers. In many ways they were worse, as they'd pretended to be on my side when, in truth, they'd only ever been on their own.

CHAPTER TWENTY-FOUR

STRENGTH

I cried on and off for the rest of that day. When my tears finally ran dry, I called my close friend Milly. She was as shocked as I was, but she knew something the police didn't – that I'd never be able to stand up in court to testify against the men. Most of them lived in the same town as me. Even worse, they still lived inside my head. Following the visit, there was only one thing I was certain of. To testify against these men would only bring more misery into my life.

Deep down I was scared, too terrified to try and unpick my past. I'd spent years since my mental breakdown and suicide attempt trying to build myself back up again. The last thing I wanted was for my life to come crashing back down. I knew I'd never be fully at peace with my past, but at least I'd made a start. I'd managed to function again both as a mother and a human being. I realised I needed to stay sharp and in a good place for my boys. It was the least they deserved.

In 2018 I was diagnosed with complex post-traumatic stress disorder and unstable personality disorder. Both are common among adults who have been sexually abused as children. I spoke to a solicitor, who filed a claim against the social services department on my behalf. I wanted to hold the department to account for its failure to care and protect me. The county council, which ran the department, admitted it had failed in its duty of care towards me. I was awarded £80,000 in compensation, but the money didn't fix me. It was – and remains – an ongoing battle.

I decided to help other children by speaking about my childhood and lived experience of CCE and CSE. I wanted to prevent other kids from being targeted and groomed into a life of crime, rape and abuse. Barnardo's charity for vulnerable children asked me to speak, and I gave my first talk to 180 teenagers. I spoke specifically to them about the dangers of grooming.

'If you're fourteen years old, ask yourself this: why would a grown man want to be your boyfriend? Why doesn't he have a partner of the same age? It isn't love – he's not in love with you – it's abuse. And, if you're under sixteen, it's not sex, it's rape.'

The hall fell deathly quiet as I continued to speak.

'I was called a child prostitute by the police, my family and by social workers. But I was fourteen. There's no such thing as a child prostitute – they don't exist – because a child cannot give consent. It's illegal. It's rape.'

By now I had the teenagers hanging on my every word.

'Ask yourself, why does this man want to be your friend? Is he your friend? Or shall we call him what he really is – your abuser?'

Although I'd initially been petrified of standing up in front of a roomful of strangers, the kids asked me such insightful questions that I realised they'd taken in everything I'd said. By the time I left I knew I'd made a difference.

After my talk, I was offered a consultancy role with a new charity to prevent CSE. Finally, I was beginning to use my horrific childhood experiences to effect real change, and I was doing it on my own terms. However, the real breakthrough moment happened in my personal life.

In 2022, unbeknownst to me, my eldest son Harry, who was then only sixteen, had been groomed and lured into so-called 'county lines' drug-running. Even though I'd always been an over-protective mum, I'd initially missed the tell-tale signs. However, when he told me he was going to meet a girl, I smelled a rat.

As a young boy, living with a diagnosis of ADHD and autism, Harry was extremely vulnerable. So when he failed to return home and rang to say he was staying overnight in a hotel, I instinctively knew something was wrong. As the night wore on I feared the worst. I knew from experience that this was how my own abuse had begun. I rang Harry's mobile repeatedly, and when he failed to answer I reported him as a missing child to the police. But they refused to act.

My worst fears were confirmed only a few hours later when my youngest son, George, showed me a picture of Harry on Snapchat, photographed inside what I can only describe as a crack house. It was in an area I'd never heard of, but at least I had a location. I searched it on Google Maps and discovered it was two hours' drive from our home. Armed with this new information I contacted the police again, but they were dismissive and refused to act. Beside myself with worry, I realised that if

I wanted Harry to be saved I'd have to do it myself. Thanks to George, I knew where his brother was being 'held', so I contacted a friend who lived nearby and asked her to post a picture of Harry on social media. The post alerted everyone who saw it to the fact that Harry was missing and had been reported as such to the police. I knew I was taking an enormous risk, exposing him like that, but I also realised it would make him 'too hot to handle', especially to those who were grooming him.

Almost immediately the situation began to snowball, and everyone started to be on the lookout for Harry. I realised he was probably running drugs for this gang, so I knew he'd be out in the community, both visible and traceable. Soon I started to receive photographs of Harry. A well-wisher sent me an image of him riding a bike I didn't recognise. Another woman – also a mother – stopped him in the street and told him to go home.

Teenagers the same age as my son contacted me to say he'd been posting stuff on social media about drugs. That's when I knew for sure that Harry was in deep trouble. With a swell of community support behind my search, Harry became too recognisable. The gang who'd groomed him decided that it didn't want or need the spotlight, so they threw him out onto the street. The police hadn't wanted to know, but I refused to shut up until, finally, they sat up and listened.

Penniless, and abandoned a few hundred miles from home, Harry called me from his mobile. I wept with relief as soon as I heard his voice because I was terrified that I'd already lost him. Along with a friend, we drove over to pick him up and bring him back home. Although he seemed a little shaken, Harry suffered no long-term effects following his ordeal. Most importantly, he was safe.

I'd acted straight away, doing what I thought was right, because I knew more than most how quickly these situations can escalate. After all, I'd lived through them.

This is why I'm telling my story. I hope that by sharing my experiences I can raise awareness and help to protect other children from suffering as I did. If I can help save just one young life, then I'll know I've made a difference.

Confidential

Medico-Legal Psychiatric Report
Report by: Professor ▮▮▮▮▮▮▮
Date: 16 June 2020

Opinion: Ms Cooper is a 34-year-old mother of two children who suffered severe abuse in her childhood and was subjected to sexual, emotional and physical abuse. She was forced into crime and drug taking. She has had an abusive relationship subsequent to this which has resulted in her being assaulted. She has had several episodes of self-harm.

Diagnosis: It is my view she is suffering from post-traumatic stress disorder and emotionally unstable personality disorder.

Causation: At the time of going into care and the breakdown of her relationship with her stepfather and mother, there were some behavioural difficulties, but things dramatically declined when she went into care. It is my view that the abuse she suffered at the hands of these men is entirely causal to her psychological difficulties. Indeed, her later relationship in choosing a violent partner is directly linked, as this is how she developed as a young teenager.

It is common for individuals with early life trauma to delay bringing claims and presenting for health as a result of avoidance symptoms part of PTSD but also, they want to avoid/block being re-traumatised. There is specific context in this case to the delay due to the father of her children being one of her abusers.

Prognosis: She has had a sustained period of abuse and rejection in her childhood. Unfortunately, later in life there have been difficulties with bad relationships, which is a consequence, in my view, of the abuse she suffered in her childhood. My estimate is that she has a 60 per cent chance of improvement in five years' time. Should she not recover then she will remain impaired with chronic PTSD symptoms that will impair her life to an extent. Specifically, it will impair her employment decisions, socialisation decisions and people she chooses to mix with due to her anxiety.

EPILOGUE

As a victim of CCE and CSE I realised I needed to navigate my own past. I needed to understand and try to address everything I'd been through, including pain, self-loathing and the patterns of my own behaviour. In short, I had to sit down and understand my own trauma.

Most people who have been abused want to believe they're okay. They just want to be a normal member of society and put the past behind them. However, when I had my own children, I truly believed I could right all the wrongs with love, understanding and a protective maternal instinct. While all these foundations are commendable, you can equally damage your children by loving them too much, especially when you still hold deep-rooted beliefs that you're not good or 'worthy' enough. You may try to fill the gap by spoiling your child. Speaking as someone who has been abused, I understand that you can retain those same people-pleasing traits. After all, these held you in good stead when trying to placate your abuser. However, a child is not a captor, a perpetrator, an abuser or a human trafficker; it's a child, and it needs strong foundations and clear boundaries to feel safe.

I gave birth to my children when I was still young and, although I've tried my best, the guilt I carry will never leave me. I tried to navigate my way out from my damaged past alongside raising my boys. However, I often worry that I may have inadvertently inflicted my trauma on them.

You wouldn't buy a car if you couldn't drive because you'd drive in the wrong lane and in the wrong gear. You wouldn't be able to read the road signs ahead and you'd generally blunder your way through until something catastrophic happened. While nothing catastrophic has happened to my children, I realise that my past has shaped them almost as much as it's shaped me. Some of the bad life choices I made along the way have had an impact on them, and this scares me. It's taken a lot of debriefing and guidance on my part to ensure that my boys grow into well-grounded young men. It's not been easy, but I feel we're finally getting there.

As a victim of child exploitation I'd advise anyone with adverse childhood trauma to address it before embarking on parenthood if at all possible. To eradicate abuse, we need to stop the cycle and smash the chains that hold us down, once and for all.

Gaia Cooper
September 2023

CHILD SEXUAL EXPLOITATION AND CHILD CRIMINAL EXPLOITATION STATISTICS*

Child sexual exploitation

The following statistics on abuse experienced in childhood in England and Wales include data on sexual abuse, physical abuse, emotional abuse and neglect. They also include statistics on child abuse and the criminal justice system.

The Crime Survey for England and Wales estimates one in five adults aged between eighteen and seventy-four have experienced at least one form of child abuse, whether emotional abuse, physical abuse, sexual abuse or witnessing domestic violence or abuse before the age of sixteen. This equates to 8.5 million people.

An estimated one in a hundred adults aged eighteen to seventy-four have experienced physical neglect before the age of sixteen (481,000 people). This includes not being taken care of or not having enough food, shelter or clothing. However, it does not cover all types of neglect.

* All data and information courtesy of the UK Office for National Statistics.

An estimated 3.1 million adults aged eighteen to seventy-four were victims of sexual abuse before the age of sixteen. This includes abuse by both adult and child perpetrators. Prevalence was higher for females than males for each type of abuse except for physical abuse, where there was no difference.

Many cases of child abuse remain hidden and do not enter the criminal justice system. Around one in seven adults who called the National Association for People Abused in Childhood's (NAPAC) helpline had not previously told anyone about their abuse.

Around 227,500 child abuse offences were recorded by the police in the year ending March 2019. Of these, around one in twenty-five (4 per cent) resulted in a charge or summons. While not all cases continue through the criminal justice system, almost four in five (79 per cent) of child abuse-flagged Crown Prosecution Service (CPS) prosecutions were successful in securing a conviction in the year ending March 2019.

Childline, the counselling service for children and young people, delivered 19,847 counselling sessions in the UK where abuse was the primary concern in the year ending March 2019; sexual abuse accounted for nearly half (45 per cent) of these and has become the most common type of abuse counselled by Childline in recent years.

As of 31 March 2019, 52,260 children in England were the subject of a child protection plan (CPP) and 2,820 children in Wales were on the child protection register (CPR) because of experience or risk of abuse or neglect. Of these, neglect was the most common category of abuse in England, and emotional abuse was the most common in Wales. As of 31 March 2019, 49,570 children in England and 4,810 children in Wales were looked after by their local authority because of experience or risk of abuse or neglect.

Around half of adults (52 per cent) who experienced abuse before the age of sixteen also experienced domestic abuse later in life. This is compared with 13 per cent of those who did not experience abuse before the age of sixteen.

Child criminal exploitation and modern slavery

'Modern slavery' is an umbrella term that covers all forms of slavery, including human trafficking and exploitation. It's a hidden crime because victims often feel unable to come forward due to fear or shame. Sometimes they're unable to leave their situation. As a result, reporting and quantifying the number of victims of modern slavery can be challenging.

There is no one data source that accurately quantifies the number of child victims in the UK. The National Referral Mechanism (NRM) currently provides the best measure of potential victims, although it is known to be an undercount.

The data for the NRM in the UK for the year ending December 2021 indicates an increase of 9 per cent in the number of potential child victims referred compared with the previous year (from 5,028 to 5,468). Of those referred, more than nine in ten (91 per cent) received a positive reasonable grounds decision (RGD), meaning they were assessed as likely to be victims. Almost four-fifths (79 per cent) of positive RGDs were for boys; this proportion has increased rapidly since the year ending March 2015.

Boys who received a positive RGD were most likely to have been criminally exploited (62 per cent), while girls were most likely to have been sexually exploited (42 per cent). Over 82 per cent of children who received a positive RGD were aged fifteen to seventeen.

Changes in police recording practices and the COVID-19 pandemic have most likely affected the number of child victims identified in recent years. Alongside data from the NRM, other data sources show an increase of 27 per cent (to 3,239) in the number of modern slavery offences involving a child victim recorded by the police in England and Wales in the year ending March 2021, compared with the previous year.

There were 16,830 episodes of need for child sexual exploitation and 2,710 for trafficking identified by the Department for Education's Children in Need census in the year ending March 2021. Both of these represent a 10 per cent decrease from the previous year, although this is probably due to a fall in referrals from schools during the pandemic. There was also a 43 per cent decrease in the number of potential child victims reported to the Modern Slavery and Exploitation Helpline in the year ending December 2021, compared with the previous year.

Between April 2016 and March 2021, the Crown Prosecution Service completed 185 modern slavery-related prosecutions involving a child victim in England and Wales – with a 51 per cent conviction rate.

Alexa Bradley of the Centre for Crime and Justice at the Office for National Statistics says: 'Child abuse is an appalling crime against some of the most vulnerable in society, but it is also something that is little discussed or understood.

'Measuring the extent and nature of child abuse is difficult because it is usually hidden from view and comes in many forms. Bringing data together from different sources helps us better understand both the nature of child abuse and the potential demand on support services.'

ACKNOWLEDGEMENTS

Thank you to Kelly Ellis and Imogen Gordon Clark from HarperCollins for allowing me to share my story.

A massive thank you to Eve White and Ludo Cinelli of Eve White Literary Agency.

My heartfelt thanks to every victim of exploitation who has brought this widespread, often unspoken, endemic into focus and kept it there. Their bravery gives a voice to future survivors so they don't feel alone and unheard.

The biggest thanks to Veronica Clark for bringing this memoir together so beautifully.